Rhetoric
in Popular Culture

Rhetoric
in Popular Culture

Barry Brummett
University of Wisconsin at Milwaukee

St. Martin's Press
New York

Editor: Edward Hutchinson
Managing editor: Patricia Mansfield-Phelan
Project editor: Alda Trabucchi
Production supervisor: Elizabeth Mosimann
Art director: Sheree Goodman
Text and cover design: Silvers Design

For information, write:

St. Martin's Press, Inc.
175 Fifth Avenue
New York, NY 10010

ISBN: 0-312-06539-6

Acknowledgments

Chapter 5 is revised and reprinted from Barry Brummett, *Rhetorical Dimensions of Popular Culture* (University of Alabama Press, 1991), by permission of the University of Alabama Press.
Part of Chapter 6 is revised and reprinted from the *Quarterly Journal of Speech*, by permission of the Speech Communication Association and Professor Margaret Carlisle Duncan.
Champion Sportswear advertisement © Champion 1992. Reprinted by permission.
Cherokee clothing advertisement © 1992 The Cherokee Group. Reprinted by permission.
Firstar advertisement reprinted by permission of Firstar Corporation.
LensCrafters advertisement reprinted by permission.
Tiffany for Men advertisement © Tiffany & Co. 1990. Reprinted by permission.

For Margaret Carlisle Duncan

Preface
● ● ● ● ● ● ● ● ●

This book joins together two vital scholarly traditions: rhetorical criticism and critical studies. There are several good textbooks, either well established or new, that cover rhetorical criticism from a fairly traditional perspective. They focus on the analysis of discursive, reason-giving texts such as public speeches. On the other hand, there are several good books of critical studies available. Some of the newer textbooks of critical studies are much improved over their predecessors in covering techniques of Marxist, feminist, and other critical approaches in ways that are accessible to students. But there is a need to apply the growing and cutting-edge methods of critical studies to the study of rhetoric, and to link these new approaches to the rhetorical tradition. That is what this book tries to do. It sees critical studies *as* rhetorical criticism, and it argues that the most exciting form of rhetorical criticism today is found in methods of critical studies.

The four chapters comprising Part I of the book are theoretical and methodological. Chapter 1, "Rhetoric and Popular Culture," introduces central concepts of rhetoric and culture. It is keyed to a concept of culture as composed of signs, artifacts, and texts, following the semiotic theory of C. S. Peirce. How signs mean, and how that meaning is rhetorical, are explained. Chapter 2, "Rhetoric and the Rhetorical Tradition," is a link to more traditional views of rhetoric. The conceptual and political bases of traditional rhetorical theory are explained, as well as why an approach linked to popular culture is an important supplement to the historical tradition. Rhetorical and political dynamics of cultures are also discussed.

Chapter 3, "Rhetorical Methods in Critical Studies," talks about what it means to be critical. It first introduces the critical process in general, and explains assumptions and techniques shared by nearly every critical method. The focus is on *choices* that the critic must make, regardless of the specific method used. In contrast, Chapter 4, "Varieties of Rhetorical Criticism," compares five specific groups of critical methods: Marxist, feminist/psychoanalytic, dramatistic/narrative, media-centered, and culture-centered. Here, the focus is on both differences and similarities among critical approaches. Throughout the first four chapters, principles are illustrated through examples and through photographs of advertisements. Chapter 4 compares and contrasts different critical methods through application to the film version of *The Wizard of Oz*. Throughout Part I, there are a number of exercises designed to reinforce concepts under discussion; these may be implemented as material for class discussion or as written assignments, at whatever degree of formality the instructor may wish.

The three chapters in Part II are critical analyses, designed to show how critical methods can be used to study the rhetoric of extended texts at length. Chapter 5, "Paradoxes of Personalization: Race Relations in Milwaukee" shows how, when political issues are linked to personal experiences, both desirable and undesirable consequences can follow. That chapter studies public discourse about race relations during a rocky two-month-period in Milwaukee, Wisconsin. Chapter 6, "Twin Peeks: Using Theory in Two Analyses of Visual Pleasure," explains the ways in which responsible criticism makes use of rhetorical theory. The importance of theory as a way to inform good criticism, as well as the importance of avoiding a "cookie-cutter" approach, are stressed in two applications: one is an analysis of watching televised football, and another is an analysis of the experience of being at shopping malls. Detine Bowers, in Chapter 7, "Afrocentrism and *Do The Right Thing*," shows how culture-centered criticism, in this case Afrocentric criticism, can reveal dimensions of a text that are not apparent from other readings. This chapter analyzes the film, *Do the Right Thing*, to show how an Afrocentric reading can be a political response to racial violence.

I would like to thank the following professional colleagues who took the time to read and comment upon the manuscript of this book: Bruce Herzberg, Bentley College; Tom Hollihan, University of Southern California; James F. Klummp, University of Maryland, College Park; John Llewellyn, Wake Forest University; Skip Rutledge, Point Loma Nazarene College; Helen Sterk, Marquette University; Barbie Zelizer, Temple University.

I am grateful to Margaret Carlisle Duncan of the University of Wisconsin–Milwaukee for her contribution to Chapter 6, and to Detine Bowers of Virginia Polytechnic Institute and State University for her authorship of Chapter 7. I would also like to thank the editorial staff of St. Martin's Press, who provided excellent guidance and support as the book progressed from mere idea to finished text. Edward Hutchinson, Jane Lambert, and Cathy Pusateri were especially helpful. Finally, thanks to my family, and to my friends and colleagues at the University of Wisconsin–Milwaukee, and to Margaret, who is both.

Barry Brummett

Contents

Part **I** Introduction to the Rhetorical
Criticism of Popular Culture
••••••••••••••••••••••••••••••••

Chapter 1

Rhetoric and Popular Culture

• •

Do you know what your blue jeans are doing to you? What kind of person do you turn into when you go to shopping malls? After a day of hard knocks at work or at school, do you try to use television to "fight back," or to escape?

If you are like most people, you are probably not in the habit of asking yourself questions like these. We may think of our clothing, favorite kinds of music, or preferred forms of recreation as ways to express ourselves or to have fun. But we might think it a little far-fetched to believe that there is any serious meaning in *Late Night with David Letterman*, or that our personalities and values are involved in checking out this spring's new swimsuits.

Although most of us realize that television ads or political commercials are designed to influence us, it may not be clear to us how the regular programming between the advertisements has the same function. A lot of us may feel that we wear our hair in certain styles for aesthetic reasons—because we like it that way. We may not often think that those styles also express certain positions in some important social and political battles. We may feel that we consistently shop at The Gap rather than at Woolworth's only for reasons of taste; we might be surprised to hear that our choice has the potential to turn us into different kinds of people.

This book asks you to think about how everyday actions, objects, and experiences affect you and others. You are probably already familiar with some of the more serious and newsworthy consequences of music, television, or films, such as the association of heavy metal rock music with teenage suicide, or rap musicians who have been arrested on obscenity charges. This book will expand on things you may already be aware of, leading you to see how *all* of popular culture works to influence the public.

The Rhetoric of Everyday Life

There are some well developed theories available for studying how such influence works. These are theories of *rhetoric*, or persuasion. The word *rhetoric* has many meanings, and we will examine more of them in more detail in the next chapter. Many people understand rhetoric to mean the ways in which words influence people. "That's just a lot of rhetoric," we say, and by that we mean that it's just so many empty but persuasive words. In this book, we will work from a different, expanded understanding of what rhetoric means: *the ways in which signs influence people.* (The term *signs* refers to the countless meaningful items, images, and so on that surround us; it will be explained more fully later in this chapter, beginning on page 6.)

In this book we will examine the *rhetorical dimension* of the everyday objects, actions, and events to which we are constantly exposed. We will also see what it means to refer to these everyday objects, actions, and events as *popular culture.* We will learn that many, even most, of the ways in which we are influenced through signs can be observed on this everyday, minute-by-minute level of popular culture. As we go through life experiencing and enjoying music, clothing, architecture, food, and so forth, we are also participating in rhetorical struggles over what kind of society we will live in and what sort of people we will be. This book will empower you to see those struggles as well, so that you will be able to find the rhetoric in rap music, the motivations in heavy metal, and the arguments in argyle socks.

To begin seeing everyday experience as alive with persuasive influences, let us begin by considering *power.* Power is *the ability to control events and meanings.* We are used to thinking that certain people, or groups, or classes of people have power and that others do not. We say that the Du Ponts, Kennedys, Rockefellers, and so forth all have power. Perhaps you have worked in offices or on committees with individuals whom you could clearly identify as powerful. Perhaps there have been other individuals who you thought were relatively lacking in power. Certainly, we might all agree that, compared with adults, children are relatively powerless for several reasons. But did you ever stop to wonder specifically when and where all this empowerment and disempowerment comes about?

Many people believe that, compared to men, women are relatively disempowered in most of Western society: Women earn lower salaries for the same jobs, fewer women have high-ranking jobs and positions of prestige, there are not as many female judges, physicians, police officers, college professors, and so forth. How does this relative empowerment of men and disempowerment of women occur? It is almost as if young males were all taken aside at a certain age and initiated into certain mysteries of dominance; it would seem as if all the men working at certain companies met in secret once a month to plan dastardly deeds of disempowerment against women. But it does not really happen during isolated moments of conspiracy. Instead, the relative disempowerment of women and empowerment of men at the workplace occurs from moment to moment during everyday experiences—in short, in popular culture. For example:

In fashion, where women often have available to them largely uncomfortable shoes and clothing designed to accentuate their bodies rather than to create ease of movement and repose;

Around the water cooler, where the preferred topics of conversation among men are often things like sports or sexual innuendo (and when the boss is a male sports nut, guess which sort of knowledge revealed in conversation is more empowering when it comes to impressing superiors);

And in social expectations, as when a male who leaves work early to pick up a sick child at school is considered responsible and sensitive, whereas a woman who does the same thing is often perceived as compromising her professional "commitment" to her career.

Of course, many women do not take these moments of disempowerment quietly. Women devise strategies of resistance, refusing the disempowerment that everyday experience often offers to them, and seeking alternative means of empowerment. Everyday actions, objects, and experiences are really battlefields, *sites of struggle* among political and social forces. We will talk more about that struggle later in this book.

Other kinds of social and political influence—empowerment and disempowerment—happen in the same way: from one moment to the next, in everyday experiences. A quick exercise will emphasize this point.

Exercise 1.1

This exercise is designed to help you see how some commonly held, even fundamental, notions are born and maintained in your everyday experiences. Pick, from among the following statements, the one that you *agree* with most strongly:

American business is suffering from unfair foreign competition.

In this country, urban problems are mainly racial problems.

It is important to look nice and to smell nice.

Pornography is a serious problem in the United States.

People should keep their houses and yards neat and trim.

Most politicians are dishonest, self-serving, or incompetent.

Now, do some thinking and reflecting on this question: Specifically when and where did you come to have that belief? Another way to ask this question would be, can you remember specific experiences that influenced you to hold that belief? To help you in your thinking, you might want to write down some specific experiences that fall under these categories:

television commercials

magazine or newspaper articles

movies

popular music

television news

television drama or comedy

a radio program

teachers

talking with friends

family discussions

other

The statements above are widely held ideas; they are a sort of "party line" for most people living in the United States today. They seem to be "common sense"—statements that "grease the wheels" of everyday social interaction, allowing it to function smoothly. Perhaps not coincidentally, these statements are also what most people who are in positions of authority or established power would want the public to believe. That is because in general, these statements maintain present arrangements of power and privilege. If it is important to smell nice, then consumers will run out and buy lots of deodorant, perfumed soap, and so on, that will keep the manufacturers of such products wealthy and powerful.

It is equally important to understand that we do not always accept what established and powerful interests want us to believe. We don't always "go with the flow" with those beliefs that seem to be most common or easiest to hold. Which of the above statements do you disagree with? If you do disagree with any of them, do you do so with the distinct feeling that you are in a minority, or bucking the tide of public opinion, in doing so? If so, use the preceding list of commercials, articles, movies, and so forth to identify how you developed your ability to *resist* a popular idea or ideas. In other words, how did you learn to struggle against some widely held ideas?

There may be an opportunity for you to discuss with your class or with friends how you acquired the beliefs that you examined above. If you are like most people, you will realize that most of what you think did not come to you in one big moment of revelation. Instead, many of your ideas were acquired through the influence of lots of transitory, everyday experiences of the kind you listed in doing this exercise.

In this book, we will come to understand the complex network of those experiences as popular culture, and we will study ways to understand the rhetoric that is embodied in popular culture. To understand how culture influences us, we need to develop an understanding of what *popular culture* is—what it is made up of, and how we live in and through it.

The Building Blocks of Culture: Signs

If we are going to think about the ways in which the things and events that we encounter in everyday experience influence us, then we need to start by thinking about how those things and events come to have *meaning*. That is because influence occurs through the management of meaning. If a bigot is persuaded to treat people of all races equally, it is because the meaning of racial difference is changed for that individual. If you are influenced to vote for Senator Smith, it is because the senator (his or her ideas, positions, and so on) has taken on a positive meaning for you. Commercials are rather explicit about the link between influence and meaning: We are urged to attach meanings of glamour and mystery to a certain perfume, for example, in hopes that we will be influenced to buy the perfume.

Let's consider the concept of a *sign* (here we will follow a very sensible scheme proposed by the American philosopher Charles Sanders Peirce). Everything is a sign. That's because a sign is something that induces you to think about *something other than itself*—and everything has that potential.

Take the book you are holding. When you see it, you do not think only about the book itself; you think about the class in which you are enrolled, about the ideas you have been reading, about the attractive person next to you in class, about how much the book cost, and so forth. Now lift your eyes from your book and look around you. For each thing you see, other thoughts associated with that thing will arise: The philodendron in that pot will remind you of the one in your family's home, the picture on the wall will lead you to think of the shopping trip on which you bought it, and so on.

Every sight and sound, every touch, smell, and taste you have, all prompt you to think about things other than, or in addition to, themselves. Therefore, everything is a sign of something else. We might also say that everything is a *signifier*, that everything *signifies* something else, or that everything has *signification*. And signification—or the other thing that is signified—is just another way of referring to *meaning*. If I say the word *professor*, and the thought of that learned individual who is teaching you pops into your head, then that thought is the meaning of the sign, "professor."

If you think about it, signification is a pretty strange fact: We hear words coming out of a friend's mouth and ideas (meanings) start jumping into our heads; we see a cap laying on a table and the sight makes us think of the soccer game we recently wore it to. How does it happen that we see and hear things, and ideas that are not the things themselves pop into our heads? Things act as signs in one or a combination of the three following ways:

Indexically (from the word *index*, referring to indexical meaning)

Iconically (from the word *icon*, referring to iconic meaning)

Symbolically (from the word *symbol*, referring to symbolic meaning)

Indexical Meaning

First, some things get you to think about something else because the "thing" (sign) and the "something else" (meaning) are linked by way of *cause* or *association*. One thing is always or often found with another thing, and so one gets you to think of the other. This kind of meaning is *indexical;* we say that the sign is an *index*, or that it is functioning *indexically*. Smoke is an index of fire; if you see smoke, it causes you to think of fire because you know that one thing is associated with (caused by, in this case), the other. A thermometer is a sign with indexical meaning: A rise in the mercury in the column means a rise in the surrounding environment's temperature. Why? Because the one thing is always associated with the other; in this case, too, the association is causal.

Every character on the television show *Northern Exposure* is an index of every other character because the members of that tight little community are associated with (though in this case, *not* caused by) each other. Some characters are more strongly indexical of certain other characters, however: O'Connell will make you think of Fleischmann more than, say, of Ed, because through various episodes of the show, O'Connell has been associated with Fleischmann more often. The same set of indexical meanings is true of other shows with groups of closely connected characters, such as *Beverly Hills 90210*.

Everyone has played the word association game in which players are supposed to say which words come into their minds upon hearing a cue word. That game can be an interesting indication of indexical meanings. The word *cat* might prompt someone to think *dog*, for instance. Does that mean that the meaning of cat is a dog? In part—indexically—it does. That linkage reveals the fact that one part of the meaning of cats really is their association, as proverbial enemies, with dogs.

Many indexical meanings are widely shared: Is there a red-blooded American, for example, who will not think about basketball upon seeing a picture of Michael Jordan? Other indexical meanings are less widespread, being limited to particular groups of people, and some indexical meanings are even private. *Sand* may induce only veterans of the Persian Gulf War of 1991 to think of Iraq; to everyone else, sand may have the indexical meaning of a day at the beach. For your author, the smell of a cigar is an indexical sign of a grandfather who could sometimes be found with one, a more private meaning (an association) unlikely to be widely shared by others outside his particular family.

Iconic Meaning

If a sign makes you think of something else because the sign *resembles* that thing, then the sign has *iconic* meaning. We would also say that the sign is an *icon*, or that it means *iconically*. The clearest example of an icon is a photograph. You look at the photograph and you think, "Aunt Griselda!" Why? Because the patterns of light and dark on the photographic paper resemble her. Some computer operating systems such as Macintosh or Windows use icons to signify the choices available to the user. Impressionists such as Billy Crystal or many of the actors on the television show *In Living Color* make their living producing icons: The combination of an inflection of the voice, a few gestures, and a stance or a way of walking, prompt the audience to think "H. Ross Perot" or "Bill Clinton," because those signs resemble the voice, gestures, and stances of the original people. Halloween is a great iconic holiday: little children, icons themselves, dress up to resemble Richard Nixon, Freddy Krueger, ghosts, and other horrors. Many words are signs with iconic meaning. Say the words *boom, bang,* and *tinkle* out loud. Part of the meaning of those words is that they resemble (by way of sound) the events to which they refer.

As with indexical meaning, signs may vary in terms of how widely their iconic meaning is shared. Your author once wore a set of nose-and-mustache glasses into class and asked the eighteen-year-old students what those glasses meant. "Halloween parties!" they all replied, giving an indexical meaning (nose glasses are found at, or associated with, Halloween parties). But this indexical meaning broke your author's heart. For him, nose glasses will forever mean Groucho Marx, because they resemble Groucho iconically. Evidently, however, the group of people who share that iconic meaning is dwindling as poor Groucho recedes into late-night television movieland. Iconic meanings can also be private; your picture of Aunt Griselda may cause only you to think of her if nobody else knows her. For others, the iconic meaning of the photo may be something more general, such as "an elderly female," because that is what the photo resembles for them.

Symbolic Meaning

Finally, signs can get you to think about something else purely because of *agreement* or *convention*, because people are in the habit of connecting a particular sign with a particular meaning. When that happens, a sign is a *symbol*, or has *symbolic* meaning, or is functioning *symbolically*. The clearest examples of symbols are words. Why does this mark:

book

mean the thing that you are holding? Only because everyone agrees that it does. People are simply in the habit of thinking of the kind of thing you are holding whenever they see that mark above, and they know that others have agreed to think the same thing. If everyone decided that this mark:

glorpus

would mean the thing you are holding, that would work just as well. Symbolic meaning comes about purely by way of what people agree to do. One way to refer to that agreement is to say that symbolic meaning is *conventional*, a product of certain *conventions*, or agreed-upon rules.

Symbolic meaning is in some ways the most difficult kind of meaning to learn, because it is not natural and because symbolic meanings vary from one group to another. Smoke naturally means fire. The photograph of your aunt naturally refers to her. There is a strong, clear, and necessary connection. Smoke also means fire in Japan, Germany, and Zimbabwe. And once you learn that indexical meaning, it does not change.

But anyone who has struggled through learning a foreign language knows that, as comedian Steve Martin said of the French, "It's like they have a different word for *everything!*" If you want to speak French, you must learn what certain signs mean for the French and assign the same meanings that they do to the words of their language. The rule for understanding symbolic meaning is to consult the group that is using the symbol to discover what the symbol means. For instance, in the inner city of Milwaukee, the expression "fall out" means to faint or to pass out. A suburban Milwaukee resident might not assign that meaning to those signs (words) unless that suburbanite checked with an inner-city resident to see what "fall out" means to him or her. The suburban dweller might assume these words refer to a long drop from a window. A nuclear strategist, on the other hand, might assume that they refer to the radioactive particles produced by a nuclear explosion. And a soldier might assume that they are an order to disperse.

Words are not the only thing with symbolic meaning. The particular pattern of red, white, and blue stars and stripes that you know as the flag of the United States *means* this country, symbolically, because the U.S. Congress has ordained it so, and people everywhere are agreed on this signification. In the U.S. Army, the figure of a golden eagle on the shoulder strap, epaulets, or collar of a uniform means a full colonel, for no other reason than that everyone in the army agrees that this is what it will mean; a figure of the sun, or a tiny Washington monument, would do just as well if everyone agreed to it.

We noted above that smoke has the indexical meaning of fire, but it can also have symbolic meaning. In the past some Native Americans used patterned puffs of smoke to send messages long distances; the people watching the smoke from miles away knew from the pattern what meanings to assign to the smoke. When the Roman Catholic Church is in need of a new pope, the College of Cardinals will meet in closed session to cast their ballots. Those who wait outside the building for news of the election watch a certain chimney. The ballots are burned in such a way that if a new pontiff has been chosen, the smoke is white; if not, the smoke is black. In this way, too, smoke has been assigned symbolic meaning; the meaning of the colors could easily be reversed, or chemicals could be added to make some other colors, as long as everyone understood which color means which outcome.

Symbolic meaning differs from iconic or indexical meaning in that it can easily be altered. Nobody can decide that smoke does not mean fire (indexically). Nobody can decide that a picture of a horse does not cause you to think of a horse (iconically). With both indexical and iconic meaning, once you learn what a sign means, the meaning simply cannot change. You can discover iconic or indexical meaning, and you can forget it, but you cannot legislate it.

But symbolic meaning changes all the time. Thirty years ago, the word *gay* meant happy and carefree. Now it refers to a particular sexual orientation. Thirty years from now it may mean something entirely different. That is the nature of symbolic meaning: You can mess with it. You can change it. And for that reason, symbolic meaning is always slippery. This changeable quality of symbolic signs (principally language), has sometimes been described as the constant "slippage" of the signified (meaning) under the signifier (word). That is, the sign (for example, "gay") holds still while the meaning, or what it signifies, slips around (from happy and carefree to homosexual and perhaps beyond). What something means is never precise, because there is never complete and total agreement among everybody as to what symbols mean. We will see that this "slippage" of symbolic meaning creates great possibilities for influence in popular culture.

Complexity of the Three Kinds of Meaning

We learned earlier that signs mean in one or more of these three ways: indexically, iconically, and symbolically. You may have noticed that we have already demonstrated how words can carry two kinds of meaning: All words are symbolic, and some words are indexical (as seen in the example of the word *smoke*). The point is worth stressing: Most signs do mean in more than one way; in fact, most signs have very rich meanings. Sometimes those meanings are widely shared, sometimes they are shared by a few groups, sometimes they are very personal. But it is a mistake to ask what one thing a sign means, or in which of the three ways it means, because signs are typically very complex in their meaning.

Pull out a dollar bill (if you have one after buying this book). This is a sign that means in all three ways. You will see some icons on it: some markings that resemble George Washington, other markings that look like a pyramid. You will find indexical meaning: You might think of shopping, or of your wallet, or of your next payday, because all those things are associated with the dollar bill. You will certainly find symbolic meanings: The bald eagle clutching arrows and an olive branch in its talons means the United States by convention; moreover, the fact that this piece of paper is worth anything at all is purely conventional and by way of agreement. Congress could pass a law tomorrow saying that pocket hand-kerchiefs will be the unit of economic trade. If that were to happen and if everyone agreed to it, then you could blow your nose on dollar bills but you would slave away at your job for handkerchiefs. The fact that a dollar bill can be exchanged for a couple of candy bars or (at this writing) most of a gallon of gasoline is only a matter of agreement and, therefore, symbolic meaning.

Exercise 1.2

Here is an exercise to help you appreciate how complicated are the meanings of signs. Review the signs listed below, and identify whether each has indexical, iconic, or symbolic meaning. Also, determine whether those meanings are shared widely, by smaller groups, or are relatively private for you or perhaps your family.

Sign	Indexical Meanings (How widely shared?)	Iconic Meanings (How widely shared?)	Symbolic Meanings (How widely shared?)
Pit bull terrier			
Rolex watch			
Skateboard			
Statue of Liberty			
Star of David			

Now, work through some examples that you or your classmates or teacher can suggest. Whenever possible, try to find at least one meaning per category.

Everything in your experience, every object, action, or event, is a sign. But that statement, although correct and important, is so broad that it does not go far enough to help us to understand how the things we experience in everyday life influence us. So we must go on to consider even more specific ways in which signs mean.

The Building Blocks of Culture: Artifacts

In this book, we will not be equally concerned with all signs. Instead, we are going to focus on a subset of signs, known as *cultural artifacts*. An artifact is

1. an action, event, or object perceived as a unified whole,

2. having widely shared meanings, and

3. manifesting group identifications to us.

This definition of an artifact is meant to be rather wide; still, however, not everything is an artifact. Let's look more closely at that definition; it will take us a little while to go through it carefully and unpack its meaning.

An Action, Event, or Object
Perceived as a Unified Whole

You may have heard the word *artifact* associated with an actual object, something you could hold in your hand. An archaeologist who digs up a pot might claim to have found an artifact of Minoan culture, for instance. That idea of an artifact as something that represents a culture will become important when we discuss the third clause of the definition ("manifesting group identifications to us") later. But in this first clause of the definition, notice that by artifact, we mean not only a material object that is tangible, but also an *event* or *action* that is perceived as a unified whole; in this sense, events and actions, occurring in the material world, are also material. Air Jordan tennis shoes are artifacts and they are concrete, physical objects. But slam dunks, stealing first base, the latest popular dance, and the Fourth of July are also artifacts.

It is also important in that first clause to notice that the artifact must be some action, event, or object that is *perceived as a unified whole*. In other words, perceptions of a whole "thing" or "happening" that has some identity or character in itself make an artifact. The bottom stripe on the United States flag is not an artifact because, although you can perceive it all by itself if you make the effort, it is not usually seen as a thing in itself, with its own separate meaning. Neither is the field of stars in the flag's upper left-hand corner. Rather, the whole flag is perceived as a unity, and that makes the flag itself an artifact.

This first clause in the definition of an artifact is based upon an old, but still controversial, idea that the reality in which humans live and move is one that is fundamentally socially created. The idea here is that people live in a world of perceptions. For instance, the French have more words for different kinds of bread and pastries than do most Americans. Bread is more important to them, and they appreciate subtle differences in size and texture of loaves. That means that they perceive differences in bread that Americans might not ("It's all baguettes to me!"). That does not mean that we cannot learn to see all those distinctions ourselves (in fact, American tourists must learn to recognize more kinds of bread so that they can order lunch more accurately). On the other hand, people living in the United States today have many different words for vehicles: Fords, Chevys, 4 by 4s, Rangers, Aerostars, RVs, Voyagers, and on and on. People in a part of the world that does not have so many vehicles may not need to perceive so many different kinds, and so may think of all vehicles as being pretty much the same thing.

We see certain things and not others because of the social contexts that we grew up in; the people around us have called our attention to certain things but not others. People organize the world in ways that fit the physical and social environment they are in. That means that perceptions are adaptive mechanisms to help us adjust to the situations in which we live. If you live next door to a snarling Doberman pinscher, your perception of the dog as dangerous is an adaptive mechanism that causes you to avoid the animal and thus live another day.

Furthermore, groups of people that live and work together try to adapt to their shared situations; thus, perceptions are also socially grounded. And so we grow up organizing the world, perceiving the world, in the ways that our social context encourages us to. For example, an important part of most Americans' situations is the need to recognize different kinds of vehicles. In addition, most Americans have the same, shared need to adapt to an environment in which vehicles are prominent. Football fans can see a bunch of people running around on a field and identify all kinds of things going on: an option play, the pass rush, and so forth. These fans have a recreational need to perceive lots of different plays, and they talk about the plays among themselves, encouraging each other to perceive the plays similarly. People who are not fans do not perceive the world of a football game in the same way because they do not need or want to; for them, a football game may look like just a bunch of people running around on a field.

. . . Having Widely Shared Meanings

To become an artifact, a sign must be more than just a perceived, unified whole. The second clause of the definition tells us that an artifact is a sign that has become charged with widely shared meaning, just like a battery that has been charged with energy.

Take the expression, "Where's the beef?" That question has an ordinary, straightforward meaning. It asks where the beef is. But in the early 1980s, it was the theme of a popular series of commercials for a fast food restaurant. In the commercial, three elderly women were examining the burger of a competitor, and one of them, Clara Peller, kept forcefully demanding to know, "Where's the beef?" Walter Mondale, the Democratic presidential nominee in 1984, picked that up as a theme in his battle for the nomination against challenger Gary Hart, implying that Hart was all style and no substance. Pretty soon, everyone was repeating the phrase with delight and applying it to all sorts of circumstances, fueled by advertisements for both the fast food restaurant and Walter Mondale.

What happened was that three words, a simple English sentence, had become charged with widely shared, additional meanings. They meant something beyond the ordinary meaning derived from just combining those words. The phrase "Where's the beef" has a definite *symbolic* meaning, stemming from the conventions of the English language. But it picked up complicated indexical meanings when it became associated with a cute television commercial, an endearing granny, Walter Mondale, and Gary Hart. Eventually, the phrase picked up iconic meanings as well, as ordinary people and television comedians went about imitating Clara Peller's exasperated query.

In another example, Michael Jackson has always meant something to his friends and family, just as you do. But you are not a cultural artifact because you are not charged with the extra meanings that Jackson has picked up as a popular music star, tabloid fodder, and notable eccentric. So one necessary condition for an ordinary sign's becoming an artifact is that it becomes charged with more meanings than it had before, and with more meanings that are widely shared.

Now, it is possible that the "Where's the beef?" example reads like ancient history to some of you. That's because this expression has by now lost its status as cultural artifact. The phrase had been out of fashion for a while by the time many of you were ready to quit watching Captain Kangaroo, and by now, nobody but scholars and trivia buffs remembers it. Of course, that three-word phrase still means something, symbolically; it asks where the beef is. But it does not have that unity as a whole and particular thing, nor the widely shared meanings, that once made it a cultural artifact.

The "Where's the beef?" example demonstrates that there is a *threshold* at which objects, events, or actions become artifacts. Furthermore, that threshold can be crossed in either direction; in other words, things, actions, and events are often in the process of either becoming, or declining as, cultural artifacts. Because perceptions change, the artifactual status of any sign must be changeable as well.

In contrast to beef, think about yellow ribbons. Before the 1970s, they had no special unity, no particular meaning in themselves beyond just being yellow ribbons. An early 1970s song by the group Tony Orlando and Dawn proposed the idea of tying a yellow ribbon around a tree to indicate to someone who has been long gone that they are still wanted back. Although the song was popular and catchy, the song itself was more of a perceptual unity, more of a cultural artifact, than was the idea of a yellow ribbon.

But when sixty-three Americans were taken hostage at the United States Embassy in Tehran, Iran, in 1979, yellow ribbons came to be used as a gesture of remembrance by the American public. They began to appear everywhere, with the specific meaning of (1) a demonstration of solidarity with those who were absent (the hostages), and (2) a desire to have them back. Since then, foreign political crises involving absent or missing Americans have repeatedly been accompanied by widespread, spontaneous sproutings of yellow ribbons around trees, lampposts, and traffic signs. They have crossed the threshold into the realm of cultural artifacts, and they are being maintained in that status by continuing social customs that encourage people to perceive them as artifacts—as things that have special meanings, as unified whole entities.

One consequence of becoming charged with widely shared meanings is that artifacts can be very complex; sometimes an artifact might even be composed of other artifacts. The Beatles were (in fact, still are) a cultural artifact as a group, but John Lennon, Paul McCartney, George Harrison, and Ringo Starr are cultural artifacts each in their own right (John Lennon, in fact, remains one even after his death). The same has been true of the New York Yankees during several periods of their history. The television show *Murphy Brown* is so popular that it is an artifact, but so are some of its more visible characters, such as the title character, who is played by actress Candice Bergen. Complex artifacts are charged with meaning, and if they comprise artifacts then those constituent artifacts are also charged with meaning. This creates some very elaborate webs of meaning, and thus of influence.

. . . *Manifesting Group Identifications to Us*

The third and final clause in the definition of a cultural artifact identifies all artifacts as *signs of group identifications*. We have noticed that the charged meanings of an artifact must be widely shared; let us turn now to a consideration of how the shared nature of an artifact's meanings relates to group identifications. Here we will learn that *artifacts are the material signs of abstract groups*.

Part of the meaning of an artifact is its connection with a group. All of us belong to many groups. Some of those groups are ethnic or racial: You might identify yourself as Italian-American, African-American, Polish-American, or Southern white, for example. Some of those groups are geographical: you are an American, a Kansan, a Brooklynite, a resident of your neighborhood. Some groups are social: You might be a member of the Vice Lords gang, of a bridge club, of a tennis team. Some groups are religious: You might be Catholic, Methodist, Rastafarian. Some groups are economic: You might be wealthy, middle class, working class. Males and females are two large group identifications. Identifications sometimes have emotional or aesthetic bases: Allegiances to particular sports teams or to clothing or product brands or designers are very often the grounding for group identifications, as with "Packer backers" or those who only buy Calvin Klein jeans.

All of us, in other words, have many different group identifications. But in fact, we very rarely see those groups in total. If you are a member of a local motorcycle club, you might very well see the whole group together at one time on occasion. But most of our other group or social "memberships" are much larger or more abstract.

Perhaps you think of yourself as a Quaker; but how, where, and when are you ever in touch with *The Quakers?* You see particular other Quakers, but never all of them, and never at once. Perhaps you think of yourself as an African American, and identify with other African Americans; but when and where does that identification occur? Another way to put this question would be, when does the "group" of African Americans touch you? When does it speak to you? How are you reminded of what to do, how to act, and what to believe, so as to identify with that group? Many of us identify ourselves as "American"—a very broad identification—but how does that identification occur? Are you being American as you sit here reading? If you stop for coffee? When does that group, "American," speak to you?

Large or abstract groups of people (and nearly all of the groups with which we identify are large and abstract) connect with us, and influence us, through cultural artifacts. There are objects, actions, and events that manifest those groups to us, that make the groups real, particular, and material. Artifacts represent groups to us, they show us what it is like to be part of or to identify with those groups, or they remind us of those groups and of what we are committed to by our identification with them. Artifacts are charged with meaning, but many of those meanings bespeak (that is, speak of or speak for) our identifications with groups. You need not be a member of a given group to understand an artifact that manifests that group identification, but it helps. That is to say, being a member of the group allows you to appreciate more of the meanings, and to understand the ways in which the artifact is standing in for the group as a whole. In that way, a cultural artifact is a sort of an "in joke." Others may understand something of what it means, but it is really the people "in the know," those who identify with the group (or groups) for which the artifact speaks, who find the richest meanings in an artifact.

Artifacts span the continuum from those that are quite obviously associated with a specific group identification to those that do not so clearly bespeak a group. Often, you may see more clearly how an artifact manifests a group identification if you are not part of that group (although then, paradoxically, you probably will not fully understand the meanings that the artifact conveys).

For instance, think about the form that cable television takes in the United States: a widely available opportunity to choose among dozens and dozens of channels, many of them with very narrow, specific purposes. Now, this artifact is part of being in that very large and abstract group, "American." Because so many of the readers of this book are part of that group, because we so rarely step outside of it or confront in any meaningful way the people who do not identify with that group, the artifacts that bespeak "being American" to us may seem natural, universal, or even invisible. Those artifacts may simply seem the only way to be. We do not notice how they create a group for us. It may take going to another country, with different patterns of television broadcast and consumption, to see American cable TV as not universal but a particular way of doing things, as our "American" way of doing things, as our sort of entertainment in-joke. Seeing alternatives to such a distinctive cultural artifact helps us to realize that cable TV is peculiarly American.

Americans are defined in many ways, and we have many points of identification with being "American," but one of them is that we are the people with ready access to that kind of cable TV. What is useful about recognizing the ways in which cultural artifacts manifest groups to us is that we can then begin understanding the meanings of the artifact, and at that point we begin to understand our groups as well. To pursue the present example a bit further, think about what all those cable choices mean, especially in terms of what it means to be an American. We can tell from what cable TV means that being American has something to do with an abundance of choices. You might consider other distinctly American experiences that display the same embarrassment of riches (such as large restaurant menus or giant supermarkets)—the availability of more choices than anyone can possibly use.

Cable TV is one of those artifacts not obviously connected to a group, yet, as we have seen, it does manifest the group identification of being "American" to us. Consider a narrower example. I once went into a small town delicatessen in a Pennsylvania Dutch county and asked for a pound of the salami that was displayed in the case. The woman behind the counter was dressed (as were all the other clerks) in the traditional long dress and hooded bonnet that the Mennonite or Amish women wear in that part of the country. She looked at me with dark suspicion: "What are you calling *salami?*" she asked. It turns out that all hard sausage there is called "bologna." What I wanted was "Lebanon bologna" (made

near Lebanon, Pennsylvania). For this store clerk, "Lebanon bologna" is an artifact that is a material sign of her group identifications, but manifests that group
so strongly and so often that she has ceased to think of that sausage as in any way
special to her group. Lebanon bologna now seems natural and universal to her.
Now, it's flatlanders like me who ask for artifacts that bespeak *our* group identifications, artifacts such as "salami."

Certain artifacts very clearly are the material signs of group identifications;
they manifest specific groups to all sorts of other people. Take African-American
hairstyles, for instance. As of 1993, certain styles are very popular among that
group. Some involve designs shaved out of the hair on the scalp or cutting the
hair into distinct shapes. And of course, elaborately braided hair, called cornrows,
has been popular for some time. Plenty of people who are not black imitate such
styles to an extent, but the artifacts of these hair styles are firmly and unchange-
ably African-American. They are styles grounded in the African heritage: African people have been using them for centuries. They are worn mainly by black
people. They are even best suited physically to the characteristics of African hair.

Let's summarize what we have covered so far. We have seen that everything
is a sign, but that not every sign is a cultural artifact. We have defined an artifact
as

1. an action, event, or object perceived as a unified whole,

2. having widely shared meanings, and

3. manifesting group identifications to us.

In elaborating on this definition, we discovered some important characteristics of
artifacts:

1. Artifacts are a socially created reality.

2. Signs become artifacts as they become charged with meaning, thus crossing a
   threshold into artifact status.

3. An artifact can be very complex, even being made up of other artifacts.

4. Artifacts are the material signs of group identifications.

Now, let's do an exercise designed to familiarize you with the concept of an
artifact. Do this exercise on your own, or according to the directions of your
instructor.

Exercise 1.3

Identify yourself as a member of at least two broad social groups [for example, Hispanic
and a union member, American Southerner and VFW (Veterans of Foreign Wars) member,
male and United Methodist]. For each group, identify

a. An artifact that "belongs" only to each of these two groups, that only members of
the group are likely to see as charged with meanings. Identify some of those meanings.
(Example: Only college professors are likely to know about and use the term *curriculum
vitae*. Ask your instructor about it.)

b. An artifact that is closely identified with each group, but one that persons outside the group know about, use, and appreciate. Identify differences in what the artifact means for those inside the group and for the public at large. (Example: What does "Mexican food" mean, for members of that ethnic group as well as for the general public? Does what is considered "Mexican food" differ between Mexicans or Mexican-Americans and the public at large?)

Definitions of Culture

In learning about signs and artifacts, we are studying the building blocks of culture. Now we need to turn to the term *culture* itself, to understand what that means. Throughout history, *culture* has been a central concept with a number of definitions. As the scholar Raymond Williams put it, "*Culture* is one of the two or three most complicated words in the English language" (1976, 76).

Elitist Meanings of Culture

Perhaps the most widely known definition of culture has an elitist flavor to it: Culture is the very best, the finest and most refined experiences, that a society or nation has to offer. This sense is found in the *Oxford English Dictionary* definition of culture, as "the training, development, and refinement of mind, tastes, and manners; the condition of being thus trained and refined; the intellectual side of civilization." This definition of culture underlies Moe's recurring complaint to Larry and Curly on *The Three Stooges:* "Mind your manners! Ain't ya got no culture? What would Emily Post say?" This idea of culture is often referred to as *high culture.*

This first, elitist sense of culture sees relatively few artifacts as making up culture. Only those objects or events having meanings associated with the very best, with high intellectual, aesthetic, or spiritual achievement, would be considered cultural artifacts under this definition. By exposing ourselves to them, we "become cultured." Those who are not exposed to those artifacts are not cultured, in this view. Some familiar artifacts that would be subsumed under this sense of culture would include the ballet, the symphony orchestra, public television, music by Bach or Beethoven, paintings by Rembrandt and Van Gogh, sculpture by Michelangelo and Rodin. Some objects or events that would certainly not be considered cultural artifacts by this first definition would include heavy metal rock, polka bands, *Bowling for Dollars, Wrestlemania,* Billy Ray Cyrus, and corn dogs.

Often, those who talk about culture with this first definition in mind have what might be called an edifying impulse. In other words, they hope to improve people (which is not necessarily a bad thing) by exposing the public to the right artifacts. For these people, there is a sense that if you listen to Brahms rather than Pearl Jam, if you see Shakespeare plays rather than *America's Funniest Home Videos,* if you eat gourmet cuisine rather than *Ho-Ho's,* you will be a better person for it (and, by extension, our country will be a better place as well). This edifying impulse has been around for centuries, and can be found in nearly every instruction from parents or teachers to do certain things because they are good for you. The edifying impulse is not necessarily limited to conservatives or those in power, either. It can also be found among certain Marxist scholars; for example, theorists such as Theodor Adorno and Herbert Marcuse (who were part of the so-called Frankfurt School around the middle of this century) thought that the pleasures to which the masses of ordinary people were addicted (things like television, pro football, or church bingo nights for us) were contributing to the oppression of those people (Adorno 1973; Modleski 1986, ix; Mukerji and Schudson 1986, 56).

On the other hand, there have been radical twists on this first definition of culture. Some people have argued that it is the radical or subversive elements of culture to which people should be exposed. This effort to "turn the Frankfurt School on its head" involves identifying experimental or alternative forms and experiences—such as guerilla theatre, alternative rock or folk music, performance theatre, and so forth—as the kinds of cultural artifacts that will liberate the common people so as "to achieve dignity and to make life full" (Buhle 1987, xx). The particular artifacts identified by this school of thought as desirable, as the right things to do or hear or see, are very different from those included in the concept of high culture. But the edifying impulse is the same. In both of these versions of what culture is, the focus is on a very limited set of artifacts, such as the objects and experiences of art, that deserve to be called culture. In its new *Supplement*, for instance, the *Oxford English Dictionary* updated its old definition of culture to emphasize "the civilization, customs, artistic achievements, etc. of a people especially at a certain stage of its development."

Exercise 1.4

Consider the following questions for individual thought or group discussion.

1. If paintings, opera, poetry readings, and so forth are the products of high culture, what is everything else? Have you heard any particular terms (such as *low culture* or *mass culture*) used to refer to everything else?
2. What kind of power is created by calling certain things high culture? Who gets to wield that power?
3. Has anyone ever tried to "improve" you by referring to the idea of culture? Think about the specific ways in which that happened.

Popular Meanings of Culture

There is a second meaning of culture that is also fairly widespread, although perhaps not as well known as the first. Raymond Williams explains that in this second meaning, " 'Culture' . . . was the growth and tending of crops and animals, and by extension the growth and tending of human faculties" (1977, 11). In other words, culture is that which sustains and nourishes those who live and move within it. We see one aspect of this meaning of culture in biological science: The *culture* within a Petri dish is what allows microorganisms to grow and multiply. It feeds them and supports them; it is by consuming the culture, by living in that culture, that the microorganisms grow.

What would this sense of culture mean for *people?* We must remember that people do not live by bread alone; unlike microorganisms, we require more than simply physical nourishment to support us. We need to be able to talk to people, to entertain and be entertained, to enjoy all kinds of diversions and distractions, to work at something we find meaningful, to meet together with other people. In short, for us culture is our "whole way of life" (Williams 1977, 17). Williams defines culture as "a very active world of everyday conversation and exchange. Jokes, idioms, characteristic forms not just of everyday dress but occasional dress, people consciously having a party, making a do, marking an occasion" (Heath and Skirrow 1986, 5). Does Williams's definition sound familiar? It should; he is really talking about the artifacts to which we are exposed.

We must be careful in how we understand the relationship between artifacts and culture, however. If you took a random collection of artifacts from all around the world and piled them in a building, you would not have a culture within the building. When Williams defines cultures as "whole ways of life," he is implying a kind of connectedness among artifacts, rather than simply a motley collection of many different artifacts. What turns a group of *artifacts* into a *culture* is that they are *systemically* related: They make up a *system* of artifacts anchored in group identifications.

Individuals identify with other people and see themselves as parts of groups, as we have already noted. Sometimes those groups are very small and completely present to the individual. More often, however, the groups are large and abstract, extending over wide geographical areas and broad reaches of time. Culture is the integrated set or system of artifacts that is linked to a group. The linkage between artifacts and a group occurs because the artifacts are how the group is manifested to its members. The artifacts are systematically linked to each other as they are linked to culture.

Culture is the system of material manifestations of our group identifications (remember that artifacts are actions and events as well as objects, and that what people do is just as material as are the objects that people can touch or see). Part of the culture of your local motorcycle club is the mangy mutt that is your mascot. Part of the culture of being Norwegian is eating *lefse* and *lutefisk*. But the club mascot is also part of a *system* of artifacts that includes your club insignia, the meeting place, certain eccentric characters who are members, the kind of motorcycles you have, your rituals and practices, and so forth. That system of artifacts, all of which are interrelated through their link to the group of the motorcycle club, is the club's culture. Similarly, *lutefisk* and *lefse* are part of a system of many other things that bespeak being Norwegian.

Exercise 1.5

This exercise is designed to help clarify the idea of culture as a system of artifacts linked to group identifications. When you read the words *sauerbraten* or *Tannenbaum*, what comes to mind? Germany, of course. Not only that group identification, however, but other artifacts that make up the interrelated (and vast) system of German culture: schnitzel, beer, lederhosen, Berlin, Munich, and so forth. To think further about culture as systems of artifacts, sort the following group of terms into what you consider the appropriate cultures:

grits   corned beef and cabbage   shillelagh   Robert E. Lee   Guinness stout catfish   leprechauns   rebel yells   the IRA   the KKK   the Mississippi the Blarney Stone   stars and bars   peat moss   Spanish moss   antebellum mansions   Catholics versus Protestants

Most likely, you had no trouble discerning that certain artifacts in this list were part of the system of Irish culture, and the rest were part of the system of Southern (United States) culture.

Popular culture refers to those systems or artifacts that most people share and that most people know about. For those who identify with playing for a symphony orchestra, there is an interrelated system of artifacts made up of rehearsals, performances, instruments, and so forth. But that culture is not popular culture because most people neither identify with symphony orchestras nor know about their systems of artifacts. But television is an immensely rich world of popular culture, as nearly everyone watches television and, even if not everyone sees the same shows, they are likely to know in general about the shows that they do not see. In speaking of popular culture, then, we are concerned with things, like television, that are part of the everyday experience of most people.

We need to refine our exploration of *meaning* now to realize that few meanings are truly individual. Instead, meaning usually comes from a cultural context. What a given sign means, especially as an artifact, is determined in large part by the system of signs (the culture, the system of artifacts) in which it is placed. For instance, what a candle means is largely shaped by the system or cultural context in which you find it. It means one thing within the system of signs that make up a movie about a haunted house, where it might flicker and then go out in the night. It means something else within the cultural system of a given religion, as a votive candle or an altar candle, for instance. And it means something else within the system of a dinner for two people in courtship, as it casts a low, warm light over the proceedings. In sum, to understand what a sign means *as an artifact,* we must consider that sign within the context of the *system* of artifacts in which it appears.

Characteristics of Cultures

The idea of a culture as an integrated system of artifacts needs further development and explanation. Let us explore three important characteristics of cultures:

1. Cultures are highly complex and overlapping.
2. Cultures entail consciousness, or ideologies.
3. Cultures are experienced through texts.

Cultures Are Highly Complex
and Overlapping

When we say that cultures are highly complex, we mean two things. First, there are a great many things that go into making up the system of artifacts that is a culture. Remember that cultures can be very broad (American) or very small (this particular monastery), but even the small ones will be made up of quite a few interrelated artifacts: the food, clothing styles, ways of walking and sitting, architecture, forms of entertainment, sayings and expressions, moral and ethical norms, religious practices, and other artifacts that are the material manifestations of the group. So when we think about cultures, we are thinking about many different artifacts that are still related to each other through being part of a system.

There is a second, more interesting way of thinking about the complexity and overlapping nature of cultures. Ordinary language usage sometimes causes us to think that we belong to only one culture. But that is not the case; we identify with many different groups through the many different cultures that nurture and support us. We can approach this second point by returning to Williams's definition of a culture as "a whole way of life." This definition is actually problematic; there really isn't a single, whole way of life for most of us today. To understand why, let's take a brief detour through history.

It probably used to be the case, many centuries ago, that any given person lived within one large, overarching culture. Such a culture may have been complex, but it was not multiple. If you had lived in Britain during the Dark Ages, for instance (say around 900 C.E.), everything around you, everything you encountered during the day, probably everything you even knew about, was part of the same system, the same group identification, and thus the same culture. You saw and spoke only to others of your own group. Different aspects of life, such as work, religion, or government, were all closely interrelated; they all manifested the same overarching culture to you. This kind of social situation may still be found in some tribal cultures around the world, where people are primarily enveloped in a small, single group of people and surrounded by the artifacts that represent that single group. Perhaps the clearest modern version of this kind of immersion in a culture would be a cloistered monastery or convent, in which the members encounter, almost exclusively, the experiences having to do with just their own, single culture.

But clearly, few of us live in such an extremely monocultural situation today. Communication and transportation have become much easier and more common, especially over long distances. We are therefore exposed to a bewildering variety of messages and signs, often originating materially in other cultures. People of many different backgrounds live with or near each other. We may now belong to a number of groups, rather than one large, overarching group that surrounds us. For instance, you can become deeply involved with computer networks, electronic "bulletin boards" that are spread out all across the country or even the world. Such a group need not have anything to do with the company you work for, which may have very little connection with where you go for recreation, which may have little to do with your ethnic or cultural identification, and so forth. In short, because there are many different groups with which you identify, you belong simultaneously to many different cultures. Because of this abundance of group identifications, many people today feel that their lives are fragmented. Some social observers have called this fragmentation the *postmodern condition*.

To return to Williams's definition, for nearly all of us in today's postmodern world, there simply are not any "whole ways of life" in which we immerse ourselves exclusively. We stand within a complex structure of ways of life, identifying with many different groups that may have very little in common with each other. This is especially likely to be true for people who travel a great deal, who associate with many different kinds of people, and who hold a variety of jobs. A person who lives in the same largely Hispanic neighborhood, attends a local, largely Hispanic Roman Catholic church, works in a local bodega, and hangs out at the nearby community center, is much closer to living within a single, overarching culture than is the person who moves out of that neighborhood, works downtown, watches French and German films, eats in Thai and African restaurants, and becomes a Buddhist. It would be a mistake to say that everyone today is one way or another; but increasing numbers of people are likely to be like the second person in this example. At any rate, the more you are like that second person—the more you move around, the more you vary your experience and your environment—the more different cultures you will find identifications with. That variety is, increasingly, the condition of most people's lives today.

It is also important to understand that our identifications with different cultures is one important source of *contradictions* in terms of what artifacts mean. For instance, if your business requires you to go into work on Sunday while your religion requires you to attend Mass, you will be torn in two directions. What it means to skip Mass will mean one thing to your business and another thing to your religion. Thus, our location in different cultures creates contradictions in what a given sign or artifact means.

Exercise 1.6

To understand where you fit into a network of cultures, you might take an inventory of yourself. If you really want to understand how cultural artifacts affect people, you need to understand what your own cultural artifacts are and how they are shaping you. On a sheet of paper, construct the chart below, leaving plenty of space to write in.

GROUPS	ARTIFACTS		
	Typical Events	Typical Objects	Other Typical Artifacts
Group 1:			
Group 2:			
Group 3:			
Group 4:			

Now, start thinking about some of the groups with which you identify the most—in other words, the cultures to which you belong. If you are like most people, there will probably be more than one. Fill in your names for these groups on the lines in the "Groups" column, and for each group, identify some of the artifacts that most clearly manifest that group for you. For example, if Group 1 for you is Native American, which typical events most clearly make that group real and material for you? Which typical objects? Which other typical artifacts? Make similar lists for several other groups of which you are a part.

Now go back and compare the groups of artifacts within each column. Do the typical events of Group 1 relate to the typical objects of Group 2 in any way? Are the events of Groups 3 and 4 connected with each other in any way? Do you find any examples of the same artifact meaning very different things as defined by different groups? In other words, do you find contradictions? To the extent that you find a lack of connectedness, your cultures are complex, fragmented, and overlapping. Later in this book, we will consider what that complexity, fragmentation, and overlap mean in terms of how power is shared and how social and political struggles are managed today.

Cultures Entail Consciousness, or Ideologies

The second important characteristic of culture is that *cultures entail consciousness, or ideologies*. Let's start with the second of these terms, *ideology*, which has traditionally been associated more closely with culture.

Ideology is a widely used term today. There are so many different uses for it that you should expect to find little agreement among scholars as to what it means. For some thinkers, such as Karl Marx, ideology referred to a false set of beliefs and perceptions that the ruling classes attempted to impose upon lower classes in an attempt to make those in lower classes cooperate in perpetuating the power of the rulers. This meaning of the term is explained in one definition given by Raymond Williams, "a system of illusory beliefs—false ideas or false consciousness—which can be contrasted with true scientific knowledge" (1977, 55). Marx's idea was to get rid of false ideas, of ideology, so that people could see things the way they really are. Then, he thought, oppressed people would see the flimsy premises upon which ruling classes built their power, and would rise up and overthrow them. For instance, if the "divine right of kings" could be revealed to be a lot of ideological humbug, then people who had been bowing to kings for centuries could be enabled to see that in reality all people are equal, and they would overthrow their kingly rulers.

That view of ideology as a system of false ideas that hide reality is still held by some, but increasingly the term has come to mean something else. Williams also gives two other definitions of the term that are now more widely used: (1) "a system of beliefs characteristic of a particular class or group," and (2) "the general process of the production of meanings and ideas" (1977, 55); furthermore, Williams suggests that these two definitions can be combined. This more recent notion of ideology is more consistent with the understanding of culture and artifacts that we have been developing here. To distinguish these senses of ideology from the older sense of false ideas, it may be more useful to think instead of the term *consciousness*, which is more clearly implied by Williams's last two definitions. To grasp what consciousness (or ideology) should mean, we need to integrate several of the ideas that we have covered so far.

First, recall that people live in a world of artifacts that are accessible only by *perceptions.* That means that people might change their perceptions, or trade some perceptions for others, but it is not possible to do away with perceptions to discover some bedrock reality underneath. To think that kings rule by divine right is one perception; to think that they do not is another. There are legitimate social and political reasons to prefer one perception over another, but because human beings can only be aware of that which we perceive, it is impossible to identify one set of perceptions as "natural" or "simply the way things are."

Second, recall that all signs are meaningful, and that artifacts in particular are signs that are charged with meaning. Third, recall that the meaning of an artifact is significantly determined by its link to groups. Finally, recall that culture is a system, or interrelated group, of artifacts. *An ideology or consciousness is an interrelated system of meanings that are generated by the system of artifacts that comprise a culture.*

To return to Williams's definitions of ideology, consciousness is a *system:* The beliefs that make up consciousness (or ideology) relate to each other; they are part of an interrelated set. Consciousness, or ideology, is a system of beliefs— not the way things "really, truly are," but what people *perceive* to be true. Consciousness is the production of meanings (through artifacts) that are "characteristic of a particular class or group." It is the system of meanings linked to a system of artifacts that is a culture.

This last idea needs some further explanation. It points to the fact that cultures, or systems of artifacts, are the locations of meanings (beliefs, values, ideas, perceptions). A sign becomes an artifact as it becomes charged with particular meanings that belong to a system. That meaning relates to the meanings of other artifacts in the cultural system; the whole group or system of those meanings is consciousness or ideology. Let's take a cross as an example. This simple sign made up of two sticks becomes charged with meanings of one sort when it is considered as a Christian artifact, or when one places it or thinks about it within that system of artifacts. The cross has one set of meanings when considered in the context of baptism, grace, communion, Christ's crucifixion, and so forth.

The cross takes on a different set of charged meanings for fans of vampire movies, although those meanings are certainly related to the meanings derived from Christianity. This smaller and less cohesive group is nevertheless a system, for the cross relates to the undead, to magical protection, to Count Dracula, and so forth. Finally, consider the meanings that the cross takes on within the system of fashion accessories. Here the sign becomes an artifact as it is linked to earrings or necklace pendants; meanings having to do with design or material (gold or cast iron, slim or stubby) become more important than they do in religious usage. It is realistic to say that the cross is perceived very differently—that, in fact, it becomes a different artifact—for the different groups that use it within their system of artifacts (Christians, vampire movie fans, fashion-conscious people). We will examine in later chapters how the meaning of an artifact can become quite complex as it shuttles back and forth among these cultural systems. But for now, it is important to understand that artifacts, such as the cross, mean what they mean according to their placement in a system of artifacts, a culture, that is the manifestation of a group.

But those meanings are also often contradictory. We noted previously that contradictions in the meaning of artifacts arise as a result of our identification with different cultures, different groups. We noted how the different meanings read into a sign by different cultures will cause contradictions in what that sign means. But even within single cultures, contradictory meanings arise. When we say that meanings of artifacts arise from groups, we are not saying that those meanings are always simple and straightforward. For instance, the Reverend Martin Luther King, Jr., is surely an American cultural artifact. But within that "American" cultural system, he means several things, some of them contradictory. He stands for racial harmony and understanding, but also for a turbulent and violent period of our nation's history. For white Americans, he is a promise that they can get along with blacks as well as a reminder of what whites have done to prevent such getting along. For African Americans, he is a moral exemplar of nonviolent civil disobedience, as well as a reminder—through his own violent death—of the frustrations that may make violence seem justifiable. Many cultural artifacts are contradictory in similar ways.

Consciousness or ideology is the sum of meanings, or the system of meanings, that is most obvious or most strongly implied by a system of artifacts. We often refer to such meanings as *preferred meanings*. These are simply the most popular, or the easiest, meanings to attach to signs. There is a Christian consciousness that is the sum of what the artifacts of Christianity mean. The meaning of baptism is linked to the meaning of grace, which is linked to the meaning of communion, and so on. To become a Christian is to enter into that system of meanings, to know them, to see their relationships. That is not to say that Christianity has no contradictions, nor that every Christian embraces the Christian consciousness wholly and completely. But it does mean that there are preferred meanings that make up the Christian consciousness. Since the meanings of many of the artifacts comprising a culture are contradictory, consciousness or ideology also contains the seeds of potential contradiction and instability.

In an earlier exercise, you were asked to identify some group that you are a part of, and to name some artifacts that materially manifest that group to you. Take a second look at that list of artifacts. Can you identify a consciousness that "fits" with a group that you are part of, a set of meanings that you use to make sense of the world, a set that would probably be different if you were part of another group?

We will see in Chapter 3 that people do not necessarily accept the consciousness of a culture to which they belong totally and uncritically. In fact, several factors that we will examine (such as contradiction) make it necessary for people to struggle over what artifacts mean, to pit the meanings of one cultural identification against another. For now, however, keep in mind that whether one accepts it wholeheartedly or not, there *is* a consciousness, or an ideology, implied for most people by the artifacts of a given culture.

Cultures Are Experienced through Texts

The third characteristic of cultures that we need to understand is that they are experienced through texts. We have learned that we hardly ever experience the whole of the groups with which we identify, and that cultural artifacts are the material manifestations of those large, abstract groups. Similarly, we rarely experience the entirety of a culture. While there is a set of artifacts that makes the large and abstract group of Polish Americans materially present for individuals within that group, the individual Polish-American person still is unlikely to experience that entire set of artifacts, and certainly never at once. Instead, we experience smaller, interrelated sets of signs and artifacts. It will be useful for us to call those sets *texts*.

The term *text* is important to the study of the rhetoric of popular culture. It is probably most familiar to you as a set of words, in the sense of a linguistic text; and in fact, very many cultural texts are linguistic, since words and expressions can also be cultural artifacts. So this textbook is a text. A newspaper article or editorial is a text. A letter is a text. We speak of the text of a poem, or of a novel.

But as we have seen, words are not the only signs, the only entities with meaning. Things other than or in addition to words can be texts as well. *A text is a set of signs related to each other insofar as their meanings all contribute to the same set of effects or functions.* All the words and parts of this book make a set, because they work together to produce certain effects in you at this moment. But a baseball game is a text, too, because all the signs you see within the game work together to produce several effects: relaxation, exhilaration, allegiance to a team, and so forth. On the other hand, a group comprising your wristwatch, the potted palm on my desk, and Axl Rose in all likelihood is not a text, because (unless something very strange is going on) their meanings are not contributing to the same effects or functions.

A text is usually a set or group of signs, as noted above, but that group can be large or small. To the extent that a single artifact is complex, comprising several signs within itself that all contribute to the same effect, a single artifact can sometimes be read as a text. Michael Jackson, for instance, is certainly a complex enough artifact to be readable as a text in his own right. More often, larger groups of signs and artifacts, contributing to the same effect, are read as texts; an entire Michael Jackson video might be analyzed in that way, for example.

A text is something that people perceive, notice, or unify in their everyday experiences; it is also something that critics or students of popular culture create. A text is something that people put together out of signs, insofar as people unify the meanings of several signs. You might go to the movies and understand the large collection of signs that you see and hear as the text of *The Crying Game* (1992), because you can see that the meanings of those signs work together to create the same set of effects in you and the rest of the audience. On the other hand, you might not think of the next meeting of a class in which you are enrolled as a text. But suppose a critic were to point out to you how the arrangement of desks, lecture techniques of the instructor, clothing styles of the students, and subject matter somehow all work together as a set of signs with interconnected meanings, all contributing to the same effects or functions. Suppose you had not thought of your class in this way before. In that case, the critic has identified the text, and having had it identified for you, now you could identify it as a text yourself. We will see later in this book that one of the primary reasons for the informed criticism of popular culture is that it can help people to identify texts of which they were not aware.

As we rarely or never experience the whole of a culture (the entire system of artifacts), we can extend our definition of a text by noting that *texts are the ways in which we experience culture*. Suppose we take the whole of rock and roll to be a culture, a system of artifacts. Music, of course, is an important part of that set of artifacts, but so are certain practices such as dancing, going to concerts, and styles of dress and grooming. In addition, there are several subcultures of rock and roll that are more specialized systems of artifacts within the larger culture; such subcultures include punk, heavy metal, folk rock, and so forth. Clearly, we might identify ourselves as "rock and rollers" and yet never experience that entire system of artifacts.

Instead, we might sit down one evening and listen to a new INXS tape; we experience that tape as a text, and that is how we experience the rock and roll culture at that moment. Or we might go to a concert. The whole experience of the concert can function as a text as well, a text made up of the crowd, the security system, dancing in the aisles, whiffs of smoke floating around, and so on. The rock and roll star Madonna herself might be perceived and studied as a text: what she does, how she dresses, how she moves, her music, her public image, her romantic affairs, and so forth.

We will see in a later chapter that for many of the texts of popular culture, it can be difficult to identify the textual boundaries. In the rock concert, for instance, where does the concert begin and end? What is and is not the concert? Some signs—such as the music being played—are clearly constituents of that text. Some signs may be questionable: Is the difficulty in finding a parking place before the concert, or the ringing in the ears after the concert, part of that concert as a unified experience, as a text? Some signs, such as the bird you see flying on your way home from the concert, may clearly not be part of the text. We will think about how to identify and define texts more carefully at a later point.

Exercise 1.7

To better understand the idea of a text, think about the following examples (two of them your own), and answer the questions (below the examples) that can help in identifying something as a text.

Your lunch today

Latest episode of *All My Children*

Local baseball game, seen live

Your own example (#1)

Your own example (#2)

Answer the following questions for each example:

1. How is this composed of a set of related signs? How do those signs work together to contribute meanings to the same effects or functions?

2. What are some artifacts that make up this text? In other words, what are its constituent artifacts?

3. How does this text "stand in for" other texts or signs in a larger cultural system? How does it represent other cultural artifacts in the same system?

Of course, if something is a text, then it can be *read*. What do we do when we read? We examine signs and artifacts and identify their meanings. That is clearly what we do when we read words. We do the same thing when we experience other kinds of artifacts, so it may be useful to retain the term *reading*, even when the texts we are examining include things other than words. A text, in other words, is something that has meaning, a meaning grounded in the culture behind the text, a meaning that can be examined and understood. We will see in later chapters that those meanings are complex and are often struggled over, since what a text means has a lot to do with power.

Because they cohere around meanings, texts are the ways in which we are exposed to consciousness. A text is the mouthpiece for a culture; it is a representative sampling of the overall system of meanings that constitute an ideology or consciousness that is linked to a group. Texts urge a consciousness on us (and thus they also contain the contradictions that are part of a consciousness). We do not always accept that consciousness in its entirety, but the urging to do so is there nonetheless.

Exercise 1.8

To understand this point, consider an example of a possible text that you considered a few pages ago: your lunch today. Think about two texts, or two lunches, that two people sitting at the same table might have.

Lunch #1	**Lunch #2**
Double martini	Hot herbal tea
Twelve-ounce T-bone steak	Pita bread sandwich, with avocado,
French fries	alfalfa sprouts, and cheese
Corn on the cob	Raw vegetables and yogurt dip
Apple pie a la mode	Simple china plate, stainless steel
Stoneware plate, bone-handled	knife and fork, cloth napkin
knife and fork, plenty of paper	
napkins	

Of course, an entire consciousness or ideology would only be absorbed after prolonged and repeated exposure to the meanings of a wide range of artifacts within a cultural system. But each of these lunches nevertheless has a "voice" of its own, and the voice speaks both to and about the diners. Would you say that either lunch shows a consistent set of meanings, beliefs, attitudes, or values? Does either lunch allow you to say something with some measure of assurance about either of the two diners? Could you make a good "educated guess" in response to any of the following questions?:

1. Which of these diners is more concerned about the environment?
2. Which of these diners is a fan of professional football?
3. Which of these diners is female and which is male?
4. Which diner is a Republican and which one is Democrat?
5. Which diner is over 55 and which one is under 40?

The purpose of posing these questions is not to perpetuate stereotypes, but to demonstrate that you probably felt that you *could* answer at least some of them. In order for you to have this sense that you could know the answers to such questions, the text of each lunch must mean something (at least approximately); each lunch must somehow fit into larger systems of artifacts and meaning.

So we have come full circle, back to the question of your blue jeans, with which this chapter began. Suppose you see a man of about age forty, wearing faded blue jeans and a tie-dyed shirt, his long hair pulled back and tied in a ponytail. Furthermore, suppose he is sitting on the hood of an aged Volkswagen Beetle plastered with Grateful Dead stickers, selling homemade jewelry from a battered display tray.

The picture just described is a unified experience—it is a text. Just like the text of an editorial in the newspaper, or the text of a speech by the president, the text of this forty-year-old man is speaking to us. It has meaning, and it is articulating a certain consciousness for us. That picture has a voice—what is it saying? What do the blue jeans this man is wearing add to that voice that would not be there if he were wearing pleated wool slacks?

These questions have to do with *rhetoric*, with how the meanings that we would find in or assign to that text are being managed so as to influence people. Rhetoric is an ancient kind of human activity, and an ancient discipline that studies that activity as well. In the next chapter we will examine that term in more detail, and arrive at a better understanding of how to apply the concept of rhetoric to the texts of popular culture.

Summary and Review

We began this chapter by posing the question, How do everyday objects, actions, and events influence people? The idea that these everyday experiences of popular culture have an important effect on people should already seem more plausible to you. Rhetoric was defined initially as the ways in which signs influence people, and in this chapter we began to understand some basic concepts that will help us to see how popular culture is rhetorical in just that way. We also briefly noted that influencing other people is a way of securing power.

To understand what culture means, we began with its building blocks: *signs*. Everything can be a sign; a sign is something that has meaning, or that gets you to think of something else. Signs mean in three ways: indexically, iconically, and symbolically. In discussing symbolic meanings, we noted that because symbols are arbitrary and conventional, their meaning is easily changed. And because they are not naturally or permanently connected to their meanings, symbols are imprecise and changeable in meaning.

We defined an *artifact* as (1) an action, event, or object perceived as a unified whole, (2) having widely shared meanings, and (3) manifesting group identifications to us. In discussing that definition, we reviewed some important characteristics that contribute to this idea of an artifact:

1. Artifacts are a socially created reality.
2. Signs become artifacts as they become charged with meaning, thus crossing a threshold into artifact status.
3. An artifact can be very complex, even being made up of other artifacts.
4. Artifacts are the material signs of group identifications.

We defined *culture* as the integrated set or system of artifacts that is linked to a group, and noted that culture in this sense is what we grow in, what supports us and sustains us. *Popular culture*, more specifically, is made up of those systems of artifacts to which most people are exposed. We noted three important characteristics of culture:

1. Cultures are highly complex and overlapping.
2. Cultures entail consciousness, or ideologies.
3. Cultures are experienced through texts.

We learned that a *text* is defined as a set of signs related to each other insofar as their meanings all contribute to the same set of effects or functions. Furthermore, *texts* are the ways in which we experience culture.

Important terms that were defined and discussed in this chapter include *rhetoric, sign, artifact, culture, popular culture, contradiction,* and *consciousness (ideology)*.

Looking Ahead

At this point, you may very well have several questions left unanswered. Let us consider some questions that *should* arise from this chapter, for your consideration and review. You might think about these questions, or discuss them in class, or use them to prepare for later chapters.

1. We have not said very much about power yet. What is at stake in the question of what artifacts mean? Why would anyone worry about that meaning?
2. We have not yet explored the idea of *struggle* very thoroughly. Are there ways in which you would say that popular culture is a site of struggle? For instance:

What happens when artifacts mean several things, or mean contradictory things? Who decides what meanings they will have?

How do artifacts come to have several meanings?

Can the assignment of meaning lead to power and disempowerment? How does that happen?

How can people resist the meanings that others try to impose on them?

How is struggle over meaning conducted? What are the tools or strategies that people use?

3. Consider the term *rhetoric*. What other meanings for *rhetoric* have you heard or read? What does the term mean to you? Are there some things or events that you would identify as definitely rhetorical, and others that you would say are definitely *not* rhetorical?

Chapter 2

Rhetoric and the Rhetorical Tradition

•••••••••••••••••••••••••••

Has popular culture always been an important site of rhetoric? Not necessarily. To understand why the conjunction of rhetoric and popular culture is especially potent today, we need to understand the history of rhetorical theory. Rhetoric has been around for centuries, both as something that people do and as a subject matter that people study. One thing that is particularly striking about rhetoric is the many different ways in which it has been defined, today and throughout history. In this chapter we will explore some of those definitions. Students of rhetoric are often frustrated with so many definitions for a term; "Why can't people just settle on a meaning?" students sometimes ask. (You may have felt a similar frustration as we discussed different meanings for culture in Chapter 1.) To anticipate that frustration, let us first think about what a *definition* is, and about *defining* as a strategy.

Definitions in General

You will recall that in Chapter 1 we discovered that the word *culture* has been defined in different ways. You probably also noticed that the ways in which you define certain terms can make a lot of difference; in fact, definitions can be a way of securing power. If you define culture as high culture—as ballet and oil paintings and symphony orchestras—for instance, that lets you reduce to second-class status everything else, including baseball games, cheeseburgers, reggae music, and Disney World. This arrangement makes a pretty nice setup for the wealthy and talented people who already control "high culture," doesn't it? If "culture" is something that people think of as generally a good thing, then being able to define some things and not others as "culture" is a source of power.

If you study history, you find that certain terms have been defined in many different ways. Throughout history there have been varying definitions of what it means to be human. Some societies defined humanity by way of race; such a definition empowered people of one race to enslave whole groups of people who did not look like them, on the theory that they were not really enslaving humans. In this century, Adolf Hitler and the Nazis in Germany attempted to define humanity along ethnic lines, portraying German Aryans as the only authentic humans. Through that definition the Nazis denied that Jews, Gypsies, and others were fully human. Women have been defined by men in different ways throughout history, generally in ways that were disempowering (as incomplete or imperfect copies of men, as inferior versions of humanity, as essentially assistants or helpers for men, and so forth).

There are many terms that can have different definitions, such as terms used in describing families or sexual orientation. But there are also many terms that do not have varying definitions. There are not widely different definitions for carrots, cats, dogs, umbrellas, or walking, for instance. What is the difference? What makes one term have lots of different definitions, while other terms seem relatively straightforward? Some words have little to do with power; you will find that these terms do not get defined in very many ways. When power and influence are at stake, the words in which power and influence (or disempowerment) are expressed or embodied will come to have lots of definitions. Settling the definition of carrots will not affect who has control over others, who has freedom to do as they will, who will have to accommodate others, and so forth.

People struggle over power; therefore, they struggle over what words that express power should mean. We may take it as a general rule that terms that have several different definitions—definitions that are controversial or argued over— are usually terms about important dimensions of human life. Such terms will have something to do with how power is created, shared, or denied. To control words is to control the world.

Exercise 2.1

The following exercise, which you can do on your own or in class with the instructions of your teacher, will help you understand what is at stake in the general strategies of definition.

One of the most important ways in which people are defined is in terms of race. Consider these questions:

1. What are the major terms for human races?
2. Are there any disagreements over what to call certain groups? Is there lack of agreement over what to call other groups?
3. What does it mean that certain groups seem to be called by only one term, with little struggle over what to call them?
4. Do different terms of races imply different definitions of people? If so, what does that have to do with power? Why are those terms struggled over? For example, in the last forty years, one group of people has "officially" been called Negroes, blacks, Afro-Americans, and African Americans. Why so many terms? What does each term have to do with empowerment and disempowerment?

We have seen how there are disagreements, and struggles for power, over how the word *culture* is defined. Now we will see that an even greater disagreement exists over how to define *rhetoric*. It seems therefore, that there must be some connection between rhetoric and power. This connection was clear from the very beginning of thinking about rhetoric in Western civilization. We are about to take a detour of some length through ancient Greece. The reason for this is that the ways that we, both the general public and rhetorical scholars together, think about and define rhetoric are grounded in the ways that the ancient Greeks thought about rhetoric. The Greek legacy to us includes some ideas about the relationship between power and rhetoric, as well as the ways in which popular culture is related to both. Let us see what the Greeks thought rhetoric was all about.

The Rhetorical Tradition: Ancient Greece

Rhetoric has been studied for centuries throughout the world, although, in this country, we are most influenced by Western traditions of rhetoric that originated in the Mediterranean world. Western civilization has historically thought that the formal study of rhetoric began in about the sixth and fifth centuries B.C.E., in the ancient city-states of Greece and their colonies. To understand what rhetoric meant to these people, how they practiced it and what they studied, we will make a quick (and therefore somewhat simplified) survey of their history.

The Rise of the City-States

Greece used to be a considerably more fertile, prosperous, and even populous land than it is now; some scholars think that poor farming and land use techniques eroded the soil. At any rate, at one time the Greek land supported a large population that was organized largely around city-states—relatively small political entities, each of which was anchored in a capital city, such as Sparta, Athens, and Mycenae. In the sixth and fifth centuries B.C.E., several important developments took place. The Greek city-states had joined together to subdue their common enemy to the east, Persia, and thus they enjoyed a period of relative peace and safety from outside dangers. Many of these city-states were on or near the sea, and they developed navies and advanced techniques of navigation. Many of them became great trading powers and began to prosper economically as a result. As is so often the case, trade brought with it new ideas about science, government, philosophy, and technology, especially from Asia and Africa. Another important development was political; many, though not all, of the city-states developed strong democratic forms of government.

A democracy requires that people govern themselves, and to the extent that people are self-governing, they must talk about common problems and devise procedures for shared decision making. When new ideas are coming quickly into a place, the people will want to talk about them, weigh them to determine their usefulness for themselves, and debate their applications. Peace gives people the freedom and leisure to participate fully in public discussions. And as economic prosperity grows, the consequences of public discussions also grow; what was decided in a prosperous city-state could have an effect on half the Mediterranean world. Do you notice the common theme in this paragraph? The ancient Greek world was an especially fertile context for the growth and development of *communication*, particularly public speaking, as an important human activity.

Nowhere was that more true than Athens, the largest and most prosperous of the city-states. This time period was known as the "Golden Age" of Athens; under leaders such as Pericles, it prospered and came to dominate many of the other city-states culturally, economically, and militarily. To understand some important assumptions that people make even today about rhetoric, we must understand how rhetoric was practiced in this important city-state.

Rhetoric in Athens

The Athenians had no lawyers, no legislators, no public relations or advertising professionals. All public decisions were made by an assembly of the citizens of Athens. We often hear of Athens as a perfect example of a democracy. In fact, it was not: Only the free, native-born, property-holding, adult males of Athens were counted as citizens. In such a cosmopolitan and rapidly changing population, that number only came to about 15 percent of the total. Still, given a population of about 150 thousand at this period for the entire city-state, it made for a sizable group of people who participated in public decisions.

From time to time, these citizens would gather at a place outside the city, and any and all issues of important public business would be raised then. When an issue was raised, it was dealt with through debate and discussion. Because such gatherings required that large groups of people be addressed at once, the discussion took the form of public speaking. That meant that every citizen needed to be able to speak in public at a moment's notice, and on any topic that might come up. If you were an olive grower and someone proposed a new law that would regulate olive growing, you had to be able to speak on that issue immediately in order to protect your livelihood. If you were a young man of the proper age for the military and someone proposed sending an army or navy on some action, you might need to speak to that issue. If you wanted some public works constructed in town, there were no city council representatives to call; you had to stand up yourself and suggest that a bridge or dam be built. If you thought your neighbor was violating the law, there were no police or district attorneys to call; you had to stand up and accuse the rascal yourself. On the other hand, someone might accuse *you* of some wrongdoing, and you would be called upon to defend yourself in an impromptu speech, on the spot.

In sum, an ability to speak, clearly and forcefully, on any subject that might come up was a vital skill for these Athenian citizens, crucial for their business and personal affairs. Today, nobody would think of starting a business without some training in accounting, business mathematics, administration, business law, and so forth. For many Athenians, the sine qua non, the most essential component, of successful business was public speaking.

Public speaking was also vital for the Athenians' political affairs. Athenians took participation in political discussion to be both a duty and an entertainment. Unlike the situation for most of us today, political decisions would be carried out by those who made them; if you voted to repair the city wall, you had to help with the planning, construction, and financing. Politics also required well-honed public speaking skills.

This need to be able to speak in public created a market for those who could teach such skills. (An analogous need today would be the great demand for training in computer competence, a demand created in just the last few decades around the world.) A class of traveling teachers of public speaking, known as the Sophists, arose to meet this need in ancient Greece. You may be familiar with the terms *sophist* or *sophistry*; today, such terms are used to refer to those who argue just for the sake of arguing, who devise empty arguments that sound good but are not sound. A sophist is, in this sense, one who is more concerned with winning an argument than with establishing the truth. But the Sophists of ancient Greece would not have defined themselves in that way. These definitions of sophistry actually arose from the viewpoint of another philosopher of ancient Greece, Plato. Let us see why.

Complaints against the Sophists

Two complaints were lodged against the Sophists. The first is that they claimed to have knowledge about public speaking, but they really did not. It would not be surprising if this complaint were true of some of them. After all, there have been quacks and charlatans in every profession throughout history. In ancient Greece, there were no accrediting agencies that could certify whether a given Sophist was a qualified teacher. So certainly, some Sophists claimed to be able to teach something that they really knew little about, though this was not true of all the Sophists.

A second complaint is more substantial, and was the primary reason for Plato's objection to the Sophists. This complaint centers on the idea that public speaking is not an art of anything in particular, because a person can speak about everything. If public speaking is not an art of anything in particular, Plato argued, then it ought not to be taught at all; instead, speakers should learn more about those things that they speak about. Certainly, it was the case for ancient Athens that people needed to be able to speak on any subject at a moment's notice, given the way that public decisions were made. People might have to speak about shipbuilding if Athens were trying to decide whether to construct a navy; about wheat farming if Athens were trying to decide what sort of agricultural laws to have; about rules of evidence under the criminal statutes, if an accusation of lawbreaking were made. The problem was, as a person learned about public speaking, that person did *not*, through those studies, learn about shipbuilding, agriculture, or law. Instead, a student of public speaking learned about introductions and conclusions, arguments, and verbal embellishments that could be applied to any topic.

Plato objected to this state of affairs because he thought it made more sense to learn the subject matters about which you would speak than to learn techniques of speaking itself (Plato discusses this idea in the dialogue called *Gorgias*). Pursuing that logic to its conclusion, Plato argued that because true democracies refer all issues to all the people and because nobody can be an expert on every issue, democracy itself was flawed because it asked people to discuss problems and issues on which they were not experts. Plato instead preferred to refer problems to experts in the appropriate subject matter, rather than to democratic decision making (see the *Republic*). He feared that democratic gatherings would be too swayed by rhetoric itself, by technique rather than substance. He therefore defined rhetoric as "pandering," as an art of the appearances rather than reality (see the *Gorgias*). Only later in his thinking did he allow some room for rhetoric, as a tool or servant of those who were already knowledgeable in a subject matter, so that these experts could better instruct their audiences (see Plato's later dialogue, *Phaedrus*).

Thus, at the very birth of thinking about rhetoric, we find disagreements over definitions. And once again we see that the struggle over different definitions has a lot to do with power. For the Sophists, rhetoric was the art of persuasion carried out through public speaking, the art of determining how to speak to popular audiences on the wide range of subjects that might come before them for review and decision. For Plato, rhetoric was an art of fooling people, of flattering them, of getting the public to make decisions based on oratorical technique rather than on knowledge or a grasp of the truth. These definitional disagreements arose precisely because power was at stake: the power to make public decisions about important public business. If the Sophists were correct in their definition, then all citizens should share in the power to speak about important decisions, to influence others, to sway the judgments of others. If Plato's definition was correct, then decisions should be made by a small group of experts in whatever subject came up, and persuasive speaking should not at all be a factor in what was decided.

So, what is rhetoric *really*? Bear in mind that any answer this book might give would have its author's own arguments for rhetoric—in other words, its author's own power issues—embedded within it. But the impulse behind asking such a question is understandable; it would indeed be useful to have some "core idea" of what rhetoric is, a basic notion underlying all of the definitions that rhetoric has accumulated over the centuries. Such a single summing up is probably not possible; but we might return to a general sense of rhetoric that we have already examined. In Chapter 1, we used an extremely broad definition of rhetoric that could underlie at least most of these other definitions: the ways in which signs influence people. A public speech, like an essay or article, consists of lots of signs (words) working together in a text; rhetoric is, very generally, the ways in which these texts influence people. Certainly, the Athenians had to use the public speaking form of communication in their assemblies in order to influence others. But what were they doing when they used those texts to influence others? What are we doing today when we use signs with rhetorical influence upon other people, or when signs influence us? How that influence is carried out, and ideas about whether that is a good thing or a bad thing to do, will be expressed more clearly in the narrower definitions that different thinkers may offer.

Two Legacies From the Greek Rhetorical Tradition

The ancient Greeks were extremely influential in the development of rhetorical theory. The Sophists and Plato initiated arguments over rhetorical theory, and Plato's pupil Aristotle wrote the most famous work on this subject, the *Rhetoric*, which in one way or another influenced all subsequent rhetorical theory. Many of the assumptions, theories, and practices of ancient Athens have had an extraordinary effect on how people have thought about rhetoric ever since. We need to evaluate what the Greeks taught us, and whether the rhetorical tradition that they began is relevant to rhetoric today. Let's examine two important legacies from that rhetorical tradition: (1) Rhetoric is conventionally equated with traditional texts, and (2) Traditional rhetoric is paradoxically linked to power management.

Equation with Traditional Texts

When the ancient Greeks spoke of rhetoric, they were referring to a particular kind of text. The Greek rhetorical legacy encourages people to assume that only the texts of public speaking had rhetorical functions. In exploring this idea further, it is useful to draw a distinction between rhetoric as a *function* and rhetoric as a certain kind of *manifestation*.

Rhetoric does certain things; it has certain *functions*. In its broadest sense rhetoric refers to the ways in which signs influence people; and through that influence, rhetoric makes things happen. When people speak, when they make television advertisements, when they write essays, they are attempting to carry out some function. What that function specifically *is*, whether it is good or bad, will vary with one's definition. The Sophists would say that the function of rhetoric is to persuade others while participating in a democratic society, while Plato would say that the function of rhetoric is to flatter or mislead people. But the *general* function—that of influence—remains the same.

On the other hand, whatever rhetoric is doing, whatever functions it is performing, it must take on some physical form that can be seen or heard. The signs that influence people come together as texts in certain forms or manifestations. In ancient Greece, the manifestation that was almost universally called "rhetoric" was public speaking. There are, of course, many different kinds of public speeches. But for the Greeks, public speeches shared four important characteristics as a form of text. These four characteristics describe what we might call *traditional rhetorical texts*. The Greek ideal of public speaking called for a text that was (1) *verbal*, (2) *expositional*, (3) *discrete*, and (4) *hierarchical*.

Public speaking is a primarily *verbal* text. Certainly, nonverbal dimensions of the experience, such as gestures or vocal expression, are important, but the words in public speaking are of primary concern. When we study the great speeches of the past, for instance, we look primarily at what was said; there is rarely any record of how the speakers moved or used the voice to emphasize certain points, how they dressed or combed their hair for maximum effect.

Public speaking is also a largely *expositional* text. Here we will draw on critic

Neil Postman's usage of the term *expositional* (1985). Postman's broad definition refers to the sort of speeches that make several claims, then defend or develop those claims by providing evidence, clarification, examples, and elaboration in carefully organized structures. Such speeches rely on evidence—especially technical, scientific, historical, or other knowledge—to make and defend points. In other words, traditional texts are based on *argument*, not in the sense of being disputatious, but in the sense of advancing and defending propositions. Expositional speaking entails lengthy development. The expression "No blood for oil" was frequently voiced as a protest against the Persian Gulf War of 1991. But this expression was not expositional in that the claim (that blood was being shed for the purposes of acquiring oil) was not developed, supported, or elaborated upon.

Public speaking is also a *discrete* text. By discrete, we mean clearly distinct and separate in time and space, surrounded by clear boundaries. Rain, for instance, is not discrete; it is here, there, all over the place, mixed in with the air and the soil, coming and going, and so forth. But a pencil is discrete. It is clearly a distinct thing, separate from the table or the paper; we have no difficulty in putting boundaries around it.

A discrete text is a unified series of artifacts that are perceived to be separate and distinct from other artifacts. Elevator music is not usually perceived to be a discrete text, because it is heard as its producers mean it to be heard: as a background noise that is merged with whatever else you happen to be doing. Traditional speeches are usually perceived as discrete texts. They begin when the speaker begins to speak, and they end as the speaker is finished. The words of a speech form the text for the most part; coughs and clearings of the throat by the speaker are not considered part of the text. Similarly, reactions by the audience—what they said and did in response to the speaker (even during the speech)—are not part of the discrete text that is the speech.

Traditional speeches are especially discrete texts in that they occur in special times and places. You go to a certain place at a certain hour to hear a speech. Speeches are not likely to be found breaking out unexpectedly in your living room. In that sense, traditional speeches are the epitome of discrete texts, texts that are distinct in time and space.

Finally, traditional public speeches are *hierarchical* texts. By that we mean that a structure of relationships is imposed on the process of using signs, of sending and receiving a message. In traditional public speaking, the structure calls for one person to speak while many people listen. One person is, therefore, put in a position of advantage over others, at least for the moment. The audience may heckle or shout approval, they may violently disagree, others may stand up to speak in agreement or opposition afterwards, but as long as a speech remains a speech (rather than turning into a riot, for instance), the roles of speaker and audience create a relative difference. It is very clear in public speaking who is the source of the message. The speech is identified with an individual, and that individual is, during the moment of speaking, put into a relatively privileged position. After all, that individual gets to claim the attention of an audience, for the duration of his or her speech. In contrast, think of how often during the day you get to command the attention of thirty, one hundred, or more people all at once.

An example of a nonhierarchical message would be graffiti. Any of us can scrawl a message on a public wall, and any of us may choose to read or not to read it. There is no structure prescribed or imposed for how we are to relate to either writers or readers of graffiti. Another example would be a highly informal, animated discussion among friends: people talk over, around, and through one another, with little attention paid to anybody having more status or more of a right to speak.

The Greek legacy tells us, then, that rhetoric occurs in traditional texts (verbal, expositional, and so on). While the mainstay of Greek rhetoric was public speaking, other kinds of texts (such as newspaper editorials) can also be traditional in form. But recall from Chapter 1 that one kind of text or manifestation that we discussed was lunch. That clearly is a different kind of manifestation than is the traditional text of a speech, essay, or editorial. In this book, we will learn that rhetoric occurs in many different manifestations. If rhetoric is using signs to influence others, then editorials, letters to the editor, advertisements, public speeches, *as well as* your lunch, your blue jeans, Ice-T's latest rap, and so forth, are all ways in which that influence is materialized, or made manifest, in the texts found in real life. The Greeks, however, did not share that understanding, nor did later theorists who wrote under their influence. In sum, the first Athenian legacy is an assumption that whatever is called rhetoric must have most or all of the four characteristics of traditional texts.

Paradoxical Linkage to Power Management

The second part of the legacy that the Greek rhetorical tradition has given us is a *paradox*. A paradox is an apparent contradiction. The paradox we inherit from the Greek legacy is that traditional texts both include and exclude people from the management of public business, and thus from positions of power. To understand this paradox, we must first clarify the idea of power management, or of managing important public business.

When we manage power, we make use of our ability to control events and meanings. Our ability to manage the decisions that we face or that influence us varies with the amount of power we have. Imagine an invalid, unable to rise out of a hospital bed. Although largely helpless and prey to the routines of hospital staff, this person will still manage what happens to him or her as well as he or she can, through the means at his or her disposal, such as use of the call button or through granting and withholding cooperation. At work, others of us might be invited to help manage decisions concerning who gets to take vacations during prime months. Other decisions, however, are managed without our involvement, such as a decision to sell our company to a foreign investor. An ability to participate in the management of decisions is empowering. Public business must similarly be managed. To the extent that we are excluded from, or included in, decisions to pave streets, finance welfare programs, or go to war, we are correspondingly empowered or disempowered.

We often manage power in one more important way. Note that power has been defined as the ability to control both events and *meaning*. Sometimes, as in the case of our imaginary invalid, the ability to control events may be sharply limited. But a kind of power can be gained by controlling the meanings of what happens to the invalid; it makes a difference whether he sees his situation as "recovery" or as "hopelessness," for instance. Similarly, the president has the power to send troops into action in the Middle East, a decision that very few might participate in managing. But the press and public do have a different kind of power insofar as they manage what the military action means: Is it a noble gesture, an act of self-defense, or the last gasp of imperialism? Given how responsive many public officials are to opinion polls, management of the meaning that results in public opinion can be a form of empowerment.

The second legacy from the Greek rhetorical tradition can best be understood by considering two aspects of the way in which rhetoric is defined. First, the more favorably rhetoric is defined, the more people it involves in managing public business. That is because rhetoric and democracy fit together naturally. When the public is officially entrusted with managing public business, they make those decisions through arguing about them together. The more decisions are made by involving people in the rhetorical exchange of open discussion, the more democracy occurs. Therefore, if rhetoric is something that people are able to do, and feel that they *should* do, and if rhetoric is the way that important public business is managed, then rhetoric is a form of communication that distributes power widely.

If, on the other hand, rhetoric is defined unfavorably as something that not everyone should do because not everyone should be persuasive, have a voice, or be influential, then public business will be managed by people who have some special status, some special claim to decision making other than being persuasive. These people will be the experts—those who are already powerful, the highly born or the specially chosen few.

Exercise 2.2

This choice between defining rhetoric (a) in order to democratize power, or (b) in order to concentrate power among a few, is one that we continue to face today. Let's leap over several centuries and think for a minute about how this choice confronts you. For each decision listed below, think about how you would prefer that the decision be made, and by whom.

Decisions	Should this decision be made democratically or by an expert few?	If democratically, who will be involved in the decision?	If by an expert few, who will the experts be?
1. How should city officials organize their filing system?			

2. Should your
   state permit con-
   struction of a
   new nuclear
   power plant?
3. What should you
   do about a lump
   that you have dis-
   covered in your
   body?
4. Is the President
   doing a good
   job?

For most of these decisions, there will be competing voices. Some will argue that the issue should be left to popular discussion and debate, others that there are experts who should be consulted instead. Some will claim that the problem is a public one, others that it is not. Note that your choice in each issue is really a choice about whether rhetoric is a good or bad instrument for managing decisions. The choices made in these kinds of decisions can either empower or disempower people.

For instance, if the issue of the nuclear power plant is defined favorably as a rhetorical issue, that definition *empowers* the general public to participate in making a decision about it. But suppose you fear that the general public may be swayed by emotional or uninformed arguments (by pandering). Suppose you do not think the public knows enough about nuclear power to be officially entrusted with the decision. If the problem is therefore referred to experts instead, that choice *disempowers* citizens of the state who will not be able to argue over it.

There are no right or wrong answers for the questions in this exercise; the point is that the ancient Athenians bequeathed to us this choice, and it is a choice over how to define rhetoric. But for each of the preceding questions, the way in which rhetoric is defined will empower some people and disempower others, thus affecting the management of public affairs.

We have learned that within the Greek rhetorical legacy, a favorable definition of rhetoric enhances the democratic management of society's important business. But paradoxically, the specific Greek understanding of rhetoric as pertaining to traditional texts—texts that are verbal, expositional, discrete, and hierarchical—is not as democratic as it might be.

There is a reason for this paradox. When people assume that democracy occurs with rhetorical discussions, but then go on to define rhetoric as referring only to verbal, expositional, discrete, and hierarchical texts, they are unable to see the democratic participation in public decision making that can occur through different kinds of texts. In ancient Greece, democracy was officially conducted within the assemblies. But after the assembly, citizens returned to the marketplace and conversed informally there. All the while, women instructed and nurtured children. Slaves and foreigners talked among themselves within their own groups. People were, of course, exposed to nonverbal signs of all sorts, and there was surely the ancient Greek version of today's blue jeans that all the younger people wore. But in the thinking and writing about rhetoric at that time, there is no mention at all of these everyday communications. There is no awareness of what is rhetorical about them, nor of how they might also be involved in the management of important public business.

Some classical theorists such as Plato were concerned about the effects of certain kinds of texts—such as music, poetry, or drama—on the public. These kinds of texts may appear to be just the sort of popular culture texts we are studying in this book. But there are actually some important differences. First, the forms of ancient Greek music, poetry, and drama were closer to traditional texts than they would be to today's texts. A Greek drama, for instance, was highly verbal, with frequent expositional passages, and not much in the way of the kinds of special effects you will find in *The Terminator*. Second, part of what was traditional about those texts was that, relatively speaking, they were experienced less in the moment-to-moment flow of everyday life than today's popular culture is. They tended to be presented as special, and thus discrete, moments of high culture, very much under the auspices of established power structures. And finally, nobody ever thought of calling those entertainments *rhetoric*.

To refer back to our very general definition of rhetoric, there was no attempt among the ancient Greeks to theorize how any and all signs might have been influencing people. Instead, we find in Greek rhetoric an assumption that the important business of the society would be conducted largely in traditional rhetorical texts. However, many everyday, moment-to-moment decisions are not made by reasoning them out through the knowledge associated with traditional rhetorical texts. We arrange dates, figure out how to get along with the new family next door, and decide which television program to watch, all using something other than traditional texts. But within the Greek legacy, experiences and decisions that people face in everyday, mundane contexts, and the ways in which those decisions are made, are all assumed to be of little consequence.

The chief result of this paradox within the Greek legacy for the study of popular culture is that traditional thinking does not recognize any important rhetoric of everyday life. If any important business of society is being conducted through the texts of everyday experience—through nonverbal signs or informal conversation, for example—then any thinking grounded in the Greek legacy will not recognize a rhetorical dimension in the management of that business. This is because Greek rhetorical theory views rhetoric as sharing the four characteristics described on pages 39–41, and everyday conversation, nonverbal signs, and ordinary social practices will probably *not* be verbal, discrete, expositional, and hierarchical. In the traditional view, texts that do not share those four characteristics have been seen as not fully rhetorical and as not fully performing rhetoric's important functions. But students of popular culture take issue with the idea that texts that do not have those four characteristics are less important and not concerned with a society's serious business.

In talking about different kinds of texts, we should not make any absolute distinctions. Clearly, many kinds of communication will have some but not all of the four characteristics of the traditional texts of public speaking. There is no sudden cutoff at which everyday, mundane business becomes public (and therefore important) business. Also, societies have a full continuum of business, from the vitally important to the trivial; the majority of a society's business probably falls somewhere in the middle. But historically, traditional rhetorical theorists have assumed that the closer a communication is to having all four characteristics of the traditional texts of public speaking, the more clearly it deserves to be called rhetoric.

Exercise 2.3

To understand the assumptions that are sometimes made about what is rhetoric and what is not, write down your reactions to the following exercise. In this exercise, you will indicate whether the texts listed below share the four characteristics of public speaking.

Is this text	verbal?	expositional?	discrete?	hierarchical?
A speech by the President of the United States				
This book				
The phone book				
A mother's routine for getting children ready for school				
Your favorite tape or CD				
A city bus going along its route				

You probably answered yes to more of the four characteristics of traditional rhetorical texts for the first two, or perhaps three, items on the list than for the later ones. Not coincidentally, most people would have no trouble identifying a speech by the president, perhaps even this book, as rhetoric—but the ways in which a city bus is a rhetorical text may not be at all clear to most people.

Now look over that list of texts again, this time asking yourself which ones are most often involved in the management of society's serious business. Which texts are composed of signs that influence people in important ways? We are likely to think that the more traditionally rhetorical texts fit that description. A list of other traditionally rhetorical texts—texts which would be likely to share all four characteristics of the texts of public speaking—would probably include most essays and articles in periodicals, and to some extent the literature of novels, poems, plays, and so forth.

In sum, the ancient Greek rhetorical legacy assumes that rhetoric means verbal, expositional, discrete, and hierarchical—that is to say, traditional—texts. This legacy links rhetoric and democracy: The more public business is decided rhetorically, the more people will be involved in managing that business. But paradoxically, the Greek conception of a traditional text places limits on the widespread management of public business. The Greek legacy does not allow for the rhetorical management of public business within popular culture. That inability to see the rhetoric of the everyday lasted for centuries beyond the time of the Greeks.

Definitions of Rhetoric after Plato

In the centuries between Plato and the present, many thinkers and writers have devised their own understandings of what rhetoric is, what functions it performs, what manifestations it takes on, and whether or how it manages important public business. This book is not meant to be a history of rhetorical theory. But it would be useful to review very briefly some of the ways in which some of these later thinkers and writers thought about rhetoric. We will see that the Greek legacy has remained strong; though there are differences, these people's ideas are fundamentally similar to those of the Greeks.

We noted earlier that Plato's student, the philosopher Aristotle, diverged from his teacher's views to write a comprehensive treatise, the *Rhetoric*. This book is a system for studying as well as doing rhetoric, and since Aristotle's time, rhetoric has been a term that can be applied both to what people do and to systems of knowledge or explanation about what people do. Thus we might say that someone delivering a speech is "doing" rhetoric. At the same time, however, there is likely to be a systematic explanation of how the introduction and conclusion to the speech are constructed, how the arguments are devised, how emotional appeals are used, and so forth; we would refer to this system of rules and practical advice as *a rhetoric*.

Aristotle broke with Plato over the subject of rhetoric because Aristotle viewed it more consistently as an activity worth doing, a subject worth studying. In Chapter 2 of Book 1 of the *Rhetoric,* Aristotle defined rhetoric as "the faculty of observing in any given case the available means of persuasion." In further defining his subject, he made it clear that he viewed rhetoric as public speaking in legal, political, and ceremonial contexts; it was in those contexts that he saw much of the important business of his society being managed. Aristotle did not include within his definition everyday conversation, bargaining in the marketplace, entertainment, religion, or other experiences of communication. His treatise is concerned with the construction of public speeches, clearly discrete and verbal texts. His focus is on expositional texts as well; how to discover and express argument is a major focus of his theory. And for Aristotle, rhetoric is also hierarchical: He envisions the classic relationship of a speaker holding the floor before an audience that has gathered to listen.

In the first century B.C.E., the Roman statesman and philosopher Cicero wrote extensively on the subject of rhetoric, most notably in *Of Oratory*. Cicero exemplified the Roman ideal at that time, which maintained that life is lived most fully when one is actively involved in public life—that is, in public debate and discussion and in public decision-making. Romans considered it both a duty and the very rationale behind life to be involved in public life, discussing the important business of their society. One of the most important ways in which that involvement occurred was through oratory, or eloquent public speaking, which is how Cicero defined rhetoric.

Cicero was a Roman senator, and at that time the senate made many of the most important decisions for the Roman Republic. It made those decisions through inspired public speaking, many examples of which are still studied as model speeches today. Cicero also valued lively and learned discussions among his fellow patricians as a profitable way to pass the time and to acquire knowledge. But he would assign the management of most of his society's public problems to rhetoric in the form of public speaking; the involvement of every citizen in public affairs, rather than the assignment of problems to experts, was his ideal. And clearly, when rhetoric was used to manage public problems, it did so through forms of public speaking that were verbal, expositional, discrete, and hierarchical.

Cicero died, the Roman Republic came to an end, and the age of the Caesars was ushered in. Within the Roman Empire, public business was managed largely by the emperor and by officials appointed by him. Although Plato would probably have disapproved of many of the people who were in charge of imperial Rome, the Roman Empire did follow Plato's model, which called for the removal of the management of public business from the hands of the people and, consequently, from rhetoric in the form of public speaking. Consistent with Greek assumptions, as democracy faded, theorists began writing as if rhetoric were also reduced in scope and importance. In the first century C.E., the Roman teacher and rhetorician Quintilian wrote a long rhetoric, called the *Institutes of Oratory*, that both prescribed a course of study for training in rhetoric and gave practical advice for its use. But Quintilian was forced to define rhetoric primarily in terms of public speaking in the courts, because that was the only important arena left in Rome in which public speaking could be exercised meaningfully. It is interesting that Quintilian did not look for rhetoric, for the ways in which signs influence people, in manifestations other than speaking; clearly, the Greek tradition was influencing him as well. This shrunken definition of rhetoric as legal public speaking reflects the relationship between rhetoric and power: As power was denied to the public and as rhetoric (public speaking) was restricted in terms of what it could control, so was the sense of what counted as "rhetoric" more narrowly defined. For Quintilian, rhetoric continued to be defined as the manifestation that is traditional public speaking, with its four key characteristics.

An important rhetorician after Quintilian was St. Augustine, Bishop of Hippo, in Africa, who lived around 400 C.E. St. Augustine took on one of the most pressing problems for the early Christian Church: what to retain and what to discard among the artifacts of the polytheistic culture that the Christians were replacing. Rhetoric especially came under suspicion, as many in the Church thought that the faithful had no business seeking to gain advantage over others through any means, including public speaking. In *On Christian Doctrine*, especially in Book IV, St. Augustine argued that rhetoric *should* be used by Christians—that, in fact, it had the high calling of inducing belief and stimulating faith in people. St. Augustine shows the influence of the Greek legacy as well, for his view of rhetoric is embodied in the written texts of the Bible and the form of public speaking that is the sermon or homily, traditional texts that embody the four characteristics very clearly (particularly the verbal and hierarchical traits). It is significant that St. Augustine does not have much to say about person-to-person witnessing or testimony, rituals and ceremonies, or nonverbal signs such as pictures, icons, and costumes, as elements of rhetoric. His writings instead reflect a sense of traditional rhetorical texts as managing the important business of the Church.

Widespread participation in public decision making was scarce in Europe for centuries after the collapse of the Roman Republic. Various forms of powerful, centralized political control succeeded one another: the Roman Empire, the Catholic Church, the feudal system with its absolute monarchies and principalities, and so forth. The important business of societies was officially being managed by priests and princes in their abbeys and castles, not by peasants and merchants. Certainly, people talked and went about their business as they had for centuries; but we can find little evidence that any thinkers thought that those everyday experiences were important in shaping society or managing its business. Significantly, because what was considered the important business of society was being managed by an elite few, and not through public speaking, rhetoric came to be defined in increasingly narrow and restrictive ways.

Between St. Augustine's time and the eighteenth century, the Greek legacy continued to hold sway. The most interesting developments in rhetorical theory were the ways in which the definition of rhetoric became limited, paralleling the highly centralized and nondemocratic forms of government and social control of the times. One way in which rhetoric was limited was its restriction to certain kinds of texts and not others. For instance, the province of letter writing was assigned to rhetoric. In the centuries after Cicero, letter writing was not unimportant; it was a major means of communication over long distances. But letter writing certainly represented a restricted scope of subject matter and contexts, compared to the days when rhetoric involved thousands of people in political, legal, and ceremonial speaking.

Another means of restricting rhetoric had to do with the kinds of strategies or techniques it used. Peter Ramus, a sixteenth-century thinker, defined rhetoric so as not to include logic or reason; those strategies he set apart as a separate field of study. Instead, he defined rhetoric more narrowly as the study and art of verbal style. Because logic was undergoing systematic development and was seen as an important tool of thought and decision making (especially in the Church and in academia), restricting the definition of rhetoric to style alone, apart from logic, was a disempowering move on the part of Ramus and his colleagues.

Rhetoric in the Eighteenth Century

We often think of the eighteenth century as the Age of Reason, as a time when nondemocratic forms of social control were rejected. It was during that century that the American and French Revolutions both took place, for instance. Significantly, the eighteenth century also saw renewed interest in rhetorical theory, especially in Great Britain. Many thinkers returned to the ancient Greek and Roman rhetoricians and reestablished that legacy. Richard Whately, for instance, extended Greek and Roman ideas of argument to include the concepts of *presumption* and *burden of proof*. But alternatives to the Greek legacy were also developed at this time. It would be inaccurate to say that any eighteenth-century rhetorician proposed a theory of rhetoric in popular culture, but a number of thinkers did propose ideas that suggest ways of going beyond the Greek legacy, thereby planting the seeds of alternative ways of thinking. Let us review briefly just a few of the people who proposed such alternatives.

Giambattista Vico was a professor in Italy during the late-seventeenth and early eighteenth centuries. Vico directly confronted the restrictive definitions of rhetoric that had limited it to style and verbal embellishment, while the more substantive areas of reason and logic were assumed to be something other than rhetoric. Rhetoric, he proposed, should be seen as the ways in which we think about probabilities and make decisions about issues that we cannot be totally certain of. Contrary to the pretensions of philosophers such as Rene Descartes of France, who thought that many if not most decisions could be made through formal reason rather than rhetoric, Vico argued that most, if not all, decisions were based on thinking about probabilities, and thus had a rhetorical dimension. He claimed that for humans, reality is a matter of what we perceive—that we create our own realities out of signs. Since reality is human-made, it must be understood by using human faculties, and rhetoric is a primary human faculty. By carefully defining both human reality and rhetoric, Vico created a possibility for thinking about our experiences of reality (including public events as well as everyday experiences) as places where rhetoric is at work, influencing us to create our realities by seeing the world as one way or another. Vico's perspective is very close to the ideas that we explored in Chapter 1, where we spoke of the world of culture as both one that is made by humans and one that has a great deal of influence bound up in the artifacts (signs) of which it is composed.

Another important departure from the Greek legacy during the eighteenth century had to do with the development of the idea of *taste* as a basis for making decisions, and for constructing and judging communication. Rhetorical theorists such as Joseph Addison and Hugh Blair began suggesting that taste, an aesthetic way of thinking and perceiving, is and should be a factor in how people communicate and in how people make decisions on the basis of that communication. Blair and other rhetoricians were primarily concerned with taste as found in traditional texts, including oratory, letters, essays, and so forth. But whereas a concern for argument, for instance, entails a restricted focus on traditional texts, a concern for taste and aesthetics enables extension of those concepts beyond rhetorical texts. If taste is acknowledged to be a reason why people might do certain things, why decisions might be made, that acknowledgement sets up ways of thinking about how taste in clothing, in grooming products, in interior decoration—in popular culture overall—might be rhetorical. If you look for rhetoric only in terms of how evidence can be mustered in support of a point, then you cannot see both a speech and a punk rocker's safety pin through the cheek as rhetorical. But if rhetoric can be defined to include aesthetic judgment, or taste, then that safety pin, too, becomes rhetorical.

The development of interest in psychology, and the application of that new human science to rhetoric, also created possibilities for envisioning the rhetoric of popular culture. British theorists such as John Locke, David Hartley, Joseph Priestly, and George Campbell began to probe into how people think, how the mind operates, during the full range of experience. Campbell developed a rhetorical theory that explained how the human understanding and imagination were addressed by others. Although Campbell also restricted his focus in practice to traditional texts, he and his colleagues opened up the possibility of thinking about ways in which people might be influenced through other things besides verbal, expositional, and discrete texts. Because they were concerned with the whole operation of the human mind, these rhetorical psychologists introduced the possibility of thinking about how the mind might be influenced by signs and artifacts found throughout everyday experience, not just during moments of reading essays or listening to speeches.

One consequence of a concern for psychology was the development of methods of criticism. By criticism we mean critiquing or analyzing, not just being contentious. Rhetorical thinkers had always been concerned with how audiences received messages and thought about them. Plato urged rhetoricians to study the different "souls" that could be found in an audience, for example, and Aristotle discussed the ways in which messages would be received and understood. But their concern was largely with offering advice for speakers, for those who would produce signs and texts, rather than for those who would see or hear them. In the eighteenth century, rhetorical thinkers such as Lord Kames and Hugh Blair began to expand their understanding of the different kinds of reactions that people might have to signs and texts, and to identify specific techniques for analyzing, or critiquing, messages, audiences, and the connections between the two.

This concern for criticism also created a possibility for thinking about the rhetoric of popular culture, because it is as critics, or as consumers, that most people confront the artifacts of popular culture. We will see later how the rhetoric of popular culture is mainly concerned with how people encounter and then use, rather than originally produce, the texts of popular culture. To begin thinking about criticism is a step in that direction.

The eighteenth century was an age of powdered wigs, of candlelit salons, Mozart and Haydn, and Voltaire. It was the dawn of modern science and industry. The eighteenth century would not seem to have much to do with Ziggy Marley and the Melody Makers or with Andre the Giant. But developments in rhetorical theory during that period laid the groundwork for understanding the rhetoric of popular culture. So far we have considered four specific developments:

1. With Vico came an understanding that rhetoric runs throughout the experiences of human reality.

2. With Blair came a concern for taste and aesthetics as a basis for decision making.

3. With Campbell came a widening understanding of the human mind and how it works in response to signs.

4. With several thinkers, including Blair, came a concern for refined methods of criticism, particularly in relation to the reception of communication.

New Theories (and New Realities) in the Twentieth Century

During all these centuries in which rhetoric was defined primarily in terms of traditional texts, people were still experiencing signs, artifacts, and texts that were not in that traditional form. Informal conversation, architecture, clothing styles, common entertainments, food—in short, the whole range of cultural artifacts other than traditional rhetorical texts—were being experienced by people, while rhetorical theorists continued to call only the traditional texts rhetoric. One purpose of this book is to demonstrate how many of today's rhetorical theorists understand the rhetorical dimension of that wider range of cultural artifacts. In other words, many theorists today would choose not to limit the rhetoric to those traditional texts (although some still would, however; see Leff and Kauffeld for an excellent review of some recent scholarship grounded in traditional texts). That shift in understanding raises the question of what changed, rhetorically, between the eighteenth century and the present. Are people being influenced by signs in different ways now, such that we must now call the texts of everyday experience rhetorical but did not need to call them that two hundred years ago? Have rhetorical theorists awakened to truths that were always there but went unrecognized until recently? In other words, does a change in thinking about what rhetoric is follow from a change in the world or a change in theory?

The answer to that final question is both. The world and our experience of the world have changed. People do things differently, new technologies alter the realities of life, environmental and political changes occur, wars come and go, and so forth. Theories, or our ways of understanding the world, also change. Often, theories change because it is felt that the old theories no longer describe experience, which has changed, accurately. But theories sometimes change for the reasons we discovered at the beginning of this chapter. A theory is a complicated way of defining something as well as explaining it, and so one important reason why rhetorical theories change is because people may have reasons to define and explain the world differently. In short, changes in theory may be part of changes in *power*.

A sampling of just a few definitions of *rhetoric* from twentieth-century rhetorical theorists will show that the seeds of the eighteenth century have grown into conceptions of rhetoric that are markedly different from that of the Greeks. In 1936, I.A. Richards defined rhetoric as "a study of misunderstanding and its remedies" (3). Richards's concern is almost exclusively with verbal texts, but his definition is important in that it places rhetoric within the contexts of everyday communication and interaction. Misunderstanding is at least as likely to occur in the give and take of conversation as in the more carefully prepared traditional texts of essays or speeches. A concern for misunderstanding also emphasizes the role of audiences or receivers of communication, and the question of how they understand and interpret texts in their everyday experience.

Perhaps the most famous definition of rhetoric in the twentieth century is that of Kenneth Burke, who defined it as "the use of language as a symbolic means of inducing cooperation in beings that by nature respond to symbols" (1969b/1950, 43). Like Richards, Burke restricts his focus to language, but his definition is more widely applicable. Many kinds of signs, in many forms and contexts, can induce cooperation. Although it does not extend directly into popular culture, Burke's definition tells us to look for how people are induced to cooperate with others, potentially in any texts, whether that be to their benefit (their empowerment) or not. Similarly, Donald C. Bryant sees rhetoric's function as "adjusting ideas to people and people to ideas" (1953, 413). Although Bryant restricts his focus to "the rationale of informative and suasory discourse," the wider idea of adjusting ideas and people to one another is descriptive of a process that can and does occur outside of traditional texts.

Although James L. Kinneavy objects to those who would define rhetoric too broadly, he himself prefers anchoring its definition in "persuasion," which encourages us to consider the ways in which many kinds of texts persuade. Kinneavy's definition is geared to the function of rhetoric, rather than to a particular kind of manifestation (1971, 216–218). Similarly, in his definition of rhetoric, Stephen Toulmin proposes a model of argument, which would seem to be largely an expositional type of text (1958). But he develops his definition from actual arguments used in court decisions and other "real life" situations. Toulmin's model has been widely used to explore the ways in which the arguments of everyday life are persuasive.

Interrelated Twentieth-Century Changes

What prompted these changes in theory and definitions of rhetoric in the twentieth century? To begin to answer that question let us examine some important ways in which the world has changed in the twentieth century. This century is, of course, significantly different from the past in a number of ways. Our concern here is with differences in how signs influence people. Some of these differences are radical, or extreme. Most, however, are relative, or matters of degree, (though still significant). In each instance, the difference has to do with a change that the Greek rhetorical legacy and its assumptions cannot fully account for; thus, these are "real life" changes that have prompted changes in theory. Furthermore, these are changes that situate rhetoric squarely within popular culture. We will review changes in interrelated areas: *population, technology, pluralism,* and *knowledge.*

Population

Little argument should be needed to establish the fact that in the twentieth century, the world population exploded. Populations grew at the greatest rate in the poorer countries of the Third World, but nearly every industrialized nation experienced the same phenomenon. Of particular interest in industrialized countries was the *pattern* of population growth: Populations first became more urbanized, then suburbanized and exurbanized as the century progressed. That is to say that the experience of living with only limited contact with others, or even of living on farms or in rural areas, became increasingly rare. Farm populations shifted to the cities during the first half of the century. During the second half, city populations began spreading out into suburbs and smaller towns on the outskirts of larger cities. The main result of these developments has been that more people are exposed to more people today than they ever were before.

This difference in population patterns is a relative one, a matter of degree. It was rarely the case that many people were completely isolated or in touch with only a few others centuries ago. Nor is it the case that no one is ever alone today. But relatively speaking, more people are living and working near more other people today than ever before. That is an important difference because it means that more people are exposed to a wider variety of cultural artifacts than before. We must note that the issue is one of greater exposure to artifacts, not just to signs. Certainly, people are no more conscious today than they ever were, nor do people have more things to perceive today than they did in the past. A person's experience is no fuller today than it was three thousand years ago. But today, a person's day *is* relatively more full of signs that are artifacts, signs that are charged with meaning and that bespeak the presence of others. This is especially true of those who live in the population- and message-dense urban areas. Ian Chambers pictures the city dweller as "caught up in the communication membrane of the metropolis, with your head in front of a cinema, TV, video or computer screen, between the headphones by the radio, among the record releases and magazines . . ." (1986, 11).

Two hypothetical cases might help to make this relative difference clear. Imagine the case of a farm family living on the Great Plains 125 years ago. What would they see and hear during the course of the day? Many of their experiences would be of nature, of signs that were not necessarily produced by humans and that did not bespeak human groups. That is not to say that their culture was impoverished, but rather that relatively speaking, their exposure to artifacts that represented others was somewhat limited. Compare that family with a family living in a city today. Certainly, the urban family encounters natural signs, but many of those might take on the status of artifacts to the extent that they were put in place by other people, such as urban landscape architects. Of more importance is the fact that as this family goes about its business during the day, it is bombarded by artifacts of every sort, by a pressure cooker of signs that bespeak other people, certainly to a greater extent than was the farm family. Most of us live somewhere in between these two extremes, but the point to remember is that in general, people today are exposed to more artifacts.

As an expanding population puts more of us in touch with more people and with the artifacts that they have produced, more of us are influenced by more signs. People have, obviously, had their everyday experiences in all times and places, but today's everyday experiences are, relatively speaking, more full of human voices than has been the case in the past. Those voices call to us from the objects and events of everyday experience. What are they saying to us? How are they influencing us? Such rhetorical questions about popular culture are more pressing today.

Exposure to artifacts produced during daily living with many more people also means that we are exposed to more artifacts and texts that are not verbal, expositional, discrete, or hierarchical. When we are surrounded by more people and thus by more signs that they have produced, artifacts come to us in a hodge podge. We are exposed to signs that come and go quickly, without time for expositional development; to signs that are nonverbal rather than verbal; and to signs that are mixed in with other signs, rather than discrete. And the clear imposition of a hierarchical relationship that is present in the experience of public speaking is much less apparent in today's signs. Instead we, as consumers of signs and artifacts, become more instrumental in structuring how those signs and artifacts are experienced and understood. How we do so, and how that influences the effects those signs and artifacts have upon us, are also rhetorical questions that are relatively more important today.

Exercise 2.4

A quick exercise will illustrate the extent to which you are surrounded by other people, and by their artifacts. Consider, either on your own or in class discussion, the following questions:

1. From where you are right now, physically, how far would you have to go to be able to see or hear any three things that were not designed, produced, or placed where they are by other people?
2. When was the last time that you were more than one minute away from the sight or sound of another person?
3. Of all the sights and sounds you have experienced in the last twenty-four hours, what percentage would you say took the form of verbal, expositional, discrete, and hierarchical texts?

Technology

A second development within "real life" in the twentieth century has been expanding *technology*. This development has been both quantitative (we are exposed to more technologies, more often, in more different experiences than people used to be) and qualitative (we are exposed to technologies that are wholly different and unprecedented in human history). Of particular interest for the rhetoric of popular culture are the technologies of communication.

In the centuries following the ancient Greeks, technologies for distributing the written word were gradually developed, most notably the printing press. Although print technologies can certainly distribute other kinds of texts, think about how well suited these technologies are for the distribution of traditional rhetorical texts (see Postman, 1985). Clearly, print is verbal; it presents words "as good as they can get," so to speak, whereas nonverbal or pictorial images in print are "still," and thus able to represent far less, proportionally, of the visual dimension of experience than words in print can of the verbal dimension. The long and careful development of arguments is very well suited to print, for print allows readers to go over difficult proofs and arguments repeatedly if they need to. Most printed texts (such as this book, for instance) are perceived as discrete texts. And printed texts establish a clear, one-way hierarchy of communication; readers cannot talk back *while* using that medium.

But radical differences in communication have occurred in the twentieth century. These differences are the products of developments of technology for the distribution and transfer of other kinds of signs and texts.

Today, the individual with a personal stereo and headphones (such as a Walkman, for example) can go through the entire day literally attached to a technology of communication. There is not a single moment of that person's day, no place of retreat at all, where technology cannot carry a message. If the personal stereo is switched to radio, that person can be reached by messages and other texts generated only an instant before anywhere in the world. If the person needs to be reached by telephone, an electronic pager can contact her anywhere she might happen to be. Cordless telephones in the home and office and cellular telephones in the car allow a person to be in voice communication with others at all times.

Elaborate messages for distribution to others can be prepared on tiny laptop computers that can be carried anywhere. Television has given people easy access to a wide range of sights and sounds that they used to have to travel to theaters to experience, and tiny portable televisions now also allow battery-powered mobility. Cable and VCR technologies have expanded this particular form of access to messages even more; a person in possession of cable television and a VCR has access every hour to more information and entertainment, to a greater volume of artifacts tumbling across the screen, than someone living a hundred years ago could have experienced in a year. A person with a computer and modem has access to a great deal of the information, and many of the artifacts, available throughout the world. Could a person one hundred years ago have sat surrounded by more books than he could have read in a lifetime? Of course; but today, a person has instant access, by way of computer networks, to an exponentially larger number of artifacts even than that.

One important result of a vastly increased number of advanced technologies in everyday life has been a vastly increased exposure to artifacts. Technologies like the Walkman allow us to fill our every moment with artifacts, should we choose to do so. More exposure to information technologies means exposure to more artifacts, and thus to more rhetorical influences in our everyday lives.

A less obvious result of the increase in information technologies has been an increase in people's reception of texts that are not verbal, expositional, discrete, and hierarchical. The lyrics of the latest country and western hit coming to us through our headphones may be verbal, but they are not likely to be expositional. The quick scrolling of numbers across a personal computer screen is not verbal, nor is much of the content of the videos on MTV. A person who switches constantly from one station to another while watching television is paying little attention to discrete texts. Instead of the more hierarchical relationship of public speaking, today's information technologies can place receivers of communications in a much more coequal relationship with the producers of communications. For example, when hooked up to a computer network via a modem, a person can respond instantly on-line to the author of a message that appears on his or her screen.

When people have more exposure to and control over a wide range of technologies in their everyday experiences, they acquire more control over how and when they experience signs and artifacts. Ultimately, the Greek rhetorical tradition is inadequate when it comes to understanding how people use and understand the wide range of signs and artifacts available to them through contemporary technologies.

Exercise 2.5

To understand the extent to which new information technologies are a fact of everyday life, consider the following questions on your own or in class discussion:

1. Name at least four information or communication technologies that you could have access to within a two-minute walk from where you are now. (extra points for naming three such technologies that you can see or hear without moving from your chair).
2. Name the last *complete* public speech, or similar traditional text, that you gained access to by using one of the electronic information technologies of information (television, radio, and so on). If you are not able to think of many, draw some conclusions about the sorts of texts that today's technologies seem best suited for.

Pluralism

A third significant development in this century is the growth of *pluralism*. This term can mean many things. Here, by pluralism, we mean the awareness of many perspectives, philosophies, points of view, codes of ethics, aesthetic sensibilities, and so forth, and the awareness of a legitimate grounding for all of these.

The growth of pluralism is directly related to the growth of population and to the spread of information technologies. If you are not directly exposed to very many people during the day, chances are the people to whom you *are* exposed are likely to be people who are just like you. The Great Plains farm family used as an example before would probably have experienced other people who were largely like them—of similar values, religion, ethnic background, and so on. They would surely have been aware of Native Americans living near them, but they would probably not have had much accurate information about them. Limited contacts with people who are different limits people's awareness of the beliefs, values, practices, and experiences of those different others.

However, increased contact with different groups of people will not necessarily increase understanding, particularly if people remain *ethnocentric,* judging different others only by the standards and perspectives of one's own group. Thus the Great Plains family might have known people who traded frequently with the Native Americans, traders who were aware of what these Native Americans thought and felt and what they did, yet who nevertheless dismissed their whole way of life as second-rate and degraded. This Great Plains family was not likely to be pluralistic, in the first case because they were not aware of a wide range of different points of view; they were not exposed to the variety of human thought and experience that there is in the world. And in the second case, neither the Great Plains family nor their trader friends were pluralistic because, whatever the differences of which they *were* aware, they probably would have seen no legitimacy for those different ideas and experiences.

But expanding population and information technologies have made for a relative change. As more and more people come to live in proximity to one another, they become more aware of their differences. The experience of immigrants clustering in American cities in the first part of the twentieth century is a good example. In this case, people from Ireland, Italy, Germany, and other countries were suddenly forced to live in relatively close proximity to each other, and thus to learn about each other. Information technologies serve the same function, allowing us to find out more about people who live even on the other side of the world, as if we were neighbors, through things like the *National Geographic* specials on public television, for example. Today, it is hard not to be aware of many other groups of people, of their habits, customs, and beliefs. (See Meyrowitz [1985] for a graphic presentation of the extent to which technologies of communication are responsible for revealing groups of people to each other today.)

An even more important dimension of pluralism, however, is a growing recognition that the beliefs and customs of other, different people have some sort of legitimacy or grounding. This is not to say that we must agree with those who are different (nor that people often do so), but rather that we are aware that others feel that they have good reasons for thinking and doing the things they do. People are becoming increasingly aware that other people have philosophical, social, religious, or other reasons for their thoughts and behavior, just as "we" do.

In the nineteenth century, for instance, people might have marvelled at stories, brought back by explorers of faraway societies, of people who put their elderly onto ice floes and cast them off into the sea; "civilized" people might have shuddered and condemned the members of such societies as hopeless "savages." Today, however, we might consider such a practice wrong, but we would at least be willing to seek to understand the reason for it; we would expect such a practice to have legitimacy for that particular society, even if we would be appalled at the thought of doing anything of the sort ourselves. This sort of understanding of difference is relatively new; such understanding has always been held by some, but is held more widely today. There is no doubt that prejudice and ethnocentrism still exist, but they exist in a curious mixture with increased knowledge of other people and of *why* others are different.

One important result of pluralism—that is, of an awareness and acknowledgement of the legitimacy of others who are different—has been a democratization of status. Prejudice, bigotry, racism, classism and sexism do still exist, of course. Nevertheless, there has been a relative increase in such pluralistic awareness in many countries over the last few decades, with the result that many different groups have been granted legal and political power, or status, that they did not have before.

At the beginning of this century, for instance, only white males could vote in the United States. Women and members of other races did not have as much of a voice as they do today. Certainly, biases against these groups still exist, but today's intentional pursuit of rights and prerogatives for all sorts of groups is practically unprecedented in history. Whereas second-class status was common for many groups in nearly all earlier times and nations, many democratic nations today try not to place any of their citizens in second-class positions. Of a different kind of importance than traditional power (such as the right to vote) is the power that comes from increased presence in the shared texts of a culture. Pick up most newspapers and turn on most television shows, and you will see, hear, and learn from and about whole groups of people who might have been, in African-American novelist Ralph Ellison's terms, "invisible" people only a few decades before.

Pluralism challenges the Greek legacy in a number of ways, two of which we will explore here. First, it legitimizes signs and texts that are not verbal, expositional, discrete, and hierarchical in the ways that traditional public speaking is. The Greek legacy is predominantly a European legacy, since European culture was strongly influenced by Greece. That European culture has been dominant in the West for centuries, of course. But people from non-European backgrounds (such as African, Asian, or Native American) who came to industrialized democracies such as the United States have developed other ways of communicating, through texts that do not share the same discrete, verbal, expositional, and hierarchical characteristics.

In his book *The Afrocentric Idea* (1987), for example, Molefi Kete Asante shows how the "Afrocentric" pattern of communicating features unity, wholeness, dialogue, and aesthetics in ways that are distinct from the structure and argumentative patterns of traditional European-based public speaking. Women, who historically had relatively less access to the forums of public speaking than did men, developed more interactional and dialogic forms of communication geared to the patterns of everyday conversation (Treichler and Kramarae 1983; Kramer 1974). Other ethnic and cultural groups have patterns of communicating rhetorically that are specific to their own heritages and that do not follow the Greek model. Pluralism demands, in other words, that we consider alternative rhetorics, other ways in which people use signs to influence others and are influenced by signs in their turn.

A second way in which pluralism challenges the Greek legacy is by creating the possibility of shifting the locus of where and when the important business of a society is conducted. In the Greek legacy, important business is conducted only by those who are officially empowered to conduct it, either members of the public, using traditional texts, or the expert few. These, of course, will be the people who are empowered generally, who are in charge within a society. If important business is only conducted by those officially empowered to do so, then only in specifically designated places and times will you find business that is considered important or valuable going on. So for the Greeks, important business happened in their assemblies, but not in their homes. In the Roman Empire, important business was done in the legal and the imperial courts, but not in the baths.

When certain groups and classes in complex societies are not empowered, or are suppressed, they become *marginalized*. Their actions, thoughts, voices, feelings, practices, and so forth are assumed not to have any part in the management of important business. Instead, these groups are moved to the "margins" of power; whatever they do, it is assumed that their actions are not part of the exercise of power taking place at the official "center" of society. In other words, society allows such groups to live and communicate only within the times and places in which that important, official business is *not* being conducted.

Of course, all of us step into the margins from time to time; for instance, if you go fishing, play cards, or watch television with your family, the Greek legacy would hold that you are not doing anything of much importance. But people who are often and repeatedly disempowered are made to occupy the margin for the long term. One outcome of such marginalizing is the assumption that whatever the group in question does must perforce be marginal, or of less value; such an assumption is the very essence of racism and sexism, for instance. This point is illustrated by the Greeks themselves: Official business was conducted by the citizens in their assembly, while women, slaves, foreigners, and so forth continued to talk and to do their business within the "margins" of society: homes, taverns, farms, and so forth. What women, slaves, foreigners, and so on did was not considered the important business of society.

But in a more pluralistic society (which nearly all industrialized democracies are now or are becoming increasingly), awareness of different groups and of the legitimacy of those groups' practices and beliefs brings an increase in the status of those practices and beliefs. And this means that what marginalized people say and do assumes more importance in terms of what happens generally in a society. Thus, the margin shrinks. People who were ignored a century ago are now publicly noticed and heard. The margin is still there and probably always will be, but pluralism makes it shrink, relatively speaking.

The challenge a shrinking margin poses to the Greek legacy has to do with the fact that traditional texts have not usually been found in that margin. Many of the signs and texts found in society's margins are not verbal, expositional, discrete or hierarchical. As noted before, people who have previously been disempowered have developed texts that differ from those traditional forms. The growth of pluralism has given rise to texts that cannot be accounted for by the Greek legacy.

Knowledge

A fourth development in this century that has worked against the Greek legacy is the incredible expansion of *knowledge,* specifically technical and scientific knowledge. It can hardly be denied that what there is to know has increased exponentially in this century. Science especially, aided by the information technologies (such as the computer) that we discussed earlier in this chapter, has amassed enormous amounts of information. So much information has been gathered and is being gathered even as you read this book that the ability to organize, understand, and gain access to that information has become a major problem, one as complicated as that of discovering new information.

Knowledge is becoming increasingly specialized. Whereas one hundred years ago one might be simply a physician, today even a specialization like internal medicine is rather broad; sub-specialties such as gastroenterology exist, and even the knowledge covered within that sub-specialty is vast. New scholarly journals and books are being churned out by the hundreds at this very moment. The explosion of knowledge is obvious and simply stated; the impact of that explosion upon the Greek legacy is significant and complex.

One effect of the knowledge explosion has to do with the relationship between knowledge and how decisions are made—that is, with the specialization of decision making. Of course, you need knowledge to make decisions. Historically, technical or scientific knowledge has been used in the decision making associated with traditional texts. By "technical or scientific knowledge" we mean knowledge based on research, public knowledge acquired through scientific methods rather than simply through personal experience. For example, when we argue expositionally, we consult facts and figures, examples, history, expert testimony, and so forth. Such knowledge has traditionally been considered more valuable than knowledge acquired simply through everyday experience or through other means. But the available technical or scientific knowledge is becoming more and more specialized as it increases in sheer volume. As such specialization happens, the location of decision making also tends to become more specialized.

The problem is that there is a limit to what decision makers can understand. As total knowledge grows, the amount that decision makers can understand stays about the same; thus, decision makers' knowledge must become more specialized, since the amount that a person can understand and control shrinks as a percentage of what is known overall. The result is that decisions based on technical or scientific knowledge are increasingly referred to specialists and experts. The general public cannot possess enough technical and scientific knowledge to argue expositionally and to make judgments about many issues that depend upon that knowledge.

Today, for instance, public decisions must be made about the issue of nuclear power: whether to build nuclear plants, where to build them, what to do with nuclear waste, and so forth. To make these decisions, knowledge is needed. But who can know enough about nuclear engineering to make a decision that is informed by technical knowledge? It is unlikely that ordinary people know very much about that subject, nor do our representatives in government. Increasingly, it is scientists in governmental or industrialized bureaucracies who are specialized enough in their knowledge to be able to make decisions about what sort of material to use in the reactor core, what the allowable ranges of radiation, temperature, and leakage should be, and so on.

But suppose you take it to be your duty to read up on nuclear power. The next issue to come along, however, is whether the state should control surrogate motherhood. Do you know all the medical and legal facts that you need to know in order to participate in making *that* decision? And so it goes.

The problem that this situation poses for the Greek legacy is rooted in the fact that the ideal of that legacy is popular participation in public decision making through public speaking. The Greek legacy is built upon the model of citizens who know enough about the issues that confront them to be able to form and develop expositional arguments about such issues, to understand the issues well enough to debate them. Traditional rhetorical texts, with their four characteristics, are designed for a rational, well-informed, step-by-step, consideration of issues. The problem is, the public can no longer confront most of the issues faced today in that way. Today's issues and problems are too vast for people to debate them rationally and expositionally, in the way envisioned by the ancient Greeks.

A number of thinkers have complained that the public is no longer able to argue expositionally and rationally (see Postman [1985], for example). The problem is actually a result of the knowledge explosion: people cannot possibly know all they need to know, and gather that knowledge into rational arguments, in order to debate public issues expositionally. It would take hours simply to recite all the studies, facts and figures, statistics, and so forth that one would need to know to be able to make a decision about most public issues. A further problem is that there are so many public issues for which there is an overabundance of specialized knowledge that the chances of an audience understanding and being able to follow a knowledgeable speaker on a technical topic are not great. This problem is true for all traditional rhetorical texts, essays and articles as well as speeches. Information has outgrown the ability of this type of text to handle it.

The explosion of knowledge confronts us with this choice: Either the public will become increasingly excluded from important decision making, as those decisions are referred to experts who understand specialized technical and scientific knowledge; or, people will find ways to understand public problems through other means besides traditional texts that rely upon scientific and technical knowledge. It may be that important public business is already being managed in ways that are not limited to texts that depend upon scientific and technical knowledge. And if that is true, then important public business is being conducted through texts other than traditional texts that are verbal, expositional, discrete, and hierarchical.

Managing Power in Popular Culture

What kind of business is managed through the texts of popular culture? That question raises the whole issue of what popular culture is, and why it is worth studying. You will recall from Chapter 1 that we learned that people grow in and are sustained by popular culture, by the artifacts and experiences of everyday life. Furthermore, we considered the idea that empowerment and disempowerment in our society do not occur only in grand, isolated moments, but are enacted in the artifacts and experiences of everyday life. Because of the growth in population, technology, pluralism, and knowledge that we have been discussing in this chapter, it is increasingly the case that public business is not being managed, and cannot be managed, in occasional, single moments of rhetoric (the "great speech," the "important essay," the "pivotal book," and so forth). Because of the growth in these four areas, more of the important business of our society is now done from moment to moment in people's experiences of popular culture.

This is a relative difference: there has always been some public business done within the realm of popular culture, even if theorists did not recognize it; and today, there is still some business conducted through the "great speech" and so on. A century ago, the business of managing the problem of racism would have depended primarily on the impact of great, occasional rhetorical efforts by leaders such as Booker T. Washington or W. E. B. DuBois. But today many of the problems of racism are managed on the television show *In Living Color*, in different styles of clothing and grooming, and in moment-to-moment interactions in public schools.

Let us pursue the example of racism further. Earlier in this chapter (pages 41–46), we discussed the meaning of the management of power. How do the ideas we explored there apply to the public problem of racism, as it is managed in popular culture? People must decide what to do and how to behave in relation to people of other races. We must also decide what cultural differences mean: for example, is it threatening or not when people of another race speak more loudly than we do, walk in a different way, stand too close to or too far from us, or use eye contact differently? Are such decisions managed, or influenced by, stirring speeches or lengthy essays today? Probably not. Instead, the problem of racism is being managed in the plots of television sitcoms and dramas that take racism as an occasional theme and urge certain audience responses to it. Racism is managed in fashion, as shirts and caps with the name or photograph of Malcolm X, or slogans of racial pride, are worn in public and seen by people of all races. And racism is managed in athletics, as people of color are elevated to heroic, even mythic, status by their exploits on the field. Racism is being managed and struggled over every time two white kids argue over whether the latest rap album is worth spending this week's allowance on. There, in the everyday texts of popular culture, is where racism is increasingly managed today.

The same holds true for the management of many other public issues. Earlier, we discussed the increasing inability of traditional texts to manage the problem of nuclear power. For the public at large, concerns for nuclear safety may be embodied in the plots of movies that urge clear stances toward the nuclear power industry. Comic books influence young minds with depictions of monsters that crawl out of contaminated swamps, and many jokes are made on the television show *The Simpsons* about the poor safety conditions at the nuclear power plant at which Homer works. On the other hand, safe nuclear power took fictional space ships to the edges of the universe in much of the science fiction of the 1950s. These texts of popular culture shape many of today's arguments over the issue of nuclear power.

If we want to understand how people are influenced on these and other issues, and how public affairs are nudged in one direction or another, we need to look more at what is happening on television than on the Senate floor. The theory of rhetoric today is increasingly recognizing the important business that is done through popular culture, as we will see in upcoming discussions in this book. In short, more important business is being done in the culture of everyday life, and theory has begun to recognize that business more fully than it ever has before.

The Texts of Popular Culture

In the next two chapters, we will look more closely at how the rhetoric of popular culture works, at how to study it and examine it. By way of preparation, though, we need to think very broadly about how the texts of popular culture differ from traditional texts. These differences can be best understood in reference to the four characteristics—verbal, expository, discrete, and hierarchical—of traditional texts.

First, in addition to verbal texts, the rhetoric of popular culture will be manifested in *nonverbal* texts. People are influenced not only through words but also through the images they see. Furthermore, the struggle over power can be conducted nonverbally as well as verbally. One person flies an American flag proudly while another person wears it on the seat of his or her pants; both are rhetorical attempts to use signs to influence others and to manage what it means to be American. A coal mining company shows pictures of a beautifully restored former strip mining pit, while mining opponents show pictures of devastation and ruin; here, too, is the use of nonverbal signs, in this case as part of the struggle over how the public business of energy and land use is to be managed.

Second, in addition to *expositional* texts, the rhetoric of popular culture will be manifested in texts that are *metonymic* and *narrative*. Metonymy is the name of a classical *trope*, or way of thinking, that means reduction. When you think about something by reducing it to a simpler, smaller, more manageable image that leaves out certain details of the larger whole, you are using metonymy. The president is a metonymy of the whole executive branch of the government, for example. The executive branch is actually many, many offices and officers, aides and advisers, all hard at work behind the scenes. But when we say "President Clinton decided that . . ." or "President Clinton sent to Congress . . ." we are using metonymy to describe this very complex institution in terms of a person. The idea of an individual president is understandable; the web of officials and offices that actually make up the executive branch, however, is much harder to grasp.

Metonymy is a reaction to the problem of the explosion of knowledge, which we have already discussed. The political problems of the Middle East, for instance, are vast and complex. It is unlikely that most of the public could claim to understand the intricacies of those problems or of the relationship of that region to the United States. Therefore, we often find metonymy at work in reducing the Middle East and its problems to images, stories, or quick explanations that allow the public to "get a grasp" on a complex situation. Metonymy is crucial to the aspect of power management that controls meaning. Part of that metonymy of the Middle East will be a focus on American or European hostages; any time one of "our people" is taken prisoner in the Middle East, the event will dominate media attention for a while. That is because our frustrations about dealing with so-called "terrorists," with a seemingly unending conflict over which we have little control, and with people who do things differently from us, can all be reduced to stories about the abduction of hostages. Through metonymy, American fears about uncontrollable political forces in the Middle East can also be reduced to images of feared leaders such as Saddam Hussein or Muammar Ghaddafi.

One of the most important ways in which metonymy is used to deal with complex issues is through *narrative,* or the telling of stories. Instead of developing complex arguments and amassing proof, as in expositional texts, many texts of popular culture either tell stories or are storylike, using both words and images. Think about the various complex social issues that have been struggled over through the means of popular films, for instance, such as race relations in *Driving Miss Daisy* and *Malcolm X,* and the disintegration of marriages in *Fatal Attraction* and *Indecent Proposal.* Television shows will often air episodes that deal with complex social issues in thirty-minute installments by turning them into stories (this week will address alcoholism, next week will take on child abuse, and so forth). Through metonymy and narrative, texts in popular culture participate in struggles over power and disempowerment, and manage issues that were (and sometimes still are) debated in lengthy, expositional arguments elsewhere.

In addition to discrete texts, the rhetoric of popular culture will be manifested in *diffuse* texts. Several points must be understood here. First, many texts of popular culture do take the form of discrete texts, although they often do not share the other characteristics of traditional texts (they are largely nonverbal, or not expositional, for example). A discrete text, you will recall, is a group of signs that is perceived to be discrete in time and space, with clear boundaries and clearly separate from its context. A diffuse text will sometimes not be recognized as a text by those who experience it, and at other times will be recognized by them as a very complex experience. A diffuse text is a collection of signs working for the same or related rhetorical influence that is not discretely separated from its context. Many of the texts of popular culture occur in diffuse form.

One good example of a diffuse text would be the whole experience of watching televised football. Most people watch televised football with other people, in small groups. Think about what typically goes on during such an experience: people talk with each other, both about the game and about issues relating to other dimensions of life; the television set is broadcasting both images of the game and an overlay of the commentators' talk about the game; people come and go between where the television is situated and other parts of the house or bar (for refreshments, bathroom breaks, and so forth); people often switch rapidly among several channels in order to check on other games as well. All of these signs and artifacts, mixed together in an incredible jumble, contribute to the same rhetorical effect of enjoyment, of involvement in football, of becoming a fan. Yet we would be hard-pressed to identify where this text begins and where it ends, to put boundaries in time and space on this system of signs. Thus, the experience of watching televised football is a diffuse text. Yet it has rhetorical influence, and because so many people are so enthusiastically involved in following football, it even manages what has become some of society's important business.

Exercise 2.6

In the preceding paragraph it was suggested that spectator sports manage some of our society's important business. On your own or in class, consider these questions carefully: When people follow their favorite sport on television, in the newspapers, or at the stadium, are some important public problems being addressed? Which problems do today's spectator sports industries help to manage? In other words, when people become sports fans are they *just* sports fans or are there wider implications to what they are doing?

The following points may help you to think about the questions posed above:

1. When the Persian Gulf War of 1991 broke out shortly before the Superbowl, there was a great deal of public discussion over whether the game should be held or not, given the gravity of world events. But the game went forth as scheduled.

2. When sports figures are involved in various scandals such as gambling, steroid use, or sexual abuse, sports commentators often sadly claim that it is especially tragic that sports figures should be involved in such activities.

3. Attempts by Japanese investors to buy the Seattle Mariners baseball team in 1992 were met by cries of anguish throughout the United States.

Finally, in addition to texts that are hierarchical, the rhetoric of popular culture is manifested in texts that are *democratic*. In the preceding example of watching televised football, who makes the text? Who puts it all together? Clearly, the fans, the viewers, the audience or receivers of communication do. Of course, a person reading a book or listening to a speech has a choice in how to experience those traditional texts to some extent; but relatively speaking, the football viewer has more choice and control. The fan is not placed in a situation where time, place, and procedures for experiencing texts are constrained as much as they are in the case of most public speeches. The fan is more actively at work assembling many related signs into a diffuse text. This is how much of the rhetoric of popular culture occurs: People walk through the crowded sea of signs that are available today (down a city street for instance), assembling diffuse texts to suit their needs and desires, in ways over which they have more choice and control.

Because the rhetoric of popular culture is (relatively) democratic, it may be found to be at work in marginalized areas of society, where traditional rhetoric was not so likely to reach. Some scholars, such as John Fiske (1989a, 1989b), even argue that popular culture springs *exclusively* from groups of people who have been oppressed and marginalized. It is true that the texts of popular culture often emerge from, and do their work among, the young, the poor, women, racial minorities, and others who have not been officially empowered. This is a relative difference as well, but a real one. The upper classes from Nob Hill watch ballet, while the disempowered from South Boston go bowling.

In general, then, texts of popular culture will be relatively more nonverbal, metonymic and narrative, diffuse, and democratic than are more traditional texts. Increasingly, because of the changes in real life conditions that we have discussed in this chapter, the important business of society is managed in those texts of popular culture. In this chapter, we have seen what the rhetorical tradition is, and why changing conditions are moving us away from it.

Summary and Review

This chapter has covered many ideas and more than two thousand years. First, we discussed the idea that definitions in general are a means to empowerment and disempowerment; how you define a term is an act of power. Some terms that have a lot to do with power have therefore been defined in many different ways throughout history; *rhetoric* is such a term.

We learned a little about the history of ancient Greece, and about how public speaking was the public's way of rhetorically managing important business. In subsequent years, this experience of the Greeks would create a legacy that strongly affected the development of rhetorical theory. This legacy comprises what we might call *traditional rhetoric*. Traditional rhetoric assumes, first, that rhetoric means a particular kind of text, the kind that is most clearly exemplified in public speaking—that is, a text that is verbal, expositional, discrete, and hierarchical. The second part of the Greek legacy for traditional rhetoric is a paradox. We learned here that the more favorably rhetoric is defined, the more it democratizes power, because widespread participation in public decisions is conducted through rhetorical discussion. But paradoxically, we also learned that because rhetoric meant traditional texts for the Greeks, the rhetorical tradition fails to see how important business might be conducted by texts that are not verbal, expositional, discrete, and hierarchical.

We saw how this Greek legacy, embodied in traditional rhetorical theory, influenced writers and thinkers for centuries. From the eighteenth through the twentieth centuries, however, the germs of new ideas were planted, new ideas that would eventually allow for the development of a rhetoric of popular culture. We also learned that "real life" developments in the twentieth century increasingly challenge the rhetorical tradition. We explored the specific developments of (1) an expanding population, (2) new technologies (especially of information), (3) pluralism, and (4) an explosion of knowledge. Because of these developments, we concluded that much of the important business of a society might not be conducted in traditional texts as exclusively as the Greek legacy would have us believe. Instead of only verbal texts, we will look for texts that also include nonverbal elements. Instead of only expositional texts, we will also look for metonymy and narrative. Instead of only discrete texts, we will also look for diffuse texts. And instead of only hierarchical texts, we will also look for democratic texts. In the next two chapters, then, we will deal more specifically with how the rhetoric of popular culture works and how to study it.

Looking Ahead

We have left many questions unanswered. So far, we have only a general idea of the basic characteristics of the texts that enact the rhetoric of popular culture. We need a clearer idea of *what to look for* in texts of popular culture. So one important question in the next chapter will be, What does the critic look for in identifying the texts of popular culture?

Critical analysis of rhetoric is never a lockstep procedure, though. Different critics will be interested in different aspects of a given subject, or will want to ask different questions about a text. So a second question for us in the next chapter will be, What choices are available to the critic of popular culture?

We also need a clearer sense of how texts work to manage society's business through popular culture. Thus, an important final question for us will be, What is it about texts that persuade people? And since most texts are complex and exert influence in several different ways, we will also want to know how to analyze texts on several different levels. These and other questions will be taken up in Chapters 3 and 4.

Chapter 3

Rhetorical Methods in Critical Studies

●●●●●●●●●●●●●●●●●●●●●●●●●●●●●

If you are an alert reader of chapter titles, you may be wondering about the title of this one. You knew that you were going to study rhetoric, but here, apparently, is a chapter that also seems to be about critical studies, whatever that may be.

There are at least two reasons for this chapter's title. First, most of those who study the ways in which popular culture influences people are working within a general approach to scholarship known as *critical studies* (although not all of these people use the term *rhetoric*). We will look at what *critical studies* means in more detail a little later on. Second, what you do when you study the rhetoric of popular culture and then share your findings with others is known as *criticism;* you will end up writing or presenting criticism, or a critique, of the particular aspect of popular culture that you are studying. The last three chapters of this book, for instance, are examples of critical studies—of race relations in Milwaukee, visual pleasure, and Afrocentricity.

This chapter is concerned with *how to think about rhetorical criticism.* It should not be taken as a set of instructions for how to march lockstep through a term paper. The different sections of this chapter, for instance, are not a "step 1, step 2" guide to how to write a critique. Preparing an actual critique or a critical study is like writing an essay, and you should proceed as you would for writing any essay or report. What is more important is understanding how to go about critiquing popular culture so that you will have something to say in your critique. That is what this chapter will equip you to do.

Texts as Sites of Struggle

Before we learn more about critiquing the rhetoric of popular culture, we need to clarify two basic principles that will underlie the critical methods explained in the rest of the book. These two principles together create a paradox about the nature of texts. First, we will learn that texts wield rhetorical influence because of the meanings that they support. In other words, people make texts so as to influence others. Second, we will learn that because texts can mean different things, they are often sites of struggle over meaning (and thus, over how and what or whom they will influence). Creation of a text may be the point of rhetorical struggle. In other words, people influence each other so as to make texts. The paradox is that a text is both a means to, and an outcome of, rhetorical struggle.

Texts Influence through Meanings

We noted earlier in this book that texts influence people to think and act in certain ways. That influence is the rhetorical dimension of texts. Here, we need to be more specific about exactly what motivates or drives that influence: the *meanings* that texts encourage people to accept. We think or act in certain ways, in response to texts, because of the meanings that the texts have for us, and the meanings that texts urge us to attribute to our experience.

Toward the end of a stellar career in professional baseball, Pete Rose was discovered to have gambled heavily on the game. A great deal of controversy arose over that discovery. Some argued that he should be banished from the game and sent to jail. Others thought he should be forbidden entry into the Baseball Hall of Fame. Many thought that his gambling was a form of illness, and that he should not be punished for it in any way. Lots of texts appeared in the popular press, and the purpose of those texts was to urge people to attribute certain meanings to Rose, to gambling, to professional baseball, and to the Baseball Hall of Fame. Some texts wanted people to think that gambling was a serious offense, especially in the context of sports. Some texts wanted people to see the Hall of Fame as a shrine of purity, a place that should not be sullied by the presence of someone convicted of a crime. Some texts argued that gambling was really an illness, that Rose himself was therefore ill, and that part of the meaning of *illness* is that it should be cured rather than punished. Why did all these texts create all these meanings, and why did they urge such meanings upon the public? Because *choices and actions* that the public might adopt *depend on meaning*. You will not vote to keep Pete Rose out of the Hall of Fame unless gambling means something criminal or wicked to you. And you will be moved to forgive and forget if Pete Rose's actions mean, to you, simply something that everybody does now and then.

Texts generate meanings about other things in the world. Texts also have meanings themselves; for example, Pete Rose himself is a text, or at least a complex artifact, with meaning. Whatever influence texts have on people's thoughts and actions arises from what those texts mean to them. Faced with a row of otherwise indistinguishable jugs of motor oil in a hardware store, you will buy the oil that has the most favorable meanings. Of course, advertisers for oil, gasoline, soap, and other largely similar products spend a great deal of money trying to attach certain meanings to their products, since those goods are hard to distinguish on the basis of their own intrinsic values. So if you pick Quaker State over Pennzoil, it is because advertisers have succeeded in causing Quaker State to mean something to you that you prefer over whatever Pennzoil has come to mean.

Texts are Sites of Struggle over Meaning

We now have to complicate the first principle we have learned, by turning to the other side of the paradox of texts. As we learned in the first chapter, meaning is rarely simple. Instead, what a given text means, what a sign or artifact means as the result of a text's persuasive influence, is often very complicated. That is because, especially in the case of symbolic meaning, meaning itself is rarely simple and straightforward. You can see this complexity in our example of Pete Rose. What he and his gambling mean is being struggled over, even today, in the texts of popular culture. Within the last decade, we have seen a dramatic change in the meaning of the states of the former Soviet Union in the minds of Americans. These states have "meant" either friend or foe as governments have come and gone, rebellions and uprisings have occurred and been crushed, and relationships to the United States have varied.

The meaning of the popular music favored by young people has always been struggled over. From Elvis to Ice-T, these artifacts have meant one thing to their fans and another thing to parents, police, and pastors or priests. In other words, people struggle over how to construct these different texts in ways that suit their own interests. Making a rap artist into one kind of text or another is therefore one goal of rhetorical struggle.

These meanings are struggled over precisely because of the first principle we discussed: Meanings are where the rhetorical power lies. The meaning of a president's decision to send troops into action against a foreign power will have enormous payoff in terms of who runs the government after the next election. Therefore, the president's political friends and enemies will spend a great deal of time and effort urging the public to adopt competing meanings about that action. Furthermore, the meanings of the very texts produced by those friends and enemies are also at stake. The whole business of so-called "spin doctors," or public opinion shapers, is to struggle over the meanings of texts themselves, so that texts can go on to influence further meanings. Scholars in the field of critical studies describe this state of affairs when they note that meanings, and therefore the texts that generate meanings, are *sites of struggle*. The idea is that struggles over power occur in the creation and reception of texts as much as (or more than) they occur at the ballot box, in the streets, or during revolutions.

The critic of the rhetoric of popular culture (which is what you, as a reader of this book, are training to become) can play an important role in those struggles. Critics are *meaning detectives;* their role is to explain what texts mean. Rarely do good critics claim to explain the only possible meaning that a text could have. Instead, the best and richest analyses show ranges of meanings, and may explain the ways in which certain texts are sites of struggle over meaning. Because meaning is the avenue through which texts wield influence, critics work directly to explain how it is that people are empowered or disempowered by the meanings of various texts.

Exercise 3.1

To better understand why meaning is the source of the influence exerted by the rhetoric of popular culture, do this quick exercise on your own or in class on the instructions of your teacher.

Think about the last article of clothing that you bought because you really liked it and wanted to own it (that is, not some socks you bought in a rush because your other gray pair had too many holes). Do some self-examination and think about what that article of clothing means to you: Does it mean physical attractiveness? Elegance? Fun in the sun? List your own meanings.

Now back up from that article of clothing and consider the meanings that you just listed. Think about other things you might do or items you might buy because of those meanings. For instance, if you bought a tank top because it meant summertime fun to you, what else will you buy or do to produce that same meaning? Sunglasses? An hour in a tanning booth? A Caribbean vacation? If you think about it, it is the *meaning* of these items or experiences that is primary; what you make of the tank top and the shades and the hour in the tanning booth—what these things *mean* to you—is what is going to stick with you.

Finally, think about the paradoxical nature of the various texts in this example. Some texts (such as ads for Caribbean cruises) urge you to accept certain meanings. But an article of clothing is a text that you yourself work over so as to make it support meanings that serve your interests.

To think about the rhetoric of popular culture, or the ways in which the texts and artifacts of popular culture influence us (along with our own participation in making meaning), we need to think about what popular culture means to people—the ways in which those meanings can be multiple and contradictory, and how those meanings are struggled over. Because critics are meaning detectives, a rhetorical criticism is an exercise in showing the influences exerted by signs through their meanings. There are many *methods* (organized, systematic, and reliable ways of thinking) for thinking about popular culture already available to you. Let's begin to consider such methods by examining the wide-ranging, loosely connected set of methods known as *critical studies*.

Three Characteristics of Critical Studies

A large number of people all around the world are studying exactly what you are learning about here (see, for example, Fiske 1989a,1989b; Kuhn 1985; Nelson and Grossberg 1988). Working as university professors, as columnists and commentators, or as independent writers of books and articles, these thinkers and scholars are studying the ways in which experiences of popular culture influence people. Their work follows many different approaches and is based on some widely differing assumptions. But taken as a group, they comprise a loosely knit school of thought or way of thinking that has been called *cultural studies* or *critical studies*. For the sake of convenience, we will use the latter term.

Critical studies is not a professional or social club with its own set of rules. It is not a tightly knit, clearly defined, precisely delineated set of principles. Many of the theories and methods used by scholars in the field of critical studies are, in fact, at odds with one another on some important issues. But there are also some principles that link these theories and methods together and help to define critical studies as a school of thought. In this chapter we will examine the principles that different branches of critical studies have in common, the theories and methods that they share. In Chapter 4, we will look more closely at some differences among a few specific branches of critical studies. Now, however, we will learn that all branches of critical studies are (1) *critical* in attitude and in method, (2) *concerned with power*, and (3) *interventionist*.

The Critical Character

One thing that characterizes the different branches of critical studies is that they are all, unsurprisingly enough, *critical*. In this sense, the term *critical* refers both to (1) an attitude and (2) a method.

Attitude: The critical *attitude* is somewhat related to the everyday, colloquial sense of the term *critical*, though without its negative connotations. If you are being critical, you are disagreeing with, or finding fault with, something. In finding fault, you take apart or dissect another's words and actions, to show their true (and pernicious) meanings. Now, critical studies is *not* exclusively negative in this sense, but it does refuse to take things at face value. It adopts an attitude of suspicion, in other words, in which it assumes that things are often other than (or more than) they seem. Again, this attitude is not intended to be hostile or destructive; it simply means that people in critical studies want to know what else is going on besides the obvious.

Critical studies is always looking beneath the surface. For instance, a critical scholar watching an episode of the television show *L.A. Law* would assume that besides being a set of interrelated stories about some lawyers on the West Coast, the show has meanings and is influencing people in a number of ways. To give another example, it is *not* being critical to say that vampire movies, such as *Dracula*, are stories about the undead who go around biting people on the neck. Such a statement has not gone beyond what is obvious, or merely on the surface. It *is* being critical, however, to say that vampire movies help people deal with problems of conformity and industrialization (Brummett 1984). An observation like that is not obvious, but it can be an interesting insight that the critic discovers and shares with readers. So in sum, the critical scholar must be prepared to dig into texts, to think about the ways that people are being influenced as well as entertained, informed, and so forth, by such texts.

Exercise 3.2

Turn to the examples of magazine ads on pages 105–109. We will refer to these ads often as illustrations of how to use cricital methods. Consider Figure 3.1, the LensCrafters advertisement. We'll think about some more specific ways to study this ad later, but for now, try to "work up some suspicions" about it. Consider these questions: What is going on here besides selling spectacles? What meanings (influences) does the ad offer in addition to considerations of price, speed of service, and style in eyewear? The following are some specific clues that could lead you to become suspicious:

There are both a man and a woman in the ad. Does the ad contain any meanings/influences having to do with differences between men and women, or with the relative status of genders?

The woman is dressed differently in the two pictures. Is the man also dressed differently? What do the woman's two sets of clothing styles mean? What does that band around her hair in the inset picture mean?

What do the two different hairstyles in the two pictures mean?

Consider the words in the ad, especially the words attributed to the woman. What kind of person is she depicted as? Why does the kind of person she is depicted as matter?

There are no absolutely right or wrong answers to these questions; the point is for you to see that for this advertisement, as for most texts, there may be some interesting meanings, or influences, at work beyond the obvious ones.

Method: Critical studies is also a *method,* a way of asking certain kinds of questions about whatever is being studied. These questions are about meaning, complexity, and evaluation.

A critical method wants to know about *meaning.* It asks, what does a text, an experience, an object, an action, and so forth mean to different people?

Rather than breaking them up into isolated parts, a critical method deals with the *complexity* of texts and experiences as they are actually experienced. Such a method asks, what are some suggested meanings in the text, what are some of their influences or effects, and how do these influences interrelate with each other?

Finally, a critical method seeks to *evaluate* that which it studies, to make some judgment about whether that object or experience's meanings and influences are good or bad, desirable or undesirable, and so forth. The methods best suited to answering these kinds of questions are sometimes called *qualitative* methods (in contrast to *quantitative* methods that rely more heavily on experimental or survey research). *Critical* is probably a clearer term than *qualitative,* however, so we will return to that usage after the following discussion of the difference between qualitative and quantitative methods.

For an example of the difference between qualitative and quantitative approaches, let's go back to the example of a critic studying *L.A. Law.* Some questions that might be asked in relation to that show are: 1) Did that aspirin commercial half-way through last night's episode increase sales of that particular product? 2) Does the show as a whole series induce more people to pursue an education in law? 3) What are the effects of the occasional violent segments in various episodes?

Now think about the best ways to answer those questions. Questions 1 and 2 are not critical questions, by and large. They might be best answered by survey research; you could simply go out and ask people about their aspirin-buying habits or their educational plans. Or they might be answered by experimental manipulation of variables, in which you compare the aspirin-buying habits and educational plans of a select group of the show's viewers against a control group that does not view the show. Clearly survey and experimental research (rather than simply sitting in a chair and musing about the answers) provide better ways to answer such questions. Both survey and experimental research are considered *quantitative* methods because many of their findings will be expressed using numbers (the numbers of those who buy more aspirin will be compared to the numbers of those who do not, and so forth).

Question 3 is a little different; it is more complex, and might be answered in more than one way. You could answer it quantitatively, by surveying people as to their reactions, or by experimentally comparing those who saw the violence with those who did not. But if you share the assumption with which we began this chapter—that an important dimension of influences and effects is meaning— then it is clear that these quantitative methods will not answer such a question adequately.

Question 3 becomes a critical question when you start to think about what a violent episode of *L.A. Law* means. This is a question that the critic must address. But asking an audience about meaning is usually not sufficient. You can ask people what the violent segment meant to them and get an answer, but that is not a sufficient and efficient way to determine meaning, for three important reasons.

First, meaning is complex. We have already discussed the idea that a given text or artifact means different things as it is considered within different contexts or cultural systems. Even within a single culture, a text will usually have many different meanings. We have noted how contradictions in meaning occur for many artifacts. Opposing meanings might be found in texts that are sites of struggle. All of this means that few people who are not accustomed to thinking about wide ranges of meaning will be able to say, comprehensively, what a text or artifact means. Texts usually have many more meanings than most people are able to see.

Second, people may not be able to articulate meanings. We learned in Chapter 1 that people participate in making meanings, but that does not mean that they can always say how they do so. A meaning detective might consider asking people to say what some text means. But some people are not very good at saying what a text means to them, even though it may mean a lot. Some meanings may be nonverbal, intuitive, or emotional, and therefore not the kind of thing that can easily be put into words. It may take a critic who is trained in talking about meaning to articulate what certain texts mean.

Third, meaning is sometimes *beyond awareness*, so that people may not consciously know what a particular text meant to them. They may not even be aware that they are being influenced by certain texts. Participation in making meaning need not be done intentionally and with full awareness. Most people do not go through the kind of conscious introspection and probing of meaning that you are becoming acquainted with in reading this book. So for many people, artifacts may have meanings of which they are unaware, and therefore meanings that they could not report.

Critical studies is qualitative because it is concerned with qualities more than quantities—and that is another way of saying that it is concerned with meanings.

The critic's job is to explore what a text or artifact means, including its different or contradictory meanings as well as the ways that meanings are struggled over, forced upon some people, and rejected by others. As critics reveal the meanings of texts and artifacts, they are simultaneously doing two things:

1. Critics are *explaining the rhetoric* of popular culture, since, as we discussed above, what texts and artifacts mean are the ways in which they influence people.

2. Critics are showing how to experience life by demonstrating how texts and artifacts might be understood, the meanings that can be found in them.

We have seen earlier in this book that people make sense of, or find meaning in, signs and artifacts as they experience them. To have an experience is to organize signs and artifacts and make them meaningful. For example, take two people watching a parade go by. One is filled with patriotic fervor at the flags and bands. The other is more cynical and not very patriotic, and every flag and band prompts her to grouse about the nation and its policies. These two people are finding very different meanings in the artifacts that go past them, and it would also be fair to say that they are constructing very different experiences for themselves.

The critic's job is to demonstrate ways of experiencing parades by explaining the different ways that parades (or films, or sporting events) mean. But the critic does not have to step into the skins of these two people and show what a given parade definitely meant to a particular person. That would be impossible to do, since nobody can see completely into another's mind. Northrop Frye (1964, 63) makes a useful distinction that explains what the critic does instead: The critic shows what people, in general, *do*, not what specific people *did*. The critic does not say, "Here is what that parade meant to Juan on that particular day." Instead the critic says, "Here is one way that this parade might be experienced (might have meaning)." In doing so, the critic shows his or her reader how meanings might be constructed and how life might be experienced.

Exercise 3.3

This exercise is designed to help you to understand the kinds of questions that are critical, that look into meaning, as opposed to the kinds of questions asked by other methods such as experimentation or survey research. You will find some questions listed below. For each question, determine (a) what methods, steps, or procedures would allow you to answer that question, and (b) whether it (or some aspect of it) can be answered critically.

1. Why do so many people think that the world is coming to an end?
2. What caused World War I?
3. Why is Michael Jackson so unusual?
4. Does my car need a tune-up?
5. Does television fairly represent all races in the United States?
6. Is television more violent than movies today?

Note: You may need to break some of these questions up into issues that can be dealt with critically and issues that cannot be. To answer some questions you may have to count, compare, or observe something as well as apply critical thinking about meaning and evaluation.

Concern with power

The second main characteristic shared by most varieties of critical studies is one that you are already familiar with: a concern for power. Critical studies examines what power is or what it has been understood to be, and how power is created, maintained, shared, lost, and seized. Critical studies acknowledges that power is often secured through the more traditional routes of elections or physical force. But within critical studies there is also an awareness, stemming from the characteristic "suspicion" that we discussed earlier in this chapter, that power is seized and maintained in other, less obvious ways: in architecture, in classroom layouts in public schools, in social norms for proper behavior during movies and sporting events—in other words, in all the experiences of popular culture. As noted at the beginning of this book, the empowerment and disempowerment of whole groups of people occurs bit by bit, drop by drop, in the moment-to-moment experiences of popular culture. The rhetoric of popular culture, or the ways in which popular culture wields its influences, therefore has a lot to do with power.

In thinking about empowerment and disempowerment, critical studies assumes that although it occurs from moment to moment in the experiences of individuals, it follows a pattern set by groups. It is as large classes that people tend to be empowered or disempowered. Of course, individuals do things that empower or disempower them individually. Being elected to the U.S. Senate is personally empowering, immoderate consumption of alcohol is personally disempowering, and so forth. But critical studies assumes that most of the time, people experience power in ways that are similar to the experiences of other members of their groups. If a child is disempowered, according to critical studies, it is because nearly all children are disempowered as a group.

The major demographic categories that have most preoccupied scholars in critical studies have been those of gender, race, and economic class. There are other categories one might consider, including age, religion, sexual/affectional orientation, body type or shape, and degree of physical ability or disability. Actually, the list of such categories is potentially endless, and may vary from one time or situation to another. But critical scholars most often focus on gender, race, and class.

Critical interventionism

We have learned that critical studies are critical in attitude and method and are concerned with power. A third and final characteristic is that they are *interventionist*. That is to say, critical studies are explicitly concerned with *intervening*, or getting involved in problems in order to change the world for the better.

The interventionist nature of critical studies is really an outgrowth of its critical attitude and method and its concern for power. We noted earlier that the field of critical studies attempts to show people how to experience life, or how to find life meaningful, in particular ways. That goal implies that people have choices among different ways to live their lives. If people have choices, then they can be influenced or taught to make sense of experience in certain ways as opposed to others. The critic's job is to show how experience might be understood, and in doing so to give people options for experiencing their lives. As a critic, you cannot help but be interventionist, because any time you show people different ways of doing things, you have intervened in their lives and changed them in some way.

For example, there are powerful social and political interests in our culture that have for decades encouraged consumption of food, fuel, consumer products, and other goods. From television ads to government and industrial press releases, we are told that it is good for the economy for us to buy as many things as we can. We are constantly urged, for example, to strive to "keep up with the Joneses."

From time to time (most recently, in the late 1960s and late 1980s), however, an ecological movement springs up that urges people to find different meanings in the process of buying and consuming. People are encouraged to see acquisition of one product after another as unnecessary and harmful to the environment. The ecologists who urge people to see consumption in this way are doing exactly what rhetorical critics do; they are saying, "Look at this plastic hamburger carton this new way, rather than that old way," and "Buying a new car every other year means a negative effect on the environment as much as it means a positive effect on the economy."

Good critics do just that sort of thing. They show us how to think about and to find meaning in certain things, how to experience certain texts and artifacts; in so doing, they try to change us. It is almost always liberating to realize that you have more options in deciding how to experience life, to be able to see and understand experience in more than one way, to be able to find many meanings in a situation. For that reason, good rhetorical criticism is liberating. It liberates you, the critic, because it gives you a chance to probe into and develop some of these other potential ways of experiencing and understanding. And good rhetorical criticism liberates your readers and listeners as they share the new insights that you have gained. Rhetorical criticism is always judged, therefore, in terms of the insights it provides into how people experience the influences of popular culture, and whether it expands the options that people have for ways of experiencing that influence.

We are now ready to consider some of the ways that critics go about thinking about the rhetoric of popular culture. This chapter will soon shift into a different mode, so be warned: The following sections do not describe steps to follow in a prescribed order, nor do they give directions for writing or presenting criticism. Rather, the actions described here are ways to think about how people experience and what their experiences mean.

In thinking about such issues, critics have to make choices or decisions about what to study, what assumptions to make about what they study, and so on.

Therefore, the rest of this chapter will lay out choices for you to make, but it will *not* tell you what to do. Critics' choices about what to study, and how to think about those objects of study, will direct their attention in different ways, thus exposing different dimensions of meaning. Thinking carefully about these choices is especially important if the texts under consideration are sites of struggle over many possible meanings; in this case, critics must decide which of those meanings to focus upon. In the next part of this chapter we will examine some of the *continua*, or ranges, of choices that are available to critics.

One important thing that rhetorical critics must consider is what the object of criticism will be. By object of criticism we mean the experience that the critic wants to analyze. These objects of criticism are usually, but not always, texts rather than single signs or artifacts. The critic must identify a text and place it in context; we will refer to this identification and placement as *positioning the text*. Obviously, a first step in positioning a text is to find, or identify, a text that you would like to study.

Finding a Text

A fundamental choice in thinking about a rhetorical criticism is that of selecting a text. You will recall from the first two chapters of this book that a text is a set of signs that work together to influence people. Another way to think of a text would be to look for a set of signs that are taken together as creating an interrelated set of meanings. It is important for you to find a text that will be exciting for you to analyze, a text that you will be able to say something about, and a text for which you have some new insights. There are two sources of texts that you should consider.

First, consider your own experience as a source of texts. What have you experienced recently, what has happened to you, what have you seen or heard, that interests you? Have you seen a film or a television show that "turned on" your critical attitude, for instance—one in which you thought that there was something going on beyond the obvious? Can you point to some complex experience, such as going to a wedding or a commencement ceremony, that might usefully be analyzed as a text? Have any of your recent experiences seemed to have something to do with power? Could you point to some magazine article or book that you recently read that worked to empower or disempower people within its own small space of influence? Finally, have you recently experienced a text that excited your interventionist impulses, or your desire to get involved somehow (for example, did you see a movie that you thought was racist in subtle ways, so that you wanted to expose that racism)? These are questions that you might ask in relation to yourself and your own experiences of texts. Remember to look widely for different kinds of texts; we will look more closely at a range of possible choices in a moment.

A second source for finding a text is theory. This term in this context will need some explaining. A *critical theory* is an abstract statement about how people construct meaningful experiences. In contrast, a *criticism* (or *critical study*) is an illustration, or modeling, of that theoretical statement. A theory explains what people do in general, how they make sense of their experiences for the most part. A critical study is an application of a theory—it says, "That generalization can be seen at work here, within this limited frame of space and time."

For example, one critical study began with a theory that said, in a nutshell: Media depictions of political candidates will influence voters by way of the personal details that are revealed about the candidates; one common and important way in which the meanings of those candidates is influenced is through reporting what they eat and drink (Brummett 1981). Notice that this theoretical statement is about how people experience: It makes an assertion about what the media show people and about the meanings that those depictions urge upon the public. Notice that the theory is also abstract or general; that is, it talks about politics overall, not about a particular race for senator or governor.

The actual critical study that was based on that theory went on to illustrate, or model, that abstract statement with some specific examples from the 1980 presidential campaign. President Carter, suffering from the assignment of meanings of weakness and vacillation, was depicted as eating fruits and salads, hardly the stuff of macho images. Ronald Reagan was successful at depicting a homespun, all-American image; he was reported to eat ribs, fried chicken, cotton candy, and of course, jelly beans. Intellectual third-party candidate John Anderson was shown consuming elitist foods like quiche and white wine (Brummett 1981).

A reader of that study should have been instructed by the study in how to use the theory to understand other experiences, in other contexts. After reading such a study, a reader might forever after be alert to references to what candidates for mayor, governor, or representative eat and drink, and to what those references mean. That reader will therefore experience news coverage of other political races more richly, noticing and understanding a little bit more of this aspect of life.

Too often, what you learn in one class is never called upon in other classes, especially across disciplines. But in using theory as a source in selecting a text for critical analysis, your own reading and prior education become valuable resources. In psychology, sociology, anthropology, English, and many other kinds of classes, you have doubtless read critical theories (even if the authors you read did not always refer to their works by that name). For example, some theories describe, in general terms, how people behave in businesses or other organizations; such theories might be illustrated with case studies of what happened at IBM corporate headquarters in New York, or at a Westinghouse plant in Indiana. Some theories describe how people in general understand poems, and will be illustrated by an analysis of a particular poem. Some theories describe the steps that people go through in grieving for the dead, and will give some concrete examples of the experiences of particular mourners.

Exercise 3.4

Think about what you have read in other classes. Describe a theory that you have encountered that describes in general what people do, how people behave, how people experience life or find it meaningful. Summarize that theory in a few sentences. When you first read the theory, was it illustrated with a critical study? Did an example come with it? How would knowing that particular theory equip you to understand other experiences beyond the example provided in that particular critical study?

In other words, suppose you read a theory in a sociology class that made some general statements about the behavior of people in nursing homes. The theory may have come with a critical application, specifically studying the behavior of people in a nursing home in a New Jersey town. Does knowing that theory allow you to make interesting connections to the ways people behave in other institutions, such as public school, summer camp, or the armed forces?

Theories are a useful source for texts because they tell you how to look for a text. For instance, you may never have thought of the stages of a personal relationship as a "text." But after reading Knapp (1984), you might well be able to see a unifying thread linking several events that have occurred in a relationship that you have had, and that unifying thread might constitute a text. Knapp argues that relationships develop or deteriorate in clear stages; his identification of those stages provides a useful system of categories for analysis. In this way, Knapp's theory of relationship stages calls your attention to a unity of influence among signs, or a text, that you might otherwise not have been fully aware of.

Whether you find a text based on your own experience alone, or one that is suggested to you by theory, you will have some important choices to make about how to identify and understand the text. Critical scholars do not always agree about how to make these choices; we will examine some of those differences among scholars in Chapter 4. Here, however, we will examine some of the ranges of choices that are available to you. We will refer to each range of choices as a *continuum*.

First you must choose the *type of text* you want to study: discrete or diffuse. As we will see, a given set of signs could be seen as either discrete or diffuse, depending on the critic's intentions. This choice may be represented on a continuum as follows:

The First Continuum: Type of Text

discrete .... diffuse

The terms *discrete* and *diffuse* should be familiar to you from Chapters 1 and 2. A discrete text is one with clear boundaries in time and space. A diffuse text is one with a perimeter that is not so clear, one that is mixed up with other signs. Whether a text is discrete or diffuse depends on how it is experienced, understood, or used. The critic must decide how he or she wants an audience to experience, understand, or use a text. A set of signs that could be seen as making up a discrete text from one perspective might also be seen as only part of a wider, more diffuse text in someone else's experience.

We are used to choosing to see some texts as discrete and some as diffuse just as a matter of habit, but good critics always consider the full range of choice available to them. The magazine ads in Figures 3.1–3.5 (pages 105–109) are usually taken as discrete texts; it is clear where they begin and end, and it is usually assumed that they will not spill over into the rest of the magazine. But a critic could choose to see each ad as only one component of a more diffuse text, such as a text comprising a dozen ads of a similar type.

The start of school might be understood as a diffuse text, including such signs and artifacts as paying tuition, meeting new friends, finding classrooms, buying books, buying clothes, going to parties and receptions, and so forth. But the critic could choose to take only the first meeting of one class as a more discrete text in its own right. On the other hand, your sister's wedding could be seen as a text with a rather discrete, concentrated core of signs made up of the actual ceremony and the reception afterward. But a critic may choose to include in the text some signs involved with preparation for, and aftermath of, the wedding, thus making it more diffuse.

It may help you in settling on a text to identify where it falls on this first continuum of discrete to diffuse. What are the consequences of choosing a more discrete or more diffuse type of text? Let's consider discrete texts first. Discrete texts are usually easier to identify because the signs that make up the text are close together in time and space; you do not have to "hunt" for them. The signs that make up the discrete text of the film *Home Alone*, for example, are all right there on the screen. Because the signs are together in time and space, people are generally accustomed to identifying such a text as a text. Both the sources and the receivers of messages that are discrete texts can count on that agreement; the people who made the large poster advertisement on the side of a city bus, for instance, know that you are likely to perceive and understand it as a text in and of itself. You do not have to work very hard to convince people that the magazine ads in Figures 3.1–3.5, the television show *Roseanne*, or a billboard are texts, each one a discrete thing or event. In dealing with discrete texts, because people are already aware of your text as a text, the insights that you will have to offer will usually be concentrated on particular details of the text. Your criticism will point to new ways to experience that text and others like it; it will call our attention to meanings that can be found in the text.

By contrast, diffuse texts are harder to identify. In fact, very diffuse texts may be impossible to identify completely—because they are so diffuse. Your task may be to indicate most of a set of signs that seem to be contributing meanings toward the same influences, without being able to identify every sign that could conceivably be part of the set. So if your diffuse text is the start of school, you may have to give an indication of what that text is by naming several of the signs that it comprises, rather than every conceivable one.

Because you have to work harder to pull together a diffuse text, people generally are less likely to identify as a text whatever you are describing as one. When texts are diffuse, people may not be consciously aware of the unity of influence going on among the several signs scattered here and there. Everyone knows that people prepare their income taxes, for instance, but not everyone may be accustomed to seeing that activity as a unity, to seeing all the steps and experiences surrounding that preparation (over weeks or months, at home and in accountants' offices) as a set or a text. Because seeing the preparation of income taxes as a text may be something new for people, the insights offered by your critique are more likely to be both about the text, and about the *existence* of the text itself. You have something interesting to say about the meanings and influences of the signs that make up the experience of preparing income taxes, but you also have something interesting to say in presenting that experience to us as a text.

We have identified a text as a set of signs that work together toward the same influences, which means toward the same meanings. *Identification of meaning* is central to finding a text. What makes a group of signs "hang together" as a text is the fact that you can say that they work together to offer those meanings. But who determines what meanings are? And how do we know what these meanings are? As critic, you also have choices in determining the sources of meanings that a text might have; these choices are represented on our second continuum, which illustrates the range of possible sources of meanings:

The Second Continuum: Sources of Meanings

broad . . . . narrow

One of the basic principles that we discussed at the beginning of this chapter is that meaning is usually complex and many-layered, and may even be self-contradictory. For that reason, it is rarely the case that a critic can completely explain the meaning of a given text. Instead, critics must narrow their focus to some of the more interesting, influential, or controversial meanings. This second continuum can help to guide a critic in making that choice of which meanings to study. This continuum reminds the critic that some meanings are widely held; we will call these *broad* meanings. Other meanings are held by only a few people, or arise only in particular circumstances; we will call these *narrow* meanings. Of course, it is important to remember that we are dealing with a continuum rather than a sharp distinction here; for most texts there is a whole range of meanings that are *more or less* widely shared, in the middle of the continuum.

For instance, what does the film *The Silence of the Lambs* mean? A critic who sets out to study that movie must choose which meanings to focus on, because they cannot all be analyzed at once. Widely agreed upon meanings would include simply what the film's basic plot or story line is. It might be widely agreed upon as a gruesome depiction of mental illness, for instance, and attitudes toward psychotics in general might shape some of the most widely shared meanings. On the other hand, there are more narrowly held meanings that might be a fruitful object of analysis as well. Residents of Milwaukee, and others who recall the 1991 saga of cannibal serial killer Jeffrey Dahmer, might see *The Silence of the Lambs* as relevant to the Dahmer case. Somewhere in the middle of the continuum might lie meanings having to do with the strength and responsibility of women, since it is Clarice, the character played by Jodie Foster, who solves the kidnapping case (though she must rely upon the help of the male Dr. Hannibal Lecter to do so). Such middle-range meanings might occur to a number of people, but not to everyone.

What are the consequences of the critic's choice of meanings to analyze? On the one hand, more widely shared meanings are often more important meanings just because they are so common. It may be important to show what most people think a text means, because meaning underlies how texts influence people. More widely shared meanings are also often easier to demonstrate in a critical analysis; they encounter less resistance because they are already understood by many people. However, because such widely shared meanings are already understood by most people, explaining them further may not go very far towards changing the thinking of those who read or hear the critical analysis. People are less likely to have their eyes and ears opened to a wider range of meaning if they are exposed only to meanings that they already know.

Less widely shared meanings do have the potential to widen the horizons of people who may never have thought of finding such meanings in a text. For instance, several university and professional sports teams have for years had Native American mascots: the Cleveland Indians, the Atlanta Braves, the Redmen of St. John's, the Florida State Seminoles, and so on. The most widely shared meanings for the texts of these mascots were fairly innocuous: They simply "meant" the teams, and occasionally they might have served as reminders of the history of a location and so forth. But critics have begun to point out that a narrower meaning, first held by Native Americans themselves, was much less innocent. For Native Americans those mascots have "meant" racial insults and a cavalier and patronizing treatment of their cultural traditions. Through choosing to reveal and analyze these narrower meanings, critics have succeeded in persuading some teams (for example, those at Stanford University) to replace their mascots (at Stanford, from Indians to Cardinal). That critical effort was not without difficulty; many people claimed to see no derisive meanings in the mascots. In fact, one consequence of choosing to focus on less widely shared meanings is that they are harder to demonstrate to a wide audience of people. But the payoff in terms of changing potentially harmful or insulting meanings that can be attributed to some texts and signs can be greater.

Paying attention to the full range of choices available to the critic, from narrow to broad, is important in revealing texts as sites of struggle. Only by showing what Indian mascots mean (narrowly) to the Menominee or Ojibway *in contrast* to what they mean (broadly) to many non-Native American sports fans could critics show how those meanings are in conflict, and how Native American mascots are therefore sites of struggle. This continuum reminds the critic of a full range of possible meanings, and thus of the likelihood that those meanings will be in conflict with each other in many texts.

Exercise 3.5

Speaking of Native American mascots, turn to Figure 3.2 (page 106), which shows an ad for Cherokee clothing. Let's start with narrow meanings. If you were of Native American descent and did not like your culture's names and pictures used to promote non-Native American enterprises, what would this ad mean to you? Think about the drawing inside the brand name: What meanings or images does the picture suggest? To someone of this cultural background, what might the presence of Americans who appear to be of European descent in the photograph mean in conjunction with the brand name? Think about meanings that a Native American would likely find in this ad that people of other ethnic backgrounds might not see.

Now consider the meanings the ad has for a broader audience. Why do you suppose this manufacturer has chosen the image of a Native American to represent its products? Does it matter that the particular tribal name, Cherokee, was chosen rather than some other, such as Paiute? What meanings does the company likely hope most consumers will attribute to a product line with the name Cherokee?

Defining a Context

Once a text has been found, the next choice the critic makes in positioning the text is to place it within a *context*. Texts do not occur, and they are not "read," in a vacuum. An important part of being rhetorical is existing in relation to some problem or situation. In other words, signs influence people for a purpose, to some end, in some context. Questions arise, then, of what causes people to construct texts, as well as who is influenced by the texts, why they are influenced, and under what circumstances. Answering these questions entails identifying a context for your text. Here, too, you as a critic have a choice, which is displayed in our third continuum:

The Third Continuum: Choice of Context

original . . . . new

Every text appears or is constructed during some first moment or range of moments in time and space. We may think of that moment (or moments) as the text's *original* context. The people who first gathered to hear Lincoln's Gettysburg Address occupied a moment of time and space that was the original context for that speech; a slightly wider, but still original, context was the nation that would learn of the speech within days by way of newspapers. The "first" use of a text may also, paradoxically, occur across many different moments of time and space. This textbook, for instance, is a text that appears in its original context every time a student picks it up to read it for the first time. The context is made up of the room or library in which it is read, the reading assignment, and so forth. This context will occur (or so the author and publisher hope) thousands of times a year, but it is nevertheless the original context each time. Original contexts are defined by the intentions of those who make or who use texts, as well as by the "real life" contingencies of when the texts, in fact, first appeared.

On the other end of the continuum, texts are often moved or appropriated into new contexts, ones that are different from those in which they originally appeared. In the film, *The Gods Must Be Crazy*, an "ordinary" soda bottle falls from its original context, an airplane, into the Kalahari Desert (a new context), where it is taken to be a message from the gods by the Bushman who find it there. Lincoln's Gettysburg Address is now studied in public schools as an example of beautiful language, succinct and efficient wording, and great ideas; the original context of commemorating a battlefield has been largely lost to the sixth grader who is being tested (that is, encounters the text in a new context) on the address next week. Of course, changing the context of a text also changes many of its meanings, though usually not all of them.

The critic has a *choice* that he or she must make about the context in which to position the text. The text may be considered in its original context, as it was first experienced by people. For instance, a critic might study the meanings that the Three Stooges film shorts had for their original audiences in the 1930s and 1940s. Or, there are two senses in which the text may be considered within a new context.

First, the critic might examine ways in which people, acting on their own initiative or through happenstance, experience texts in new context. For example, the critic might think about how the meanings of Three Stooges shorts change as they appear in the 1990s, as television reruns or on videotape.

Second, the critic might propose a new context for consideration by the readers of the criticism, even if the text has not actually been experienced by these readers in that context. By suggesting that a text be seen in an entirely new context of the critic's proposing, the critic can often fulfill the important function of showing people more of the ways in which life is made meaningful. For instance, the critic might suggest to her or his audience that they think about the Three Stooges reruns as political commentary on the present presidential administration. Clearly, this is nothing like the original context. But if the reader begins to think about how those short features might be understood (or found meaningful) as being about the president, new insights about politics and our present situation might be opened up to that reader. The placement of the Stooges, or any text, in a radically new context like this should not be done capriciously or simply for fun. The new context and text should "fit," and the new placement should teach us more about what both text and context can mean.

In a more serious vein, it would be interesting and insightful for a critic to ask readers to think about Lincoln's Gettysburg Address as being about the Persian Gulf War of 1991—the desert battlefield of that particular war, and those who fell in that conflict. The critic can, in a sense, ask Lincoln to speak across the years and miles to a new context. We might learn a great deal about what war means to Americans and how Americans experience war, by placing that text in this new context. Correspondingly, we learn more about the text of the speech itself by observing the additional dimensions of meaning that are highlighted in a new context. For many people, the meaning of the speech's original purpose (dedicating a battlefield) has been lost; meaning might be restored to the speech by repositioning it in relation to a new battlefield.

Choosing to place a text at one end or the other of the continuum, or somewhere in between, entails certain consequences. To consider a text within its original context, the critic must do some historical work first, by discovering what the source of the text (the writer, speaker, film producers, and the like) and the original audiences were thinking about. If we are to think about the film *Gone With The Wind* as a rhetorical text in its *original* context, then we will have to look at the concerns of American moviegoers in 1939 and examine the meanings that the film may have had in that context. It may be illuminating, for instance, to think about the characters and events of the film in light of growing fears over war and destruction in Europe and Japan, and to ask how the film influenced the audience through the meanings it offered, given the context of the outbreak of World War II.

A second consequence of placing a text within its original context is that historical accuracy becomes an important criterion for judging a criticism. Whether a criticism faithfully reports the meanings that a text had in its original context is an important consideration when that context is where the critic places the text. Today's readers of the criticism will learn about how to experience and to find meanings in life if they can understand the patterns of meaning that were followed at different times in the past.

If the critic chooses to place a text in a new context, especially if it is a context entirely of the critic's choosing, different consequences result. The context will be suggested more by the critic and the critic's insights than by historical research. Historical accuracy becomes much less of an issue, and instead, the quality of the critic's insight becomes a criterion for judging the criticism. What does it teach us, one might ask, to think of the Three Stooges films as being about today's political context? Clearly, accuracy is not the issue in that case, as no one is claiming that those films either addressed, or intended to address, today's politics. What matters is whether or not there are insights to be gained; unless placement of a text in a new context is enlightening, it becomes just a game that is best avoided by serious critics.

Exercise 3.6

This exercise asks you to become a collage artist. A *collage* is a work of art formed by pasting together many clippings of words or images taken by the artist from other sources such as magazines or newspapers. In a sense, collage art is the art of choosing to see texts in new contexts.

Look at the Champion sportswear advertisement in Figure 3.3 (page 107). Think about the meanings that this ad had in its original context (attempting to sell sportswear in a popular magazine). Think about the meanings offered in this ad that would be attractive to most general readers.

Now let's place that ad in an entirely new context, one of our own making. Suppose, for example, you were a collage artist and you wanted to make a visual statement about the limited opportunities that women have to become great athletes. What images or words would you cut out from this ad to place in the new context of your collage art? Try to think of other words, images, or ideas that this ad might seem to refute or contradict. What meanings does the ad offer in the context of these new words, images, or ideas? To whom would such an ad appeal, and how would those meanings influence people? Why would a critic choose to examine a new context of this kind?

The last issue that we will consider in thinking about how to position a text is the *relationship between text and context*, and how that relationship works.

There is no single way to view that relationship; the choices that are available to you are explained in the fourth continuum:

The Fourth Continuum: Text-Context Relationship

reactive . . . . proactive

Sometimes, texts may be analyzed for the ways in which they *react* to a context, which is the left side of the continuum. People have a clear perception that certain challenges, problems, or possibilities exist (creating a context), and that texts are devised so as to react to that context. People may be out of work, racial tensions may be high in a certain locale, perhaps there is a hole in the ozone, and so forth. Under such circumstances, texts are designed or are used so as to react to these perceptions of a preexisting difficulty. For instance, during a period in which there was great international concern over apartheid in South Africa, the film *Cry Freedom* appeared and attempted to influence many people to oppose apartheid, to assign negative meanings to that system. A presidential election is a clearly perceived context for most people, many of whom choose texts in the forms of lapel pins, bumper stickers, and yard signs that react to that context and urge certain meanings upon others.

At the other end of the continuum is the possibility that texts might be analyzed for the ways in which they are *proactive*—that is, the ways in which they create their own contexts. That is not to say that these texts appear spontaneously or for no reason. Rather, the most important or interesting context within which to consider them is the context that they create themselves. Much advertising works this way. For example, many products, such as the Frisbee, hula hoop, or Salad Shooter, are simply not needed; they respond to no real life problems. Instead, they *create* a context of need for themselves, proactively.

Politics often generates texts that are most interesting for the contexts they create. In the 1992 Senate confirmation hearings for U.S. Supreme Court Justice Clarence Thomas, for instance, issues of Justice Thomas's character and integrity were, by and large, not part of the context—until Professor Anita Hill's accusations of sexual harassment were made public. Hill's text of harassment instantly created a context of concerns over Thomas's character. What was especially interesting about this event was the proactive creation, through Hill's text, of a national context of anger, concern, and discussion over the problem of sexual harassment in general.

Most texts in and of themselves are both reactive and proactive, just as a debater's speech both responds to an earlier statement and in turn becomes the basis for the opponent's reply. A critic must choose which sort of text-context relationship to feature in his or her analysis. But an analysis might address a mixture of both kinds of relationships (a point in the middle of the continuum).

For example, racial conflict is usually a preexisting context of some level of importance in our country, although it varies in terms of immediacy and the amount of attention paid to it. Since the late 1980s, a series of films, such as *Do the Right Thing, Mississippi Burning, Driving Miss Daisy, Jungle Fever, Malcolm*

X, and *Falling Down*, have both responded to that perennial context *and* ignited a new and intensified context of racial concerns. This new context has generated more widespread public discussion of racial issues. The consequences of choosing whether to identify texts as reactive or proactive to their contexts are important. As a result of that choice, the critic must look either backward or forward—back to a context to which a text or texts react, or forward to determine new contexts that texts create.

Exercise 3.7

As noted in the preceding section, many advertisements create new contexts that will influence people to buy the products. For this exercise, pick up almost any newspaper or popular magazine and look for ads for electronics, such computers, audio or video equipment, and so forth. If you wanted to analyze the sales appeal of these ads, would you choose to show how such ads react to a preexisting context, or how they proactively create a new one? If you are more interested in an ad's reactive relationship to a context, what would that context be? If you choose instead to focus on the ad as proactive, what new context does it create?

Note: In doing this exercise, bear in mind that ads for many high tech products stress the idea that their particular products replace obsolescent competitors (ones that are rapidly declining in use). But the idea of obsolescence itself is an interesting context for a purchasing decision because it can have either a reactive or a proactive relationship to a text, or both at the same time. For example, we might be urged to buy a high definition television (HDTV) because conventional television is really, truly obsolete. On the other hand, however, the texts of HDTV ads might go a long way toward creating that very "obsolescence" of conventional TV.

We have discussed ways to find a text and a context. This has been a process of both discovering a text and positioning it so that we can think about it more usefully—think, that is, about what the text is, what it is trying to do, and the things to which it responds. In every case, the critic must make choices about the most interesting questions to ask about texts in context. Now we are ready to think more carefully about the text itself, and about how its component signs work together; for that, we must go further "into" the text.

"Inside" the Text

How can we think about what a text is *doing*? How do texts urge meanings on people, and how do people accept, reject, or struggle over those meanings? We will build our discussion of the dimensions of the "inside" of texts around three categories: (1) direct tactics, (2) implied strategies, and (3) structures. These three categories can be usefully displayed as ranging across our fifth, and last, continuum:

The Fifth Continuum: From Surface to Deep Reading

Direct tactics . . . . Implied strategies . . . . Structure

A word of explanation regarding this continuum is in order. This continuum, like the others, represents *choices* that a critic can make in thinking about critiquing a text. This fifth continuum represents whether, or how far, a critic wishes to go beyond studying the explicit and straightforward appeals that a text makes, into an analysis of more indirect and less obvious appeals.

Most texts make certain explicit appeals, which we will call *direct tactics*. Texts also have *implied strategies*, which are subtler and not always consciously intended or perceived; these implied strategies are often the implications of some of the direct tactics that are used. And finally, any text is put together or organized in certain ways, and its various parts have relationships among themselves. These parts and their relationships make up the text's *structure*. Direct tactics, implied strategies, and structures are the sources or storehouses of meaning in a text. Which of these levels of appeals will the critic focus on? That is the choice offered by the continuum. The choice is a continuum because, although we have identified three levels at which texts appeal, the levels are not radically distinct; rather, they merge into each other.

Direct Tactics

Direct tactics reveal the system of meanings, the consciousness, offered by a text most explicitly. A direct tactic is any straightforward request or prompting for you to think or behave in a certain way. It is often accompanied by a reason or rationale for you to think or act as urged. If someone says to you, "Order the steak; the lobster isn't fresh," it is clear that a direct attempt to influence you is being made. The direct tactics used in the rhetoric of popular culture are, in many ways, closest to the reasoned arguments of expositional texts that we studied in Chapter 2. Explicit claims, reasons given in support of the claims, visual images with a clear message in terms of what you are being asked to do or not to do— these are all direct tactics that you might find in popular culture.

Our fifth continuum represents a range of appeals that the critic would choose to analyze. Of all the possible choices on the continuum, direct tactics are probably the easiest appeals to find within a text. Many advertisements are full of direct tactics. A rap song urging people to fight oppression, or a rock and roll song telling people to stay off drugs, is also using direct tactics.

But not all texts have direct tactics, whereas all texts do at least have implied strategies and structures. In fact, some texts seem almost devoid of direct tactics. We have all seen our share of ads that make no explicit claim upon us, ads that comprise nothing but a brand or company name and an ambiguous visual image. Many soft drink commercials show only the product and images of happy people having fun. Similarly, a street gang's preferred hat style is usually devoid of direct tactics.

Perfume advertisements provide especially vivid examples of this lack of direct tactics. Among the examples included in this chapter, the Tiffany ad in Figure 3.4 (page 108) comes closest to a complete lack of direct tactics. This ad shows a group of desirable products, but no argument is offered as to why one should buy them.

Because direct tactics are on the surface of the text, the critic who chooses to focus on them should first simply note what the appeals are, make a list of them, and identify what is being urged and why. The critic should think about what support or reasons were given for the direct appeals, remembering that such support might be visual as well as verbal or expositional. Finally, the critic should think about the most likely audience for the appeals, and then assess the likelihood of the appeals succeeding with that group.

Exercise 3.8

The Lenscrafters advertisement in Figure 3.1 (page 105) is the closest to a traditional text included in this chapter; it is also the one with the most direct tactics in evidence. Let us examine some of these direct tactics, using the following procedures:

1. Note specific appeals in the ad. Try to isolate particular claims or requests that the ad makes.
2. What support or evidence is given for the claims? Try to construct a diagram linking claims with support.
3. Who is the likely audience for the ad? Who is likely to buy the product? Who might have been reading *People* magazine, where the ad was found? Try to assess whether the ad's appeals are well matched to that likely audience.

Implied Strategies

If critics are not satisfied with examining direct tactics alone (or if few, if any, such direct tactics exist), other choices are available to them. They can examine the implications of the signs, the relationships among them, how they are arranged, and so forth. It may be a little difficult to understand exactly what critics are looking for in examining implied strategies, and how such strategies differ from direct tactics. Perhaps a hypothetical example will help. Suppose you had a friend who was working at a bank. Suppose that every time you met that friend, his conversation would be punctuated by statements such as, "Embezzling really isn't such a bad thing"; "Gee, I think they probably don't catch embezzlers very often, especially if, you know, they don't really take very much"; "I've often thought that really smart people could get away with taking their employer's money"; and the like.

The "direct tactics," so to speak, in the text of your friend's conversation are rather straightforward; these are simple statements about the subject of embezzling. But if you only considered direct tactics, you would probably miss something else that is going on with your friend. Most people would probably realize that the *implications* of your friend's words are far-reaching; they might mean that your friend is swindling the bank where he works (or at least considering doing so), perhaps that he is even in serious trouble. You would arrive at that conclusion because your friend is saying things that you would not ordinarily expect, and repeating certain things more than is quite normal for conversation. There are oddities and peculiarities, interesting things that call attention to themselves, in what your friend is saying. So acting as an everyday rhetorical critic in this situation, most of us would probably do an informal critique of this friend's text and either warn him sternly or turn him in to the police.

Every text has similar interesting quirks and peculiarities—things missing or things too much in evidence—that convey meanings in and of themselves. A critic must choose to focus on these implied strategies. Following the work of Kenneth Burke, we will look at three categories of implied strategies, each of which suggests a question that you can ask about texts: (1) *association* (What goes with what?), (2) *implication* (What leads to what?), and (3) *conflict or absence* (What is against what?). These categories overlap somewhat, as we will see. The three questions accompanying them are the basis for how a critic probes a text for implied strategies.

Association: What Goes with What? In answering this question, the critic considers the signs that are linked together in a text. Such linkage may occur when signs are placed in the same place or within the same image, so that they seem to go together naturally. The linkage may also occur when signs appear together repeatedly; every time one sign occurs, the other sign occurs as well. For signs that are linked in such ways, the meanings that would usually be assigned to one sign are transferred to the other, and vice versa. Linking signs becomes a strategy of borrowing meaning, of moving signification from one sign to another.

Exercise 3.9

Look again at the Champion sportswear ad in Figure 3.3 (page 107). Think about the ways that most of the signs in this ad fit together: We see a basketball, a distant chain link fence, and an expression of high-powered intensity; we also see that the people in the ad are African Americans. Together, these signs tend to suggest an urban environment; you might consider which signs would have to change in order for the ad to suggest a rural environment.

Now consider that into this set of linked signs the advertiser has inserted two other elements: The key player in a group that seems to be largely male is a woman, and she is wearing a Champion shirt. Is the reader of this ad likely to accept the insinuation of these two additional signs into this mix? If so, what effect will the inclusion of the two new signs have? Why did the advertiser choose to add these two signs?

Implication: What Leads to What? Often, several of the elements of a text will suggest, or lead to, some other element. That element may not even be the most frequently recurring sign in the text, so long as the other signs consistently imply, suggest, or refer to it. We call that a *keystone* sign within a text, and close examination of that sign can tell us a lot about what the text in general means.

For instance, Bart Simpson seems to be a keystone sign in the television show *The Simpsons*. The show's attitude and many of its plot developments lead to Bart Simpson, and they keep returning to him as a key figure. Bart's contrary character can then be taken as an indication of the tone of the show and of why it is popular. In a sadder example, when the space shuttle *Challenger* exploded in 1986, killing all aboard, most of the texts commenting on the disaster seemed to be keyed to the teacher, Christa McAuliffe, who was on board. The nation's sense of tragic loss, and of an end of innocence in what had been a largely accident-free space program, was reflected in texts that were keyed to this particular passenger.

Another way in which one sign leads to another is by way of *transformation,* or the "standing in" of one sign for another (this transformation can be detected in the iconic, indexical, and symbolic meanings of signs, discussed in Chapter 1). In thinking about the meaning of these signs within the text, the critic should ask why one sign was chosen to stand in for another in the first place, and what meanings are conveyed by such a transformation. For instance, a recurring feature of Clint Eastwood's "Dirty Harry" movies was an enormous Smith and Wesson .44 magnum pistol, with which the character Dirty Harry dispatched his victims. The gun was of a size and clumsiness to make it an unlikely "real life" police weapon. So the question arises, what was such a gun doing in the films— why was that gun used and not a more realistic one? A critic might propose that the gun was really standing in for an intense hatred of criminals on the audience's part, and a desire to do such criminals great harm; the gun looked awesome and destructive enough to be a transformation of that desire. In the movie *Jaws,* most of the film's action leads to the shark. It is also interesting to ask what the shark is standing in for in the film. Various critics have suggested that the shark actually represents fear of the forces of nature; others point to concerns over crime and lawlessness.

Exercise 3.10

In this exercise we will examine two signs within the texts of two of the magazine ads included at the end of this chapter. First, consider the picture in the Tiffany ad in Figure 3.4 (page 108). Where is your eye led when looking at the ad? What are you encouraged to look at? The word "Tiffany," of course, occurs several places throughout the ad and serves to guide the viewer's gaze. What meanings does that word have for most people, or more specifically, for the readers of *Rolling Stone* (the original audience for this ad)? You might think of the associations the term "Tiffany" has—that is, the indexical meanings that it signals. Now look at the watch that is being offered for sale in the picture. How does that watch fit with the meanings of "Tiffany"? What does the watch itself stand for?

Now consider the LensCrafters ad in Figure 3.1 (page 105). Two key words that the text of this ad repeatedly leads the reader to are "accident" and "choice." Think of the ideas of "accident" and "choice" as standing in for many of the other elements of the ad. Note that in the small, "accident" picture, for instance, the woman is informally dressed. She also has a braided band around her head, and an odd, rather helpless expression on her face. Compare that with the larger, "choice" picture. Here she is professionally dressed and groomed, with a confident, straightforward expression. Can this ad be understood as using the terms "accident" and "choice" to stand in for the ideas of a lack of control and control? Examine the rest of the prose in this ad with an eye toward how the words of the ad can lead to meanings having to do with control.

Conflict or Absence: What Is against What? The critic who asks this question looks for ways in which the text keeps certain signs apart. Texts do this in two ways. First, texts may *omit* certain signs. To locate such omitted signs, we ask what the text did not say and compare that with what it did say. We look for what is missing, especially for signs that should be there but are not.

Second, texts may show certain signs in *conflict*. Within such texts we see explicit pairings of concepts in opposition to each other. Sometimes those oppositions are in the form of contradictions, such as include signs that would not typically go with the other signs that they appear with in the text. Note that in texts of this kind, signs which are usually against or apart from each other have been paired; this unusual combination prompts us to think about the meanings that the odd pairing generates.

Almost any night of ordinary television viewing will yield many examples of "what is against what" in the first sense of certain signs that are omitted. For example, women are routinely omitted as players or commentators from professional sports broadcasts. Thus, over time the meaning that "Women are not athletic" is built up. Consider also the relative absence of people of color on your television screen. Gradually, more African Americans are appearing on television, though their representation is still low overall. Think about the virtual absence, however, of Asian or Hispanic people on television, despite their rapidly growing populations in this country. When texts rarely link people of color with everyday roles such as store clerks, business office workers, plumbers, and so forth, such texts serve to further a false image of nonwhites as uninvolved in the everyday life of our country.

In other words, if ninety-nine percent of the successful professionals in the United States (such as doctors and lawyers) are *not* African-American, Asian, or Hispanic (as television shows would seem to indicate) what does that seem to say about realistic career aspirations for people of color? As the public increasingly depends on television for entertainment—indeed, for a description of reality— what meanings does such an underrepresentation of people of color convey to the public? What effect might those meanings have on the members of minority populations themselves?

One major absence on television is a realistic concern about money. On most television programs, you will notice that when people are finished eating in restaurants, they simply get up and leave. In reality, however, people in restaurants divide the bill among themselves, argue over who ate what, ponder about the tip, and so forth. When the people on television programs *do* pay for something (such as when they are getting out of a cab), it is done with a hurried grab for whatever is there in their purses or pockets. In reality, of course, people count their bills carefully, rub them to make sure two are not stuck together, wait for change, and so forth.

Television's silence about money becomes most obvious in commercials. Commercials are rarely specific about what anything costs; in fact, most of the time the fact that a product costs anything at all is simply not mentioned. There seems to be an assumption that everyone can afford anything; all sorts of products are depicted as being affordable by people from all walks of life.

The second way in which signs are placed against other signs, the depiction of *conflict*, is clear and straightforward. Dramatic television series almost always depict certain groups as in conflict. Terrorists are nearly always presented as Middle Eastern (specifically Arab or Palestinian) and are shown in conflict with Europeans or Americans. The popularity of Iranian or Iraqi "bad guys" on television has grown as the plausibility of Russian enemies (a former TV favorite) slips; spies on television shows now come from the Middle East instead of from the former Soviet Union. Such oppositions, or conflicts, urge upon the television audience a particular view of how the world order is structured.

The unexpected conjunction of signs that would usually be set apart from or against each other is also fairly common. In any election year, for example, we see powerful and wealthy politicians don overalls and flannel shirts to show up at county fairs and eat fried chicken and corn on the cob. The president rarely goes to 4-H shows in Duluth, Minnesota; thus, when he *does* attend such a show, the intended meaning becomes interesting and noteworthy. Television commercials often show cheap and ordinary products in contexts of great wealth. Consider the series of commercials for Grey Poupon mustard, in which the occupant of, let us say, a Bentley limousine leans out of the window to ask the occupant of a Mercedes-Benz limousine for the loan of some Grey Poupon. Here, then, is an ad for a product that is assumed to be affordable for all, being sold with the argument that it is desired and purchased by the very rich.

Exercise 3.11

Consider the Firstar ad in Figure 3.5 (page 109). It may help your understanding of this ad to know that in the original version, the picture was black and white, but with bright, almost fluorescent, orange and yellow stripes on the sneakers to make them stand out. The interesting thing about this ad is the unexpected conjunction of the conservative business attire and serious demeanor of the model with the flashy athletic shoes. What is the ad saying about the financial company in putting together these signs? Take the headline term "performance." How does other wording link together the ideas of financial performance and athletic performance? Also consider the first line of the ad's text: "In business . . . a little conservatism now and then is a good idea." What meaning do you think the advertisers intend to create by juxtaposing that line with this image?

We have been learning about three *implied strategies:* (1) *association* (What goes with what?), (2) *implication* (What leads to what?), and (3) *conflict or absence* (What is against what?). It may have already become clear to you that these categories sometimes overlap or blend into one another. One thing might "go with" another thing by "leading" to it, for instance, and being "against" one thing will often imply being "with" another thing. As noted at the beginning of this chapter, the categories and questions presented in this chapter are ways to think about the rhetoric of popular culture, and such thinking about real experiences rarely falls into tidy categories. Returning to our fifth continuum, we will now turn to the third choice critics make once "inside" texts: whether to analyze those texts' *structures*.

Structures

When a critic chooses to analyze a text's structure, he or she is dealing with the pattern, the form, the bare bones or organization of that text. Recall that we are considering choices, on the fifth continuum, from surface to deep reading. With structures, we have arrived at the level of form or pattern. Here, we do not ask what is said or shown in the rhetoric of popular culture, but rather what forms or patterns we can discern beneath the things that are said and shown. At this end of the continuum, signs and texts are examined to discover the most fundamental patterns that organize them, and the broad categories to which their elements belong. There are two concepts that a critic might choose to focus on that have to do with structures: *narrative* and *subject positions.*

Narrative: A number of scholars have suggested that texts can be usefully studied by thinking of them as *narratives,* or stories (see Jameson 1981; Fisher 1984, 1985). This is obviously true for texts that do in fact tell a story, as most films do for instance. But clearly, a number of texts (perhaps most of them) are not narratives or stories on the surface. So what can these scholars mean by suggesting a narrative approach to the criticism of these nonnarrative texts?

They mean that critics can treat these texts *as if* they were narratives. For texts that are not narratives on the surface, this means that the deeper form or structure of the texts should be analyzed, because it is at that deeper formal level that the characteristics of narrative will be found. What does the critic look for in examining a text for its narrative qualities?

The essence of all narrative is *form, pattern,* or *structure.* The phrase "The proud African warrior" is only the germ or nub of a story because it does not flow forward; it suggests but does not follow through on any pattern. But, "The proud African warrior looked out across the grasslands as he set out on his quest" is already patterned, in two ways. First, it follows a *syntagmatic* pattern. A *syntagm* is a chain, something that extends itself in a line. We can think of syntagmatic patterns as *horizontal,* as moving in time and space. That kind of movement is what narratives do; a plot is nothing but a pattern chaining out horizontally in time and space, a series of expectations that arise and are either met or frustrated. Our sentence about "the proud African warrior" asks us to start imagining that warrior as being on a journey, in pursuit of some noble goal. We might imagine what that goal is, foresee dangers, and so forth. These expected developments will be revealed to us (or not) as the story moves on.

A second kind of pattern that this sentence follows is called *paradigmatic.* In contrast to syntagmatic structure, paradigmatic structure is *vertical;* it looks at structures or patterns derived by comparing and contrasting a given sign or text with other signs or texts that are like it. We already know that our African warrior is in a quest story; thus his story can be compared to similar quest stories: (medieval knights in search of the Holy Grail, astronauts going to the moon, and so on). Much of what this African warrior means comes from that sort of implied comparison.

In a baseball game, to take another example, what develops when first Smith

Table 3.1 Syntagmatic and Paradigmatic Forms

↑ Paradigmatic Comparisons ↓		
What Smith did in the last game	What Jones did in the last game	What Brown did in the last game
What Smith did last time up in this game	What Jones did last time up in this game	What Brown did last time up in this game
SMITH GROUNDS OUT→	**JONES HITS A DOUBLE→**	**BROWN SINGLES JONES IN**
What Rivera (of the opposing team) did last time up	What Johnson (of the opposing) team did last time up	What White (of the opposing team) did last time up
What the leadoff batter did in that movie you saw last weekend	What the second batter did in that movie you saw last weekend	What the third batter did in that movie you saw last weekend

The Syntagmatic Flow→

goes up to bat, then Jones, then Brown, will follow a syntagmatic pattern; events will follow each other in a forward-moving narrative sequence. But when a given batter is up, we might compare that batter's statistics to those of other batters, to see how this batter's performance fits into the pattern of other hitters. That second kind of pattern is paradigmatic; we are considering the *paradigm*, or category, of batters. The relationship between syntagmatic and paradigmatic forms is illustrated in Table 3.1.

There are really two levels of paradigmatic form, and one of them we have already examined in considering direct tactics and implied strategies. When we took a given sign and asked what it went with or went against, we were thinking paradigmatically. A second level of paradigmatic form is the level of structure. We can identify the flow, or pattern, of a given text syntagmatically. But we can also take that pattern as a unified whole and move vertically, to comparing and contrasting it with the patterns underlying other texts so as to construct a paradigm. For instance, one can examine any television newscast syntagmatically to identify the pattern that is followed: headline story, remote broadcast from a reporter, next news story, personal interest story, the weather, and so on. But we can also compare the entire pattern of a particular station's news broadcast paradigmatically with those of other stations, in an effort to identify the overall pattern or structure that tends to underlie *all* newscasts. Often, this construction of a paradigm or vertical form is also referred to as the construction of a *genre*.

Identification of form or structure entails asking the sorts of questions that we might ask of good stories:

1. Is the pattern *cohesive*, and if not, why not? What influence or meaning occurs when the pattern is broken? Humor is often the intended result of deliberate disruptions in narrative patterns that seemed to be following the

accustomed groove; examples of such humorous disruptions can be seen in many skits on the television shows *Saturday Night Live* and *In Living Color*.

2. Is the pattern *recognizable?* What other texts seem to follow the same pattern, and what does their presence in that genre, group, or paradigm tell us about the meanings and influences of particular texts? A number of observers noted, for instance, that the texts of the speeches, press conferences, and photo opportunities generated by President Ronald Reagan followed the form of the movies in which he had starred in his early life. These critics might have derived a way to understand Reagan's presidency by analyzing his various texts within the paradigm of Hollywood (see, for example, Rogin 1987).

Exercise 3.12

We have already examined the magazine ads at the end of this chapter in terms of paradigmatic structure. Still, or unmoving, visual images such as those found in magazines can also be examined syntagmatically, but such examination can be difficult, and usually involves placing oneself in the position of the reader as he or she "moves through" the ad. So in this exercise we will depart from the magazine ad to consider some films, books, and television shows.

This is one form, pattern, or structure that might underlie a text:

(a) People occupy a distinct space

(b) that they are not free to leave;

(c) hostile external forces attempt to attack or infiltrate the space, and

(d) they must be repelled or subverted.

Examine, on your own or in class, all of the films, books, and television shows from the following list with which you are familiar. You will find that all share the structure described in items *a* through *d* above. For each film, book, or TV show, identify the *surface* features (actual events, characters, and so on) that match the elements of *structure* listed in *a* through *d* above.

Film, TV Show, or Book	a	b	c	d
The Swiss Family Robinson				
Battlestar Galactica				
Alien				
Home Alone				
Robinson Crusoe				
any *Star Trek* movie				
20,000 Leagues under the Sea				
(your own example)				

What can you learn about the meanings and influences of these texts of popular culture by examining their structures? How does clarifying the "bare bones" of texts, both syntagmatically and paradigmatically, help you to understand the ways that those texts might influence people?

A different structure underlies the following texts. This time *you* supply the description of the structure underlying all of these texts. Then identify the surface features in each that match the elements of the structure you come up with.

My Fair Lady

Diff'rent Strokes

The Fresh Prince of Bel Air

Alf

Webster

E.T.

Subject Positions

The Marxist scholar Louis Althusser (1971) and others (for example, Hall 1985) have argued that texts ask those who read them to be certain kinds of *subjects*. To be a certain kind of subject is to take on a sort of role or character; these theorists argue that rather than having any single, stable, easily located identity, we do nothing but move from one *subject position* to another. In a sense, then, the power that a text has over you has a lot to do with what kinds of subject positions it encourages (or forces) you to inhabit.

Whether or not you agree with such a claim, an interesting question that can be asked of texts is, Who was this text made for—who would fit into the role of audience for this text most easily? Note that a subject position is *not* a character in the text itself. Instead, a subject position is who the text encourages you to be as you, the reader or audience, experience that text. Rarely will a text explicitly announce its preferred subject position for the members of its audience. Instead, a subject position, like narrative, is part of the *structure* of a text. You can think of a subject position as the missing perspective, the point of view, required for the text to make sense.

You can also think of some subject positions as *subversive stances*, positions taken deliberately by the reader in opposition to the "preferred" subject position suggested most strongly by the text. For instance, almost without exception, old "Cowboy and Indian" movies strongly encourage a white, law and order–based, pro-establishment subject position—in other words, one that will root for the cowboys. It is easier to see such films from this perspective; the films are structured toward that end. But one can also root for the Indians by refusing that subject position and taking an alternative, or subversive, one. In this way, subject positions can often become sites of struggle.

Another instance of the possibility of a subversive subject position can be seen in relation to the film *Fatal Attraction*. Clearly, the viewer of that film is intended to see the film from a male perspective, one in sympathy with the lead male character played by Michael Douglas. It is easier to see *Fatal Attraction* from a position of growing outrage, even hatred, toward the female lead character, played by Glenn Close. But it is also possible to see the film from the subversive perspective of that female character herself—to become angered by the leading male character's assumptions about relationships and his attitudes toward his own responsibility for her pregnancy. Depending upon how deeply you inhabit this alternative subject position, you may even identify with the female character's attitude toward the safe, sanitary nuclear family unit in which the male character seeks security; that is, you might see that family unit as founded on hypocrisy and deserving of disruption. Furthermore, if you are pro-choice on the issue of abortion and are frustrated by the ways in which many men feel entitled to force their own reproductive preferences on women, you might also relish the ironic turning of the tables in this film, in which the man desperately wants an abortion to take place and the woman refuses to let him disengage himself from the dilemma of an unwanted pregnancy.

Now the film itself appears to be trying very hard not to allow you this alternative position; by the end, the filmmakers have pulled out all the stops to make you see the female character as evil incarnate, someone who richly deserves a violent death. But because every text has a preferred subject position in which it is trying to place you, it is always possible, at least in principle, to find an alternative one. Doing so may yield some interesting insights into that text.

Subject positions are defined by the type or category of person that is called to by the text: male or female, old or young, and so on. Subject positions also imply certain characteristics, such as happy or unhappy, active or passive, and the like. Finally, subject positions imply a *consciousness*, which, as we learned before, is a system of meanings linked to a group identification. Thus there is a feminist subject position that entails the adoption of a feminist consciousness, for example.

We have already considered some of these issues earlier, in our examination of the idea of context, or audience, for the magazine ads in Figures 3.1–3.5 (pages 105–109). Recall that we asked who the ads seemed to be speaking to, but we also considered alternative, or oppositional, stances that an audience might take. For instance, it seems clear that the Tiffany ad in Figure 3.4 (page 108) is calling to a financially comfortable person, probably a male. That would appear to be the preferred subject position, the one most obviously and easily entered into, in order to read this text. But with some effort, one could take an oppositional subject position in order to read this text. How, for example, would someone who adopted the subject position of advocate for the homeless read this text differently than someone who adopted the preferred subject position?

Exercise 3.13

You have been reading this book for nearly three chapters by now. That much immersion in any text will certainly call forth a subject position. Consider the following questions:

1. What subject position is the preferred one for this book? That is
to say, who does this book "call
to"? What kind of person, role,
or character would find it easiest
to read this book? What sort of
characteristics or consciousness
are associated with that subject
position?

2. Think about yourself as you read
this book. You have to adopt a
certain subject position in order
to read it. How does that subject
position differ from the subject
positions that other texts—such
as the text of a party you attended recently, the text of *Saturday Night Live,* or the text of the
latest Eddie Murphy movie—call
you to?

3. Suppose you hated this book,
hated the class it has been assigned for, hated the whole subject. Think of an alternative, subversive subject position you
could take in reading the book,
one its author clearly did not
hope for. What difference would
that alternative subject position
make in terms of the meanings
of particular passages, examples,
or exercises?

We have been learning optional ways to think about texts, once you, as a rhetorical critic, have positioned them. The kinds of close and careful examinations of texts that we have demonstrated in this chapter have provided choices in consider-ing *direct tactics, implied strategies,* or *structures.* Only one more set of choices is necessary to consider before you can begin to produce the actual rhetorical criti-cism. We will now consider different ways to step back out of the text and to think about how the meanings you have discovered do social and political work.

The Text in Context: Metonymy, Power, Judgment

Actually, the ways that we have gone about thinking about texts have always asked you to keep one eye on what is outside the text, on the real world within which texts do their work. So this next group of questions will serve largely as a way of review-ing what you have already learned about texts. In considering, generally, what in-fluence texts have in the social and political world, you will need to choose whether to focus on (1) *metonymies,* (2) *empowerment/disempowerment,* or (3) *judgment.*

Metonymies

What texts do is, as we have discovered, very complex. All the ads that we have examined in this chapter are, for example, trying to influence the meanings that people assign to certain products, in order to sell those products. But critics, you will recall, are concerned with power, and with how public business is managed in the rhetoric of popular culture. So in addition to noting how ads sell cigarettes, critics will also ask about the ways in which ads, or any texts, manipulate the distribution of power as they manage public business. (Recall that the management of public business occurs in popular culture as texts influence decisions and sway meanings about important issues.)

You will recall that for reasons of increasing population, technology, pluralism, and perhaps most of all, knowledge, public issues must be reduced or *metonymized* into the signs, artifacts, and texts of popular culture. Only in that reduced form can people participate in the management of public issues, by helping to determine what those issues and their components mean. Therefore, once you have thought about what the texts of popular culture *mean*, it is important to ask how those particular meanings *metonymize* public issues.

An interesting example of the use of metonymies in attempts to manage a public issue that occurred during the 1992 presidential campaign. Vice President Dan Quayle, attempting to win conservative, family-oriented voters, criticized the television comedy series *Murphy Brown* for its positive portrayal of an unwed mother (Murphy Brown, played by Candice Bergen). Later that fall, the series aired an episode in which the fictional characters responded to the "real life" attack by Quayle as if the show itself were real, as if Quayle had attacked a real television newscaster who was unwed, and not simply a television production.

This remarkable exchange illustrates metonymies. The problem of unwed mothers, or fatherless families, has received a great deal of public attention in recent years. By featuring Murphy Brown's unwed state, the show metonymized that complex problem within its own narrative. Brown and the other characters could then urge the audience to adopt certain meanings and attitudes about unwed mothers. The vice president wanted the public to attach different, more negative meanings to unwed mothers; but it is significant that Quayle, too, metonymized the problem by picking the television character Murphy Brown as the focus of his remarks, rather than by discussing the vastly more complex "real life" problem. The show's response to the vice president was a commentary on its own and Quayle's metonymies. Real life and fictional representations of real life intertwined in a clear illustration of how popular culture uses narratives to manage the meanings of complex or sensitive issues to the general public.

Empowerment/Disempowerment

The category of empowerment/disempowerment is fairly straightforward. It asks us to consider who is empowered and who is disempowered by the meanings that might be assigned to or generated by the text. Remember that empowerment and disempowerment mainly befall large groups of people rather than isolated individuals. Recall also that power is managed in moment-to-moment, everyday experiences (including popular culture) far more often than it is in single, grand events. How does that empowerment or disempowerment result from the way that public issues are metonymized?

In the case of the *Murphy Brown* controversy, it would appear that the vice president found it worth his while to criticize a television show precisely because, in his view, the effect of the show would be to empower family units that do not conform to the traditional, nuclear, two-parents-plus-offspring model. The thrust of such empowerment would be to make divergences from that model seem more "normal," more a part of the mainstream, and less a cause for shame than Quayle's conservative constituency thought suitable. Certainly, the creators of *Murphy Brown* took Quayle's attack as a blatant attempt to disempower not only themselves, but single mothers everywhere who might find strength in Murphy Brown as a role model. Producer Diane English said as much during a speech she made while accepting an Emmy award for the show. "To all you mothers out there who are raising your children alone either by choice or necessity," said English, "don't let anyone tell you you're not a family."

Of course, it was also noted at the time (even by some who disagreed with Vice President Quayle) that the character Murphy Brown was a well-paid media professional in a financial position that would allow her to raise her child comfortably—hardly a realistic picture of single motherhood for most women. However, realism may or may not be the most important issue here.

After decades of almost complete absence, African Americans began appearing on television in much greater numbers during the 1980s and 1990s, often taking center stage in situation comedies such as *The Cosby Show* and *Family Matters*. These television texts metonymized the life experiences of African Americans into thirty-minute episodes. A number of critics raised the issue of whether the shows were realistic or not. But metonymy, because it is a reduction, is hardly ever completely realistic. Perhaps more important questions would be, Who is empowered and who is disempowered by these shows? Are they for the benefit of blacks or of whites? Do they tend to perpetuate the established system, the way things presently are, or do they encourage alternative distributions of power?

Judgment

The critic is not only concerned about power; he or she is interventionist as well. The critic has some purpose or goal in mind in doing rhetorical criticism—as we noted before, the critic is on a mission. That means that for the critic, judgment of the text is inevitable and unavoidable.

Judgment runs throughout all the insights offered by the critic. In suggesting that a text means this or that, the critic is also judging it. That is because to claim that a text means a certain thing, or calls for a certain subject position, or encourages a certain consciousness, is to take a stand about what the text is doing in the world.

Objectivity is not possible for the rhetorical critic. That is not to say that merely expressing personal opinions is an acceptable alternative for such a critic. All the categories and questions covered in this chapter guard against making criticism merely an expression of personal opinion; instead, they lead the critic into making well-supported *judgments* about the material that is being studied. Such categories and questions direct the critic to give reasons for her or his judgment. Thus, the choices that the critic makes, as illustrated in the five continua presented earlier in this chapter, are not made at random, or simply for fun. They are choices that the critic must support with good reasons and evidence, in an attempt to persuade the audience who will read or hear the criticism that the meanings the critic asserts are in certain texts are really there.

Summary and Review

The purpose of this chapter has been to help you learn how to think like a critic. In discussing the many things that rhetorical critics think about, we have covered quite a lot of concepts and terms. Does the critic have to use every term and concept included in this chapter in doing criticism? Certainly not. Remember, we have been explaining choices that are available to the critic. What should guide those choices? The critic should ask those questions that help to reveal the meanings that he or she finds most interesting and important. Let's go over some of the more important ideas in this chapter once more in a quick summary.

We began by reviewing two basic principles: that texts wield their rhetorical influence by affecting the meanings that people attribute to the world, and that because meaning is complex, texts are often sites of struggle over what the world means. Therefore, critics are meaning detectives, and their chief task is to show what signs and texts mean, and the meanings they urge upon their audiences.

Critics, working within the framework of critical studies, display three characteristics as they go about explaining meaning. We learned that critics are critical in both *attitude* and *method*; that is, they refuse to accept easy answers to the question of what texts mean, and the kinds of questions they ask about texts generally are not best answered through quantifying social scientific methods. We learned that because meaning is complex, difficult to articulate, and often beyond awareness, the specially trained critic is in the best position to say what texts mean. In explaining meaning, the critic shows people new ways to experience life and helps people to expand the ways they have of finding meaning.

Second, we learned that critics have the characteristic of being *concerned with power*. And third, we learned that critics are *interventionist*; they want to change people by changing how they understand the world and the meanings they see in the texts they encounter in everyday life.

Having arrived at an understanding of what critical studies do in general, we explored a number of choices that are available to the critic as she or he approaches the study of a text. First, we learned that the critic must position the text. This involves finding a text, for which the critic may consult her or his own experience or theories about texts. One major choice confronting the critic is to settle on a text that is either *discrete* or *diffuse*, or somewhere in the middle of this first continuum. We also learned that the critic cannot study all the meanings of a text, and is therefore faced with the choice of focusing on either broad or narrow meanings, or analyzing the text as a site of struggle over meanings. The third choice the critic must make in positioning the text is to focus upon an *original* or *new* context in which to place the text. We learned that the critic may study original or new contexts in which others have placed the text, or may propose a new context of his or her own if doing so will help to illuminate what the text or context means. The critic's final choice in positioning the text involves examining the text-context relationship, and deciding whether to feature *reactive* or *proactive* relationships between text and context, or perhaps a mixed relationship between the two ends of that continuum.

Once the text is positioned, we followed the critic further "into" the text. Here we saw that the critic's choice is whether to analyze a text's *direct tactics, implied strategies,* or *structure.* We saw that direct tactics are straightforward appeals and urgings for an audience to feel or act in a certain way. Implied strategies are subtler and more indirect, and are revealed by asking the questions associated with the categories of (1) *association* (What goes with what?), (2) *implication* (What leads to what?), and (3) *conflict or absence* (What is against what?). Structure is a consideration of the basic form or pattern of a text. Here, the critic examines both *narrative* and *subject positions* so as to reveal the underlying structures of texts.

Has this seemed like an overwhelming number of categories and concepts to consider? It probably has. Yet you should remember that we have been focusing on a critic's choices for just that reason—to illustrate the vast number of choices and options available to the rhetorical critic. No single critical analysis can possibly take into consideration all of the concepts we have reviewed in this chapter. Instead, the critic must make specific choices for how to think about texts and their relationship to the world, and then confront the consequences that follow from those choices.

Looking Ahead

This chapter has reflected the strong conviction that critics are deeply involved in helping their audiences to see certain meanings in texts. We began the chapter by arguing that meanings are the basis for rhetorical appeal, and one clear implication of that argument is the idea that critics are also rhetoricians. Rhetoricians argue for particular perspectives and views, often against other perspectives and views.

One might finish this chapter wondering whether critics are in agreement over which meanings to reveal to an audience. This particular chapter has had very little to say about disagreements among critics. And although we have focused on a critic's choices, we have not shown one of the most important choices that critics cannot avoid—the choice of which sorts of "real life" concerns and commitments to urge upon an audience in revealing the meaning of texts. In Chapter 4, we will turn to a discussion of the particular schools of thought within which critics work. Consider these questions as you prepare to begin the next chapter:

1. What are the different perspectives or schools of thought that critics work within as they reveal meanings?

2. What specific kinds of changes or new meanings do some critics want to instill in their audiences?

3. How can criticism serve "real life" politics and social movements, so as to help people who are in need of liberation?

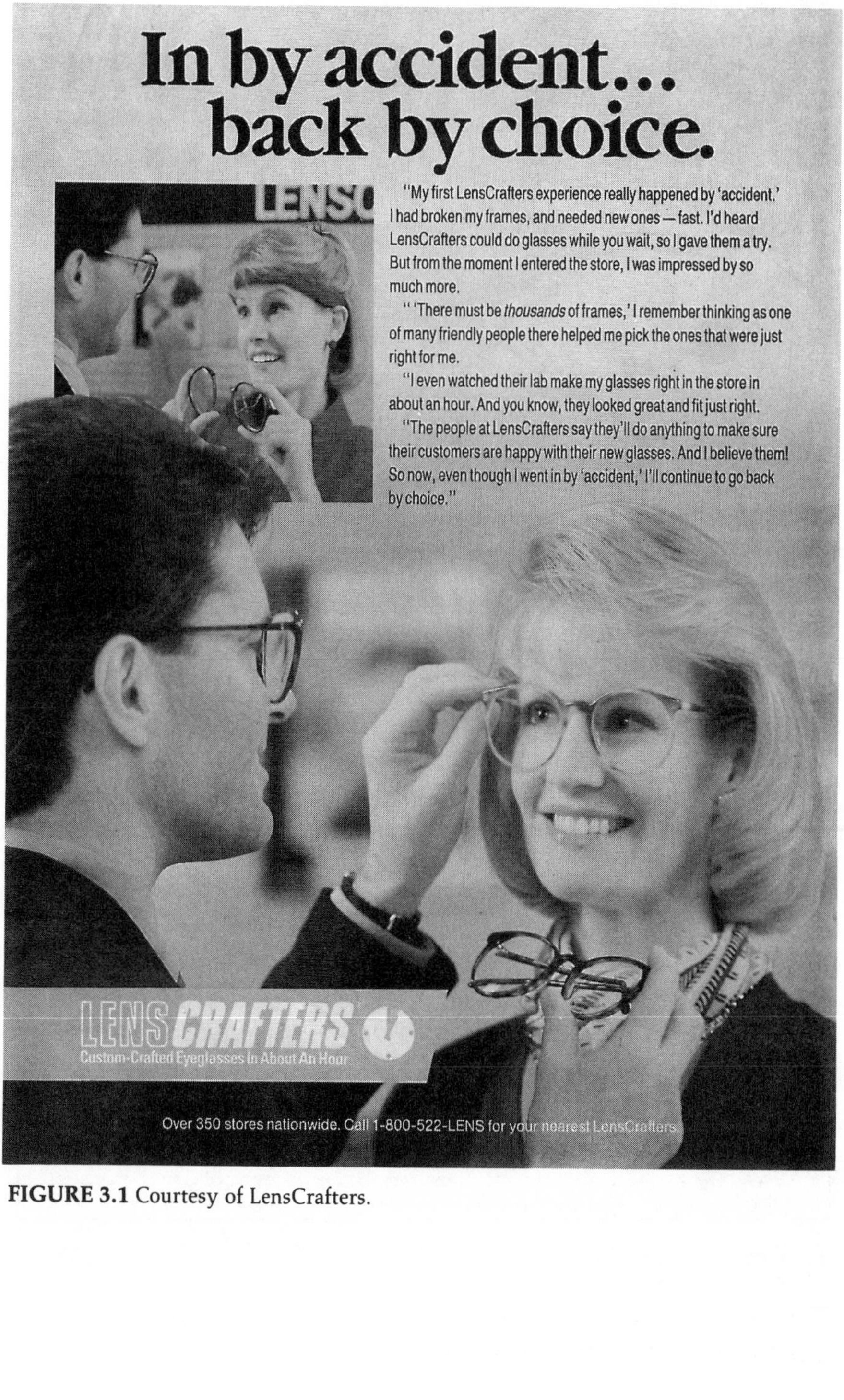

FIGURE 3.1 Courtesy of LensCrafters.

FIGURE 3.2 Reprinted by permission of the Cherokee Group.

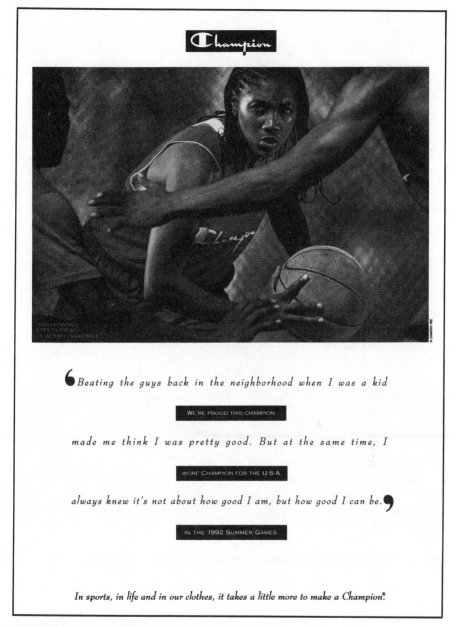

FIGURE 3.3 Reprinted by permission of Champion.

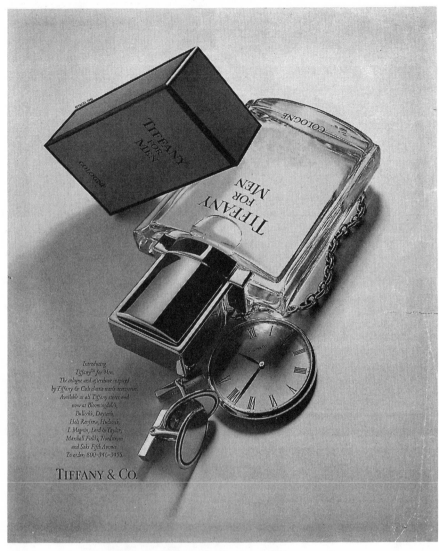

FIGURE 3.4 Reprinted by permission of Tiffany & Co.

Investment strategies for top performance.

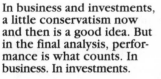

In business and investments, a little conservatism now and then is a good idea. But in the final analysis, performance is what counts. In business. In investments.

At Firstar Trust Company we pay sharp attention to the details to achieve the performance you want for your investments.

Paying attention. Being in the right place at the right time. Decisive action. The qualities that keep you ahead in business. The qualities that make Firstar Trust an investment leader.

Call Carl Silvestri at 765-4777; or Phil Hardacre at 765-5080.

More experience for your money.

FIGURE 3.5 Reprinted by permission of Firstar Corporation.

Chapter 4

Varieties of Rhetorical Criticism

•••••••••••••••••••••

In Chapter 3 we learned that critics who are trying to understand the rhetoric of popular culture are confronted with choices about the texts that they study. These critics are in search of what texts mean, and of how those meanings influence people. We have looked at some of the concerns and questions that most rhetorical critics have in common.

But within the last chapter, the choices that critics make were presented along continua, as evidence that not all critics make the same choices or study texts in the same ways. Texts inevitably have many meanings, and critics may disagree about which meanings and which influences are the most important. Similarly, critics may disagree about which meanings are most influential; in trying to explain why people do what they do and why the world is the way it is, some critics of popular culture will point to some meanings and other critics will point to other meanings. These differences reflect unavoidable differences in taste and philosophy. People simply disagree, and while some think that the world turns because of power, others think that it turns because of biochemistry, or sex, or God, or economics, or race, and so forth.

An Introduction to Critical Perspectives

Another way to express these differences is to say that while we were concerned with *how* texts mean in Chapter 3, in this chapter we will consider five different perspectives on *what* texts mean. There is always more controversy over the latter (*what* texts mean) than the former.

In this chapter we will look at five groups of critics, or five schools of thought in the rhetorical criticism of popular culture: (1) Marxist, (2) psychoanalytic and feminist, (3) dramatistic/narrative, (4) media-centered, and (5) culture-centered. You can think of these different approaches as different sets of questions for a critic to ask, different categories within which to think, different critical tools, different kinds of meanings to which critics call our attention, and different ideas of what to study in a text.

Before we start thinking about specific approaches, however, we need to make three observations about them. First, within each school of thought are wide differences of opinion, despite the sharing of a general approach to criticism. Indeed, there is not even universal agreement about the labels that are used to denote the five groups. (Works included in the reading list at the end of the book will allow you to investigate these differences further.)

Second, there is significant overlap among the five schools of thought. The fact that one critic might be labeled a Marxist and another a feminist does not mean that they are at odds. Indeed, critical studies often employ more than one approach in combination. So our first two observations could be summed up by noting that any identification of any number of approaches to rhetorical criticism must be somewhat arbitrary, and that the boundaries between various approaches are not firm.

Third, not all approaches to the rhetorical criticism of popular culture are discussed in this chapter. As suggested above, we will deal with only some of the many methods used within each particular school of thought. And some schools of thought, such as deconstruction, will not be developed here at all. Because our space is limited, we will look only at those approaches that seem most fruitful for revealing rhetorical influences, rather than other dimensions, of popular culture.

You have already noticed how important illustrations and examples are for demonstrating how theoretical and methodological concepts relate to our experiences of popular culture. In this chapter we will often use as an example an experience that is surely familiar to anyone who has lived in the United States for more than a couple of years: watching the 1939 film *The Wizard of Oz*. That movie, broadcast every year on television and widely available on videotape, comes as close as anything to a universally shared experience of popular culture within the United States.

Marxist Criticism

Right away we are in trouble with terms and their connotations, because there is not widespread agreement about what to call this perspective. On the one hand, some people think of this school of thought solely in terms of ideological, or class- and power-based rhetoric. On the other hand, Marxism has far more negative connotations for many people (bringing to mind images of people in Eastern Europe, standing in line for hours to buy bread, for example).

We align ourselves with the first group, viewing Marxism as an approach that is concerned with ideology, with class, and with the distribution of power in society. Many of the methods and assumptions with which we think about those issues were first proposed by the German philosopher Karl Marx in the nineteenth century. That is why we label this approach *Marxist*. The term is a handy "umbrella" word, covering all of those concerns and more.

The association of the term *Marxist* with repressive Communist governments is understandable, but not that relevant to our concerns in this book. The political system in the People's Republic of China, for example (as well as those of the former Soviet Union and Eastern Bloc nations), bears little resemblance to the system of government that Marx actually proposed. Similarly, there is very little connection between those specific governments or economies and Marxist theory as a way to think about the rhetoric of popular culture. Marxism, in the sense in which we will use the term, is a method, or a set of assumptions. So when we refer to Marxist critics, we are referring to people who draw on Marx's theories (regarding class, power, and ideology) in analyzing the rhetoric of popular culture.

Actually, you have already been exposed to many of the methods and principles of Marxist criticism. This approach is one of the most common, and the most mixable, of the five that we will examine. Therefore, it is the source of many of the ideas and terms to which you have already been introduced. Some of those ideas will be reintroduced here, in the context of a discussion of Marxism as a particular approach in rhetorical criticism.

Materialism, Bases, and Superstructure

The philosophy underlying Marxist approaches to criticism is called *materialism*. This philosophy holds that ideas, rules, laws, customs, social arrangements—in short, everything belonging to the world of ideas or concepts—grows from material conditions and practices. That world of ideas is a vitally important one; it includes our ideas of who should govern whom, of who is more or less valuable, of law and morals, of aesthetics and taste in art and entertainment, and so forth. But materialism holds that those ideas are what they are because of real, concrete, observable actions, practices, and objects. Materialism stands in sharp contrast to *idealism*, a way of thinking that argues that the world is the way it is because of abstract ideas and concepts. Marxist materialism argues just the reverse.

As an example, take the idea of free choice, which many of us value and believe that we exercise. An idealist would argue that free choice is a powerful idea that exerts influence in the real world, and that because it is such a compelling idea, people come to arrange their affairs, their governments, and their everyday practices so as to make the idea of free choice a concrete reality. Marxists, on the other hand, would argue that the present economic and political arrangement of capitalism requires that individuals make purchasing decisions on the basis of their own desires, without thinking about the larger good of the community. In other words, our economic system depends on people going out to buy stereos because they want them as individuals, not because they think that doing so is good for others. Because the economic base of our society functions on that model of making "free," individual decisions, Marxists would say that the whole idea of free choice grows out of that economic base, that it is derived from those economic conditions. Were we living under a different economic system, so the thinking goes, the idea of free choice might never occur to us, or at least not as such a powerful and central idea in our understanding of our social and economic lives.

Different versions of Marxism have developed different versions of materialism. An early, very basic form of Marxism (now not as commonly held by critics) argued that a *base* of economic conditions (who owns what, working conditions, trading practices, and so forth) simply produced a *superstructure* of everything else: culture (including television, films, and books), ideological institutions (including churches and schools), politics, and so forth. The superstructure of ideas and culture was said to be *determined* by the economic base.

Most Marxists, however, now recognize that churches, rock concerts, schools (and all that happens there) are just as material as the economic system is. So, for example, the Marxist theorist Louis Althusser has argued that other systems within a society (such as the political and ideological systems), as well as the economic system, operate relatively autonomously; that is, they are all material and they all generate ideas and concepts (1971). In trying to explain why people think what they do, why certain ideas become current (including ideas of who should rule, who is valuable, and so forth), Marxists now would more commonly say that those ideas are *overdetermined*, or caused by several material forces acting simultaneously (rather than just the economic forces).

Today, Marxists such as John Fiske expand the idea of what is material to include all the objects, conditions, and practices of everyday experience, arguing that ideas, concepts, customs, and the like grow from the material, day-to-day experiences of everyday life (1989a, 1989b). More explicitly (and more radically), some Marxists would argue that ideas themselves are embedded in, and take form in, everyday experiences. This view of ideas is essentially the position taken in this book. That is why we have been looking so closely at the "little" experiences of reading magazine advertisements, for instance: because ideas of who has power and who does not have power stem from, take shape in, and are worked out in just such "little," everyday experiences. It is these two concerns—*materialism*, and the way material affects *power*—that together form the core of Marxist analysis.

Our chief example of popular culture in this chapter can help us see the kind of general approach that Marxism takes. The film version of *The Wizard of Oz* with which we are all familiar first appeared on the screen in 1939, toward the end of the Great Depression, when economic conditions (especially in "dust bowl" states such as Kansas) were still grave. The year 1939 also saw the beginning of World War II, with Germany's invasion of Poland and France, and the beginning of hostilities between Germany and Great Britain. *The Wizard of Oz* is an extraordinarily rich text, bearing many meanings within the guise of a pleasant children's story. Let's examine just one theme in this movie, considering how critical approaches that are specifically Marxist might approach that theme: the idea of *home*.

"Home" is the last word uttered in the film ("There's no place like . . ."), and it is the place to which Dorothy is going at the very start of the film (fleeing the evil Miss Gulch). After her one ill-fated attempt to run away from home and her untimely return during the tornado, poor Dorothy spends the entire movie trying to get back home: trying to get into the storm cellar as the tornado approaches, and then trying to get from Oz back to Kansas. Home is a central term, or a central value, in the film.

Marxists might take at least two related approaches to understanding *home* in this movie. First, they would try to understand the idea of home and how it is expressed in *The Wizard of Oz* as a symptom or expression of the economic conditions of 1939. They might note the peculiar intensity with which Dorothy wants to return to her hardscrabble farm; she is not lured for long by the attractions of Professor Marvel's alleged globe-trotting, nor by the technicolor beauty of Oz.

Dorothy's desire to return to black and white Kansas would be understood by these critics as tied in with the economic difficulties of 1939. The economic system needed workers to be happy with home, wherever that was. Home is a metaphor for the established system; it is the job you have, the income you already make. It was important for the public to maintain faith in the economic system and to keep working within it, even though it had failed them. The growth of labor unions also threatened to disrupt traditional economic arrangements, as working people acquired the means to demand changes in working conditions and distribution of income. Dorothy finds out that a desire for change, even from desperate conditions, results in disaster. The idea of home as the place to be, as the primary object of all desires, is an idea growing out of the established economic system's need, in 1939, to keep workers loyal and complacent, despite an itch to "roam."

Second, Marxists might see *The Wizard of Oz* as an argument for isolationism, or against foreign entanglements (such as a war in Europe); this was the official United States policy and practice in 1939, even as Hitler was gaining power. These critics would note that troubles begin when Dorothy's dog is allowed to run wild in Miss Gulch's yard and grow worse when Dorothy herself goes to foreign parts (Oz). Dorothy learns at the end of the movie to stay "in [her] own backyard." The theme of home as the confines of North America would thus be read by Marxists as emerging from the prevailing isolationist tendencies in the United States at that time.

The idea of home is part of the meaning of *The Wizard of Oz*, and part of how its rhetoric works. Marxists point out that any economic or political system not only *produces* goods, products, practices, and ideas, but also *reproduces* the conditions under which it produces those things. The tactics by which such an economic or political system induces people to allow it to continue as it is are clearly rhetorical. So part of the rhetoric of *The Wizard of Oz* is the way in which it reproduces its conditions of production—that is, the economic system of capitalism and the political system of isolationism. It encourages workers to stay on the job, dismal though it may be, and it encourages Americans to stay at home and "mind their own business" politically.

The film's meanings are rhetorical because they work to influence the ways that workers regard their jobs and the ways that the general public regards overseas conflicts. Marxists today would argue that it is in this movie, as in countless other experiences of popular culture (on the job site, in schools) that both economic and political systems are made. In other words, foreign entanglement *is* the trouble that Dorothy gets into, accepted as a truth by the audience of this film, and added to other, similar meanings encountered in other everyday experiences.

Economic Metaphors, Commodities, and Signs

Today, Marxists look for material causes that go beyond the narrowly economic. But because the history of the Marxist approach began with an attempt to link ideas, culture, power arrangements, and so forth to economic conditions, Marxist critics often retain *economic metaphors* for how culture works. For instance, Marxists often regard meanings as if they were commodities, and discuss the ways in which they are exchanged, traded, bought, or sold. This metaphorical approach can be a fruitful way to think about how artifacts of popular culture are used, since most of those artifacts are in fact bought and sold and possess some dollar value. Marxists supplement the idea of the cash value of artifacts with a notion of their value in terms of *signification*, or meaning.

Take, for instance, a simple stud earring. Suppose you make and sell earrings as a hobby, buying the materials for one dollar and selling the earrings at three dollars a pair. You are enriched by two dollars per pair. Your customers have three dollars less, but presumably they feel that the commodity, the earring, is equal in value to that amount.

But consider the ways in which an earring can also pick up value as a sign, value that can then "enrich" its users, that can even, in a sense, be "traded." What does it mean, for instance, for a man to wear such an earring? The meanings are not as charged as they once were (when, for example, the choice of which ear to wear the ring in was supposed to be a sign of whether or not a man was gay—a system that collapsed due to widespread confusion and instability in that particular meaning). But even now, an earring in a man's ear picks up some added symbolic value. It enriches the man who wears it with different meanings: He suddenly has "daring" or "slightly different" or "stylish" added to his other meanings.

Think also about a stud earring worn in the nose. What meanings would that "add" to the "symbolic wealth" of the wearer? We can also think in terms of the exchange value of those signs (just as we might think of the exchange value of money, of labor, or of commodities). To consider exchange value, think about what it would say about you if you were to date, or become friends with, someone wearing a nose ring; what meanings would you have "bought" through such an association? Of course, besides having exchange value, all these meanings should also be thought of as rhetorical; you can clearly influence someone by using a sign in ways that are charged with certain meanings, such as wearing a ring in the nose.

Another example of the exchange value of signs can be found in a rap music group that tried to achieve fame and stardom amid controversy during the early 1990s: Young Black Teenagers. The members of this group were certainly teenagers, and therefore young, but every one of them was white. But of course the sign "black" refers to more than simply skin color. As this group appropriated the sign (or took it as their own), they tried to make it refer to even more than a particular culture, narrowly defined. Young Black Teenagers tried to make the sign "Black" mean an attitude, a political stance, a set of experiences in life, certain associations with people and places. The controversy arose over their right to appropriate the sign of "Black" in that way, and to enrich themselves symbolically with meanings that they were unlikely ever to have owned in real life.

And as a final example, the film *The Wizard of Oz* also contains numerous signs that have picked up meanings that give them a kind of value. Marxists might study the film as a source of such signs, and they might study the ways in which people appropriate those signs so as to spend them and exchange them. The term "Munchkin" has been extracted from the film to serve as a derogatory term, for example. I like to tell people that I can infallibly discover when a certain coworker will come to the office in a bad mood by looking out the window to see if "Surrender Dorothy" is written in the sky. In certain bohemian neighborhoods of cities like New York or San Francisco, you can find T-shirts saying, "Toto, I Don't Think We're in Kansas Anymore." And if you are going to the zoo with a child, and the child asks whether you will be seeing lions, you might find yourself adding "and tigers and bears" (to which the child might respond "Oh my!"). The list goes on and on; *The Wizard of Oz* is a bank of signs to "spend"—to use as wit, as insult, as fun. The ways in which these meanings can be "spent," or used strategically, are an important part of their rhetoric. Such uses are part of the way in which these meanings influence others.

Many Marxist critics look beyond the narrowly economic to identify the ways in which actual artifacts, objects, events, and practices influence power arrangements. Power is, then, perhaps the strongest interest of Marxists. Marxist critics study the ways in which large groups of people are empowered or disempowered. They assume that every society has power structures that privilege some groups while placing others in a relatively disadvantaged position. Such differences in power need not be intentionally planned by any group, nor do they need to be startlingly obvious. But such differences *will* be consistent throughout most of the experiences within a culture. So in the United States today, for instance, second- and third-generation citizens are relatively empowered and recent immigrants are relatively disempowered, men are more empowered than women, and so on. These differences in empowerment are found consistently throughout the culture in everyday, ongoing experiences—because they are created there.

Preferred and Oppositional Readings

More and more Marxist theorists are coming to see the practice of reading texts as a sort of material experience with ideological consequences. One way in which already empowered or established groups and interests maintain their power is through the ways in which the texts within a given culture are read. By "reading," Marxist theorists mean the discovery and attribution of meaning in a text or artifact. Every text, every artifact, according to Marxists, has a *preferred reading*. This is a reading that is the easiest, most obvious one—the one that seems to be *common sense* within a given culture. When the evening news reports that a police officer was wounded in a shootout with an armed robbery suspect, for instance, the public is generally encouraged to assume that the police were in the right and the suspect in the wrong. But notice that this reading perpetuates a system of power in which the already empowered enjoy more police protection than do poor or disreputable people within that system.

In contrast to preferred readings are *oppositional readings.* These are meanings found in a text that are different from, or even opposed to, the easiest preferred meanings. Marxists identify two sorts of oppositional readings: inflections and subversions. An *inflection* is a bending of the preferred meaning to suit one's own needs and situations, rather than an outright rejection of those meanings. One possible inflected reading of the preceding example (the officer wounded in a fight with an armed robbery suspect) might come from a National Rifle Association firearms enthusiast who saw the story as evidence of a need for all citizens to be armed. Such a person might "read" this story as showing that armed citizens could have deterred the suspect in the first place, or could have aided the officer with additional firepower.

A *subversion* is a reversal, an active undermining or rejection, of the preferred meaning. One clear subversion of the robbery example would be to read the situation as one in which the officer had used too much force, thus forcing the suspect to defend himself. The whole structure of who is right and who is wrong in this story is thus reversed, and the meanings upon which established views of law and order rest are subverted. Note that no given text must be read with preferred meanings; nor must it be understood oppositionally. Inflections and subversions are simply different ways of attributing meanings to the signs that make up texts.

We have already discussed one of the preferred readings of *The Wizard of Oz* in terms of the concept of home. Let us think about some of the other ways in which the movie is "easiest" to read (we should stress that these are but a few of the possible ways to read the film). There is a tension in the movie between the value of fairness and open dealing on the one hand, and on the other, a respect for law and order. The preferred reading seems to be that law and order should be obeyed, even if such obedience is difficult or repugnant, because fairness and honesty will eventually triumph. The wicked Miss Gulch arrives at the farm with all the force of law behind her ("I've been to the Sheriff. . . . I'll bring a lawsuit that'll take your whole farm!"). She has a legal instrument in hand, allowing her to take the dog, Toto. "We can't go against the law, Dorothy," says Auntie Em in resignation. Dorothy *does* try to do just that by running away with Toto to Professor Marvel's camp, and she pays for it with an injury to the head.

When Dorothy reaches Oz, it becomes clear that a structure of law works there as well. "Rubbish," Glinda the Good Witch tells the Wicked Witch, who threatens Dorothy with mischief; "your magic has no power here." Dorothy's companions follow the Wizard's instructions for obtaining the broomstick, even though they seem hopelessly unfair. But the Wizard, in turn, gets his comeuppance when he is exposed as a fraud. The virtue of the four companions who have been following his "contract" to obtain the Witch's broomstick triumphs at last. Clearly, even a grudging respect for law and order supports the present system of power and resource distribution. Dorothy and her friends teach the audience to respect that system, even when it puts them at a disadvantage, promising that justice will triumph in the end if we "don't make waves."

One of the movie's easier readings sees it also as a celebration of the value of work. Dorothy is something of a nuisance on the farm at the start of the film because she is the only one with no clear job to do. Everyone else is running around frantically doing chores. "I know three shiftless farm hands that'll be out of a job," warns Auntie Em, to spur the help on to greater efforts. The whole context of the action in Oz is a quest—doing something or working hard, so as to earn passage home. At the end, Glinda reveals to Dorothy that she could have gone home at anytime, simply by tapping her ruby slippers, but that she "had to learn it for [her]self." Dorothy and her three companions think nothing of the Wizard's setting them various tasks to do in order to win "some brains, a heart, the nerve," and a trip back to Kansas. Although it is in his power to grant their wishes (or so they think), they accept the need to *earn* those gifts. For an audience eager to find work in the Great Depression, the preferred reading of the value of work would certainly have been easy to swallow. But the continuation of the established capitalist economy also depended on that desire to put up with a failed economy until its health should be restored; thus an emphasis on the value of work encouraged people to continue seeking what the system could not, at that time, give them enough of.

When people read, or draw meaning out of, texts by drawing on a preferred reading, they participate in one of those everyday, material experiences that perpetuate the existing system of empowerment. The tendency of people to turn first to preferred readings is a product of *hegemony.* We would say that a group exercises hegemony in society when their preferred meanings, the readings of a text that would keep them in power, come to be the meanings that other, even disempowered, groups tend to turn to first. Hegemony is a remarkable phenomenon; because of it, oppressed people not only accept but often participate in their own oppression. How is it that some women go about saying that men ought to be "in charge"? How is it that some gays feel contempt for themselves, and see their lifestyles as degraded and somehow wrong? Marxists critics are very concerned to examine the ways in which preferred readings induce oppressed people themselves to participate in such oppression.

Marxist theorists note that many of the subtlest means by which power maintains itself are disguised—that is, they do not display themselves as sources or means of power. These theorists would say that the tools of ideology and hegemony tend to be *occluded* (or hidden) as such. In other words, people are not aware of the ways in which they are empowered and disempowered. Clearly, most casual observers of *The Wizard of Oz* would not be aware of the deeper meanings that it is urging upon them, or of the ways in which it supports the established system. Marxists therefore tend to be highly interventionist (as we defined that term in Chapter 3), in eager pursuit of the goal of showing people how empowerment works. (See pp. 76–78.)

Marxists tend to see many flaws in the present established system, and to seek changes in it. Therefore, they also try to understand the ways in which texts offer resources for making meaning differently, for being understood in different ways. They do so by encouraging oppositional readings. When texts contain resources for both preferred and other, alternative readings (as nearly all texts do), these texts can be seen as *sites of struggle* (as discussed in Chapter 3).

The economic metaphor (discussed on page 115) is often used to clarify the ways in which people construct oppositional readings. Participating within an economic system in legitimate ways (through running a business or buying products, for example) is sometimes likened to choosing the preferred meaning of a text. In that case, oppositional readings become a sort of "black market" of signification, a way of "stealing" signs and using them for one's own purposes.

For instance, there are very clear preferred meanings for a baseball cap; list a few such meanings in your mind. Now, for a gang member to wear a cap in different positions is to steal that sign, the cap, and make it mean something else—in fact, to make it mean something specifically designed to *offend* the established order and its preferred meanings. The same is true of pop star Madonna's use of signs that are, in the preferred reading, religious artifacts; she makes them mean something else entirely. Marxists argue that to turn signs against their preferred usage is a refusal of hegemony, of established power structures.

Let us think of some of the ways in which *The Wizard of Oz* can be read oppositionally. The film has within it the resources to be read in ways that are, in fact, *critical* of the established system. Authority can certainly be read as suspect in the movie. Glinda the Good Witch appears to be the only unambiguously good authority figure in the film, yet even she is fooled by the Wizard, describing him to Dorothy as "very powerful, but very mysterious." Glinda can, however, be read as unfair and even threatening in the way she submits Dorothy and her friends to what might have been a fatal adventure (when she could have told Dorothy from the start how to get back to Kansas). Her power can be read as capricious and arbitrary, apparently exercised for its own sake.

Although there is certainly a preferred reading for male dominance, the movie also has the potential for feminist readings. It centers around a heroine, Dorothy. Two of the most powerful figures, Glinda and the Wicked Witch, are female. Auntie Em is clearly in control on the farm back home in Kansas. All of the adult male figures in Oz are weak, silly, or incompetent. The film is about the quest of a young woman who finds at the end that the resources she was looking for all along were within herself. So, against the dominant male ideology of 1939, it is possible to find resources for female empowerment in *The Wizard of Oz*.

Subject Positions

Another important part of the meanings of texts, also referred to in Chapter 3, is the *subject position*. Just as every text has a preferred reader that it implies or "calls to" (or, in Althusser's terms, interpellates), so there are *negotiated* or *oppositional* subject positions. Marxist critics try to discover the kinds of roles or characters, or subject positions, that are most strongly suggested by texts; but they also try to identify the resources within texts and within people's experiences that would enable the construction of inflected or oppositional subject positions.

From our discussion of preferred readings, it should already be clear to whom *The Wizard of Oz* "calls." It is easiest to watch the movie as an honest, hard worker, as one who admires fair dealing and openness, as one who values doggedness and determination, and as a good citizen who obeys even unjust authority. From that subject position, one does not find it strange that Dorothy risks her life so as to earn passage back to the dreary workaday world of Kansas. That subject position makes it easy to despise the false Wizard at the end. The "good citizen" subject called to by this film will go along reluctantly with the decision to hand Toto over to Miss Gulch, while hating her for throwing her weight around. The "good citizen" will not be surprised when Dorothy and her companions sorrowfully turn to leave the Wizard's palace after first being rudely turned away. Much of the rhetoric of the film lies in these subject positions; they were recognizable to much of the film's original audience, and easy for these people to step into. The preferred readings of the text felt comfortable for many people, and the meanings found in those readings were easily accepted by them.

There is much more to Marxist rhetorical criticism than we have space to explore here. The Marxist critic is concerned with the ways in which popular culture influences people to accept established arrangements of power and economics, and it tries to discover ways in which people find resources for influencing themselves and others to change undesirable power and economic arrangements. One of the most important ways in which power and goods are distributed is by attention to a person's *gender*. Feminist/psychoanalytic criticism is a close cousin of Marxist analysis; we will explore that approach in the next section.

Psychoanalytic and Feminist Criticism

This method of rhetorical criticism has such a lengthy name because it really begins with psychoanalysis and moves to feminism. We will make the same move, in an effort to find out what this method is concerned with and how it works.

Psychoanalysis

Psychoanalysis began as a method for analyzing and treating mental illness. It was founded by the Viennese psychiatrist Sigmund Freud in the late nineteenth and early twentieth centuries. Today, not all psychiatrists use Freud's methods rigorously, as their main approach to treating mental illness. But rhetorical and cultural critics have found Freud's approach very useful in explaining certain things about culture in general. Today, the term *psychoanalysis* is used more broadly, in reference to a theory about how the individual mind, personality, or psyche is constructed.

Of all the methods of critical studies, the psychoanalytic may be the most "suspicious," for it takes nothing at face value. Psychoanalytic criticism assumes that all the artifacts of popular culture—in fact, all signification whatsoever—has something "behind" it, some other reality or significance beyond just itself. Those deeper meanings, the ones that psychoanalytic critics are especially interested in, have to do with the ways in which the mind is constructed. Let's examine a few of the basic principles of psychoanalytic theory.

Desire and Repression: Newborn babies only experience pure and uncontrolled *desire.* When they want something, they cry for it, reach for it, or crawl for it. They have no self-control, nor do they know about social inhibitions. When they are hungry, they want to eat then and there; when they wish to urinate or defecate, they do so at once, no matter where they are. If they are angry, they express that anger at once. Infants live for gratification of desire; Freud called this characteristic of infancy the *pleasure principle.*

Yet from the moment of birth, inhibitions and controls also begin at once to curb the infant's actions and expressions. The child learns that there are times and places to be fed, that not everything may be grasped, that the elimination of waste must be strictly controlled, and so forth. In contrast to the pleasure principle, the child comes to learn the *reality principle:* that the world will disapprove of and even punish certain actions. And so the child comes to *repress* more and more of its desire for gratifications, so that its behavior is acceptable and it can live with others in a society. Such repression is widely regarded as a necessary step in human development. People, being social creatures, cannot go about seeking gratification in totally uncontrolled ways and still live with others in civilized groups. It is "common sense" that adults cannot go about eating, defecating, and urinating whenever and wherever they please.

The *psyche*—the mental equipment that everyone has, the mind in all its complexity—is a product of both desires and the ways in which desires are repressed. Who we are, how we think, what we come to value, and so forth, are all created by what our parents and society at large tell us that we can and cannot do, think, or feel—but also by our powerful desires to do, think, and feel those things nevertheless.

The desire for gratification, although repressed in favor of reality, never goes away. Instead, in its repressed state it takes on a different form, the structure within the psyche that Freud called the *unconscious.* The unconscious is formed by the process of repression. The unconscious keeps trying to make its desire for gratifications felt; it keeps trying to break through to conscious awareness and action, all the while remaining continually repressed. Despite this repression, the unconscious exercises enormous influence on how we think and feel, how we act, and how we relate to other people.

Let us consider one example of psychoanalytic explanations for behavior. Infants, of course, want to defecate—and to be honest, the experience of defecation remains mildly pleasurable for adults as well. But that desire must also be repressed at certain times. The question is, how is it to be repressed? Some psychologists argue that young children should be praised for the production of feces in appropriate times and places (and anyone who has raised a child knows how proud they are to be able to learn how to use the toilet). But more important, some psychoanalytic theorists argue that this particular method of repressing desire—the use of high praise—results in adults who are highly productive in many ways, people who freely and confidently produce whatever counts as production in their respective fields (sales records, art works, engine blocks, and so forth). In other words, the key to happiness and productivity lies in the way in which the desire to defecate was repressed; productivity at work is in part the result, within the psyche, of proper toilet training.

Cultural Repressions of Desire: One major theme of psychoanalytic criticism is the ways in which particular cultures repress desire. Desire repressed makes up the unconscious, and much can be learned about why people do what they do by studying the patterns of repression that are peculiar to their particular cultures. Some cultures may disapprove more of some desires than of others, and the ways in which infants are taught to repress certain desires will also affect the development of the unconscious.

Psychoanalytic theory strives to explain certain characteristics that seem to be common to most members of a culture. Taking the idea of American culture very broadly, for example, it has often been observed that ours is a highly pragmatic and highly competitive culture. Getting ahead and doing whatever it takes to maximize the bottom line is a theme that has always been strong among most Americans. Practical results often count more than do self-improvement, ethics, or other principles. Psychoanalytic theory would try to locate the sources of this distinctively American trait in the ways in which the unconscious is built out of repressed desires.

Such an explanation is also a rhetorical theory, however, for it explains what is desirable, or what is sought after, within a particular culture. And of course, what is desirable and sought after is what will be influential, or rhetorical. A psychoanalytic theory of American competitiveness, for instance, could explain why certain films, such as Oliver Stone's *Wall Street* or *The Terminator*, achieve tremendous financial success at the box office in this country, while films celebrating unambitious, unassuming characters—the type who would never succeed in business—often find only moderate audiences (such as *Little Man Tate,* or *Curly Sue*).

Childhood Sources of Desire: Another major theme of psychoanalysis is a return to the experience of infancy as a source of continuing desire among adults. For the adult, the experience of desire will never be as uncontrolled and the satisfaction of desire will never be as complete as it was for the infant. Friendships will never equal the intensity of bonding with a parent. No food or drink will ever be as completely satisfying as is the milk or formula of infancy. Psychoanalytic critics argue that the appeal of many experiences in adult life, including those of popular culture, can be illuminated by showing how these experiences mirror or parallel the early experiences of childhood.

Explaining the appeal of popular culture in this way is an important aspect of the psychoanalytic understanding of the rhetoric of popular culture. For instance, a very popular use of this theory is to argue that the experience of watching a film in a movie theater is very much like the young child's experience of discovering the mirror. Psychoanalytic theory argues that an important stage in child development is the child's learning about images or representations, and that one way in which this happens is by the child's discovering its own reflection in a mirror. The child is delighted to find that when it moves, the image or representation of itself moves. In other words, the child learns about connections between images and reality.

From that knowledge, the child learns how to use and understand signs, which are also images of reality. Much of the appeal of all signs, whether television, film, words, or objects, is that they remind the adult of that pleasurable mirror experience of childhood. But part of the frustration of experiencing signs for the adult is that no other signs so perfectly match the things to which they refer as the mirror image matches the original object. In other words, the sign "dog" does not match that furry thing you have at home nearly as well as the mirror image of a face matches the original face.

The experience of watching a film, however, comes close to duplicating that mirror stage. The film viewer is "cradled" in a soft and comfortable chair, much like a parent's arms. The darkness of the theater is also comforting and soothing. And finally, most films that we see today are examples of what has been called *realist cinema;* that is, they are designed to put the viewer into the actual action of the movie. You may or may not know that when a movie is being filmed only small pieces of it are filmed at a time. For instance, if Jack and Jane are talking to each other, all the shots of Jane's speaking might be filmed at once, with the camera standing where Jack would have been standing, and then all the shots of Jack's speaking might be filmed with the camera in Jane's position; the film is then edited to give the illusion of Jack and Jane speaking back and forth. That technique has the effect, psychoanalytic theorists argue, of *suturing,* or binding, the audience into the actual film itself: Jack and Jane appear to be talking to you, the viewer, as well. Furthermore, psychoanalytic theorists argue, that experience of finding yourself "sewn up" within these images on the screen parallels the child's delightful discovery of appearing in the mirror's image; this, they argue, is why film is so rhetorically appealing and influential.

Just as a side note, one area of interest within the study of popular culture is the ways in which the *apparatus,* or specific physical means of production, of a particular medium works to create influences and effects, and psychoanalytic theory is often called upon to explain those influences (see, for example, Cha 1980). For example, television shows must be taped in a hurry to meet the industry's voracious need for programs, and so its cameras are usually placed out front, where a stage audience would be, so that the actors can simply play their parts once through. Psychoanalytic theorists argue that television is therefore less influential and less appealing than is film, because the audience is merely a spectator rather than sutured into the image itself.

Sexual Repressions: A third major theme of psychoanalytic criticism is the particular desires that are repressed by human beings, especially sexual desires.

Sexual desire is among the most intense of human yearnings, and also among the most repressed. There are more social rules and taboos having to do with where, when, how, and under what circumstances, a person may gratify his or her sexual desires than for any other form of desire. Sexuality is therefore a major area of concern and analysis for psychoanalytic critics.

Furthermore, because sexuality is the source of such significant desire and repression, psychoanalytic theorists argue that differences based on sexuality are the root of some of our most important contemporary problems. Psychoanalysis observes that sexual differences between men and women are the basis for some of the strongest, most interesting, most enduring, and most troubling social and political conflicts. So critics who are interested in psychoanalysis put that interest to work in trying to show, for example, how power imbalances between men and women occur, are maintained or justified, and can be reversed.

Feminism

Thus, from Freud's interest in repressed desire we have come to sex, *the* repressed desire, and from sex to gender and the ways that actual men and women are empowered or disempowered. This last concern, of course, is the province of psychoanalytic *feminist criticism*, which draws on psychoanalytic theory to explain the empowerment and disempowerment of the sexes.

Varieties of Feminist Criticism: We discovered that Marxist critics believe that there is an established system of power already in place in any society, and that the system tries to perpetuate itself even as some people try to oppose it. Feminist critics make a similar assumption; they argue that there is a male-dominant system of power in place, and they call that system *patriarchy.*

Of course, many observations about the inequities between men and women can be made on the basis of fairly obvious evidence. In general, men are paid more, they hold more positions of governmental or corporate power, and so on. The critical approach that draws attention to these kinds of inequities between men and women is often called *liberal feminism. Liberal,* in this sense, means attempting to increase participation within a democratic system. Thus, the liberals of nineteenth century politics tried to change the laws so that more people could vote within the already established political system. And liberal feminists today are concerned with involving more women in the already empowered echelons of business and government. Some rhetorical critics do adopt a liberal feminist perspective in order to study the ways in which inequities are created and maintained in a patriarchal system.

But as we have discovered, critics do their most uniquely valuable work in revealing what is not obvious. And that which is "not obvious" is the whole business of the unconscious: Because the desires that form the unconscious are repressed, they come out in disguised form. They are expressed in behaviors, thoughts, and objects that are signs of what has been repressed and the ways it has been repressed. Therefore, many feminist critics use psychoanalytic theory to explain ways in which inequities between men and women are grounded in the unconscious, or created in early patterns of repression. These feminist rhetorical critics, then, study the ways in which patriarchal systems in society and in politics are a product of the repression of desire and the creation of the unconscious.

One branch of feminism, *radical feminism*, is often allied with the kind of psychoanalytic feminism that we are discussing here. Radical feminist critics point out that it matters little whether a female executive gets the same salary as a male executive if deeper inequities are built in to the very social being of men and women. These critics assume that the most important, and most fundamental, bases of inequities are to be found in the creation of the psyche, in the unconscious and its repression. Radical feminists thus use psychoanalytic theory to point out how the present system itself *creates* men and women inequitably. But this inequitable "creation" occurs through the repression of desire in the unconscious; in other words, it happens in ways that are "beneath the surface," and thus require the efforts of critics to reveal them.

Using Gender Differences in Criticism: Let's examine a couple of the kinds of gender-based differences that psychoanalytic feminist theorists might study. One very broad generalization that is made about women within most cultures is that they have a *lack*; specifically, they lack a penis. The more internal and less easily observed female sexual organs do not count, so to speak, when it comes to serving as signs, simply because they are not immediately visible. Our culture, which privileges sight as a route to knowledge, tends not to value what it cannot see; hence this symbolic strike against women. The idea of a lack is then translated into other traits stereotypically attributed to women, traits that parallel a lack. Passivity is a lack of activity, docility is a lack of initiative and command, and so on. Of course, these critics are not arguing that women universally or naturally have such traits. Rather, they are pointing out that such traits are attributed to women, or more precisely to the female role, under a system of patriarchy.

Now consider a second and more complicated example. We noted above that films suture the audience into their story line by putting the camera, and thus the viewer, into the space occupied by Jack and by Jane, the characters in a film. However, the audience is more often encouraged to occupy Jack's space. This is because, as feminist critics would note, popular culture much more often makes women into *objects* rather than *subjects*. That is to say, women become something to be looked at, talked about, worried over, desired, and so on. Men, on the other hand, are more typically made into the lookers, the talkers, the worriers, the ones who desire—in short, into subjects. (As another way of thinking about this distinction, consider the grammatical roles of the *subject* and the *object* in a sentence, for example.)

In terms of the position of the camera, the story line, and the audience's sympathies, movies more often present a situation that assumes, or suggests to the audience, that men are subjects and women are objects—that men act, desire, and decide, while women are acted upon, desired, and decided about. This is not only true of film, feminists argue; feminist critics point to many different texts of popular culture to illustrate this subject-object distinction. Of course, women *are* occasionally portrayed as subjects in some texts; but in these cases they are often punished for occupying such a position. In the film *Thelma & Louise,* for example, much (though not all) of the story is told from a female subject's point of view; but the two lead women end up going off the deep end (literally) at the end of the movie.

The real rhetorical effect of this ingrained subject-object distinction, argue feminist theorists, is to encourage men to act mainly as subjects, and women to act mainly as objects. The rhetoric of popular culture occurs daily, from moment to moment, as first children and then adults are taught how to be men (subjects) and women (objects). The work of psychoanalytic feminist critics involves locating that subject-object distinction (and many others as well) in the experiences of the texts of popular culture.

Signs of Gender Difference: Feminist critics argue that under patriarchal systems, culture will be organized around signs that are *phallic:* signs that represent the penis and the male sexual function. You may have heard the term *phallus,* or *phallic symbol,* before. We refer to the phallus as a symbol or sign, rather than to the actual penis itself, as a way of referring to a wide group of signs that *represent* the penis and the male sexual function (including, for example, rockets, skyscrapers, guns, oil wells, the Eiffel Tower, and so forth).

Signs that are phallic will be more favored or valued; signs that are linked to female sexuality will be less valued. Relationships between signs that express male or female sexuality will mirror the relationships that the culture favors between men and women. That is because those real, cultural relationships are already in place when the infant is born, so the repression of aspects of male and female sexuality follows those cultural patterns. The system of patriarchy (like the economic and political system as understood by Marxists) reproduces itself by creating in the individual unconscious the patterns of empowerment between the sexes that are found in actual practice.

Thus popular culture has a sort of dual function of both production and reproduction. It produces signs of the unconscious, and it comprises those signs as they are produced. But popular culture also perpetuates culturally shared ways of organizing the unconscious through repression. As an example, think about swimwear that is intentionally designed to be sexually alluring. Skimpy men's and women's swimsuits are balanced finely between desire and its suppression. They do so by both featuring and hiding body parts that signal presence (rather than a lack). Specifically, male genitalia and female breasts are emphasized by tight fabric at the same time that they are hidden, or repressed, by the swimsuits.

Accounting for Differences: There is a branch of feminist criticism that is not directly linked to psychoanalytic theory, a branch that might be called *foundationalist* or *essentialist.* Liberal feminism sometimes takes this form. This school of thought argues that there are a number of desirable characteristics that are essentially female, regardless of the culture in which one lives. Essentialist feminists maintain that these characteristics need to be reclaimed in a world dominated by undesirable male characteristics. They argue that it is fundamentally female to be communal (rather than individual), noncompetitive, and nonviolent; these desirable characteristics are perceived as inborn, part of the nature of being female.

Psychoanalytic feminist theory, in contrast, maintains that every different society creates people in its own image, by way of the powerful unconscious, and that noncompetitiveness, for instance, is a female trait only if a society creates that trait in women. Psychoanalytic feminism could be said to be concerned with how men and women are created as male and female by different social systems.

However, the arguments of essentialist or foundationalist critics do pose some challenges for feminist criticism. One challenge is whether to account for sex-specific actions and behaviors as a product of cultural conditioning or a product of nature. Answering this challenge involves trying to determine whether there are characteristics that are common to all men and to all women in every culture; if there are, such characteristics must be physically or genetically based. For example, are women everywhere and in every culture more nurturing, more supportive of the young, than are men? If so, that suggests that there may be some physical basis for differences between male and female psyches.

Psychoanalytic feminism must also clarify two other issues. First, while acknowledging that it owes much to Freud, psychoanalytic feminism must determine whether Freud's ideas about how the psyche is formed apply universally to everyone, or are true only for the society in which he lived. Freud was, after all, a rather sexist individual living in a sexist society. Feminists who admire psychoanalysis often argue that some of the sexist elements in Freud's theory are there because of the patriarchal society that created Freud himself. But Freud presented his ideas as universally true, and not specific just to his cultural context.

Finally, psychoanalysis has a lot to say about how the psyche is created in childhood. But feminists are interventionists as well: They want to change people. So psychoanalytic feminism must also try to sort out which elements of the psyche are permanently etched during childhood and which are still changeable in adults. None of these challenges or issues has been adequately answered yet.

The Imaginary and the Symbolic: Many psychoanalytic feminists have found the work of French psychoanalyst Jacques Lacan helpful in settling at least the question of which characteristics of the psyche are "natural" and which can be attributed to patriarchal culture. Although his work is far too complicated to explain fully here, we will note the distinction Lacan makes between the *Imaginary* and the *Symbolic*. The *Imaginary* is the pattern through which the psyche is organized for everyone, regardless of culture. It includes very basic structures of perception and experience; the "mirror stage" (referred to on page 123), in which children learn how images and representations work, is one component of the imaginary.

Lacan refers to the ways in which particular repressions are carried out, or the particular issues that one culture worries about, as the *Symbolic*. The symbolic varies from one culture to another. It is the set of parameters available within a given culture for making individual psyches. This concept is important, because psychoanalytic feminists identify all of patriarchy as being within the realm of the symbolic. By doing so, these theorists are saying that an ability to recognize images, for instance, is something that people in all times and places must acquire (and therefore part of the imaginary). But the repression of desire does not *have* to occur in such a way as to privilege phallic signs; that particular form of repression, a patriarchal problematic, occurs in some but not all societies (through the symbolic of the particular culture in which it occurs).

What would psychoanalytic feminist criticism show us in *The Wizard of Oz?* A number of psychoanalytic feminist readings could be made of the film; let's examine just a few examples of insights that this method might bring us. Some interesting observations can be made about the movie by thinking about shapes: elongated or pointed phallic signs, and rounded signs that remind us more of the relatively rounded contours of the female body (of the ovum, the breasts, and so forth). Glinda the Good Witch, the ruling female of the film, comes and goes inside a giant round bubble, for instance. One instrument of the Wicked Witch's power is the crystal ball, in which we see mainly women (Auntie Em, the Witch herself). The false Wizard, exposed largely by the female Dorothy, is whisked away at the end of the movie in a round, hot air balloon that he cannot control ("I don't know how it works!").

In contrast to these and other female shapes are the film's phallic signs. A sign of great power is, of course, the tornado that takes Dorothy to Oz, a possible phallic sign. The city of Oz rises up in elongated form on the horizon as the travelers draw near to it; in it they will find the supposedly powerful male Wizard. The Wicked Witch, of course, is a somewhat problematic female. She has stepped outside the bounds of acceptable power for women; she is bony and angular and entirely outside conventional standards of female beauty. Her castle is also phallic, and Dorothy and her friends are finally trapped by the Witch's soldiers in a guard tower, rising erect above a wall of the castle. The ruby slippers themselves, although a blood-red (menses?), are both elongated and the source of the power that Dorothy was seeking all along. Think for a moment about the effects or influences created in the audience by the interplay of these male and female symbols. What do they say about differences between men and women, and about the status of women?

Let us consider one more set of signs in the film. As noted above, the tornado is rather clearly a phallic sign: long and sinuous, snaking its way across the plains of Kansas, doing violence. Dorothy is taken up into the tornado and is eventually expelled from it. She lands in a place populated by child-sized Munchkins. Is it possible to find a link between Dorothy's dramatic expulsion (ejaculation?) from a phallic sign and the sudden presence of children? Dorothy is the focal point of a struggle between a good woman (Glinda) and a bad woman (the Wicked Witch) for the rest of the film; but in her experiences, she meets men almost exclusively. Those experiences constitute a quest, a yearning, to arrive at the place that she has deemed to be right for her. What can you make of this structure of the film as a quest story, given the signs of sexuality and procreation that began Dorothy's journey in Oz? What meanings do these signs offer within the context of a quest? Does it mean anything that Dorothy ends the film lying in a sickbed? For instance, one might read that final scene, in the context of other sexual imagery in the film, as a suggestion that Dorothy has experienced childbirth—that the acquisition of sexual knowledge and maturity is the real payoff of her journey.

Psychoanalytic feminist criticism uses theories first developed by Sigmund Freud to call attention to meanings that have to do with differences between men and women. If Freud's theory is right, those differences are powerfully grounded, having been formed as individual personalities and minds were formed. But this method also argues that the ways in which our culture signifies can be changed, especially if we can become aware of how signification perpetuates certain structures in the unconscious.

Dramatistic/Narrative Criticism

The third perspective on the rhetorical criticism of popular culture is a broad, loosely connected school of thought. Many different critics and theorists have worked within the field of dramatistic/narrative criticism. What unifies this approach is a shared understanding of basic human reality and motivation.

The first two perspectives that we have studied, as well as most others, have an understanding of what "makes the world go around" in terms of human reality, perception, and motivation. Marxists see material, economic conditions as fundamental, as the reason for why we see the world as we see it, and why we are motivated as we are. Feminist/psychoanalytic theorists would argue that early childhood experiences, especially those based on sexual difference, make people do what they do in later life.

Language as a Ground for Motives

Dramatistic/narrative critics believe that *language and other sign systems* are the grounding for human reality and motivation. We have seen earlier in this book how signs, especially as they function symbolically, take on a life of their own. They can impart meanings that are not connected in a necessary, one-to-one relationship to any material objects or actions. Critics using a dramatistic/narrative approach (which we will abbreviate as D/N throughout this discussion) argue that we see the world in certain ways, and react to it with certain motivations, because of and through the symbols that we use. In other words, the most fundamental reality is the symbols we use, especially the larger structures, such as *drama* or *narrative*, into which these symbols are arranged.

Pursuing that idea further, these critics go on to examine the ways that signs (especially symbols) change, interrelate with one another, lead from one to another, and suggest or discourage linkages to other signs. They study those symbolic operations because they assume that they are the sources of perception and motivation. They argue that the "dances" that signs go through because of their intrinsic characteristics are the same moves that perception and motivation go through. For instance, the intrinsic similarity of the words *God, guide,* and *guard* cause us to see them as linked in terms of their meaning or motivation.

Because language and other symbol systems are so complicated, D/N critics use many critical tools that call attention to the many meaning- and motive-generating functions that language performs. Here we can review only a few of the major categories of analysis. We will turn chiefly to the great dramatistic theorist, Kenneth Burke, for the ideas that we will study here.

D/N critics assume that people create and use texts so as to help them understand and formulate responses to problems that they encounter in life. An author, poet, or political speaker puts symbols together in an essay, poem, movie, oration, or other text as a way of trying to understand and respond to certain problems in life. Once a way of understanding and reacting to a problem is encoded in a text, that text becomes a place to which others may also turn for motivation and perceptions. Readers, film and television viewers, and others who share similar problems may use the same texts for help in confronting those problems. In Kenneth Burke's phrase, D/N critics assume that "literature is equipment for living" (1973, 293–304).

Because the source of perceptions and motivations is the symbols themselves, it is assumed that anyone who understands the symbols and how they work within a given system will have access to the perceptions and motivations that they generate. If one is unhappy with one's present life, dramatists would argue, it is because one is using a dysfunctional set of symbols; the key is to find different motivations by using a different set of symbols. To quote Burke again, "motives are shorthand terms for situations"—if you want a different situation, use different "shorthand terms" (1965, 29). The label of "evil empire" for the former Soviet Union once summed up widespread American motives toward that country. Descriptions of Russia or the Ukraine as "impoverished," "struggling," or having a "crumbling economy" are shorthand terms that describe our new motives and new perceptions of lands that were once part of the U.S.S.R.

Sometimes, the focus of D/N analysis is at the level of the individual symbol, sentence, or other small unit. You have already studied some of the critical methods used by D/N analysis in Chapter 3, especially in the section on "implied strategies," in which you were urged to consider "what leads to what," "what goes with what," and so on. As we discussed in that section, the fact that a given word leads to another word indicates that the motivations suggested by that word lead to the motivations suggested by the next word. This kind of critical strategy is very much in keeping with the principles of D/N criticism.

Terministic Screens: In studying individual symbols, or sets of them, a central concept for D/N criticism is that of *terministic screens.* The idea here is that the vocabularies that people typically use allow them to think and to do certain things, but prevent them from thinking and doing certain other things. Therefore a terministic screen is, in Burke's words, a "trained incapacity" as much as it is an enabler to see the world in certain ways (1965, 7).

To see this point in one quick example, consider how, in the United States today, our ways of talking about the success of people or groups tend always to be embodied in terms having to do with money. The success of movies, for instance, is measured in box office sales as expressed in the total dollar amount. This practice leads us to see contemporary films such as *E.T.* or *Home Alone*, (with a ticket price of six dollars or so) as doing very well when compared to movies (such as *Gone with the Wind*, for example) that first came out when admission to theaters cost far less. We are simply not attuned to talking, when it comes to films, in terms of numbers of viewers; instead, we talk in terms of total dollars. In a related example, we are quite accustomed to measuring a person's career success in terms of salary dollars; but we simply have no convenient way to talk about success in terms of personal satisfaction, low levels of stress, and so forth. We must talk around those points, or talk about them at great length, while it is much quicker and easier for us to talk about salary figures.

Teleology: When D/N critics examine individual symbols, another important concept that they use is *teleology,* or the idea of the development of a symbol (Burke 1966, 16–20). Teleology refers to the perfection of a thing—the idea that within every concept or representation of a dog, for instance, is the concept of a perfect dog, which is the *telos* of that dog. One important thing that any narrative or drama does is to develop symbols, often in the direction of its telos. The great Russian playwright Anton Chekhov, for instance, once said that if a gun appears in the first scenes of a play, it must be used by the end of the play. That is because a gun is not perfected until it is fired; the shooting gun is the telos of the gun lying on the table. That idea or symbol of a gun yearns to be fired. This idea of development, or teleology, comes from the characteristics of the symbol, not from any material reality itself. The gun lying on a table, as far as it is concerned, can stay there until it rusts. It is the human idea that guns tend toward a perfection in being fired that calls for its firing.

D/N critics would therefore look for key individual symbols in a text to track their development throughout a narrative or drama, and to show how that development happened as it did because of teleology. Because such texts are "equipment for living," D/N critics would explain ways in which the teleology of symbols intersects with real life problems and solutions. For instance, nuclear weapons are the perfection of harm. They are the worst thing that can be done to a person or people or place. It is interesting to note the times when the texts of popular culture call for the use of nuclear weapons against enemies, and when they do not. South Africa, for instance, has often been viewed with abhorrence by people in the United States because of its racist system of apartheid; but no one has called for its nuclear destruction. Yet conflicts with Iran, Iraq, and Libya have repeatedly been dealt with in popular culture by invoking this perfect symbol of harm, the nuclear weapon.

Because we have already discussed some of the other principles of D/N criticism in relation to individual symbols, vocabularies, and other small units of discourse in Chapter 3, here we will focus on understanding larger units of texts within D/N criticism. Sometimes D/N critics focus on the whole structure of a text, on the forms and patterns within it, the type of text that it is, and the ways in which the structures within the text relate to one another. We will turn now to just a few of the major categories of analysis that D/N critics follow in looking at how larger structures of texts work.

Narrative Genres

D/N critics view texts as *stories* or *dramas*, even if a given text is not explicitly such, because they argue that the characteristics of stories and dramas underlie all symbolic behavior. Stories and dramas usually occur as examples of types, or *genres*. A story might be a mystery, or a romance, or a spy thriller, for instance. The text will include indications of which sort of genre or type it belongs to, leading the reader to have certain *generic expectations.* For instance, if a detective and a murder appear within the first twenty pages of a book, the book is in a way "asking" to be considered a mystery. Sometimes some parts of the context of the text will alert us as to its genre or type. If you are attending a college graduation, you know that the genre of a "commencement address" is likely to be the type of speech that you will hear from the featured speaker, and you will expect the speech to include some sort of uplifting advice for people about to enter the world outside of academia. Another part of a text's context might be the person or people who had a hand in producing it. If you hear that Stephen King has a new book out, you can make a pretty good guess as to the genre that book will fit into.

All texts of popular culture can be viewed in this way, by placing them within a genre. It is important to understand that a genre describes a set of expectations that an audience might have about how a text will interface with the audience in a certain situation. A genre does *not* describe a set of hard and fast rules that texts must follow. For instance, if you are at a dance and are told that the D.J. will next play the latest song from the group Metallica, you will certainly expect a hard-driving, loud, heavy metal tune. That is not to say that you will, without any exception, get such a thing. Suppose Metallica's latest song is a soft ballad done to singing violins. In this case, the idea of genre would still be useful, because it would describe the expectations that such a song would *violate.* The people at the dance may find the song a wonderful and interesting change, or they may shout it down. But their reasons for doing one or the other are likely to be influenced strongly by their generic expectations.

Comedy and Tragedy

In several of his books Kenneth Burke takes the idea of genre a step further to argue that the standard, classical genres of literature underlie all texts that one might encounter (even those of popular culture) and that those standard genres provide important but unsuspected "equipment for living" to their audiences (1937, I). Burke reviews many genres such as the epic, the satire, the burlesque, the ode, and other classical categories of literature. Two categories particularly well developed in Burke's analysis are the two broad categories of *comedy* and *tragedy*.

To understand what Burke means by comedy and tragedy, we must understand some of his views about the real life problems that people face (1969a, 1969b). Burke argues that people are threatened by differences. We do not like to think that others are strange and alien, and when we perceive differences between ourselves and others, we work to overcome them. The condition of being different and estranged from others is referred to as *mystery,* and Burke argues that we try to overcome mystery.

Differences are overcome by entering into relationships that are organized around certain rules and principles; these relationships are called *hierarchies.* By "playing by the rules" of the hierarchy, we find common ground between ourselves and others, and we are able to keep mystery at bay. The common ground that is established in hierarchies is a way to achieve *identification* with others, which is something that people generally want. For instance, the rule-bound and highly structured organizations within the business world provide a way for people from different racial, religious, ethnic, and age groups to relate to one another. Similarly, people may be from very different backgrounds, but if they are attending the same football game together, the structure of watching the game in the stands is a source of identification for them. And a man and woman may be different from each other, but through the structure of a marriage they can achieve identification.

The problem is, nobody can follow the rules of any hierarchy all the time. We are always violating the rules, or at least thinking of violating them. Such violations create feelings of guilt, and the violations must somehow be dealt with so that the hierarchy may be restored. Sometimes we observe others violating the rules, and those violations must also be dealt with so that others do not destroy the hierarchies that ground identification and keep mystery at bay.

So the question becomes how to handle the inevitably recurring guilt that comes with living in hierarchies. This guilt is an inevitable, real life problem. For example, we may think racist thoughts and feel guilty because we know that those thoughts violate the principles of equality that many of our hierarchies insist upon. We realize that we are not working as hard as we have agreed to at our jobs, and feel guilty because we know that we are violating the rules of that particular business hierarchy. What can we do?

Burke says that discourses (by which he means the texts of popular culture, among other things) are available for people to turn to in devising means of dealing with guilt. Guilt may be handled in three ways. The first way is through *transcendence:* to see our guilt-inducing action as not truly a source of guilt because it is required by a different, higher or nobler hierarchy. If you need to work late every night of the week, for instance, your family may complain and you may realize that you are guilty of violating expectations that you will come home at a reasonable hour. But one way of dealing with that guilt is to say, to yourself and to your family, that by working late you are earning more money for *their* benefit, for the greater ultimate good of all. In another example, a president may deal with the guilt of having lied to Congress by saying that he did so because the higher considerations of national security compelled him to do so.

A second way of dealing with guilt is to punish it in one's self. This simple and straightforward method Burke calls *mortification*. Sometimes, the guilty party finds a way to punish his or her own guilt through some related, atoning action. This way of dealing with guilt, through punishment, is, of course, common in religious faiths: a particular sexual sin, for instance, might be punished by some form of penance such as fasting, prayer vigils, or giving money to the poor.

The third way of managing guilt is described as *victimage* by Burke; it involves finding some other party that can represent one's guilt, and then attacking the guilt in that other form. (You may be more familiar with this general phenomenon under the name of "scapegoating.") Of course, if one is concerned about the guilt of others in the first place, then victimage is a convenient way to handle their guilt as well. And now we come back to *comedy* and *tragedy*, two kinds of texts that illustrate the two forms victimage may take.

Comedy is a kind of text that pictures the guilty act in question (either one's own or another's) as being committed by a *comic fool*. The text treats this misbehaving individual as mistaken, and embarrasses him or her by revealing the error of the action to all. Comedy also typically shows its audience that the guilty act was inevitable insofar as it was a common human failing. In this way, the comic fool is reintegrated into the social hierarchy. But more important, if the fool's guilt mirrors a person's own guilt, then by experiencing the comic text, that person has vicariously reintegrated himself or herself back into the community, and the hierarchy, as well.

Tragedy is a kind of text that pictures the guilty act in question as being done by a *tragic hero* (*Hero* is simply a technical term here, and need not mean a "good guy"; in fact, some tragic heroes are rather objectionable). According to a tragic text, the guilty action is something that needs to be punished, as, by extension, does the tragic hero. The hero is depicted as engaging in actions that are inevitable insofar as they arise out of situations or character flaws that members of the audience might have as well. But instead of treating the guilty hero as simply mistaken and in need of correction, tragedy treats the hero as in need of punishment or even destruction. When audience members experience a tragic text, then, they see their own guilt purged by seeing it punished and destroyed.

This theory of comedy and tragedy, as well as Burke's theories of other categories of literature (the epic, the ode, and so on), may sound rather esoteric, but is meant to explain how people experience all kinds of discourses and texts, including those of popular culture. To see the relevance of this theory, consider the television series *M*A*S*H*, which is now widely seen in syndicated reruns. Nearly every episode of *M*A*S*H* finds Frank Burns doing something outrageous that threatens to destroy the camaraderie of the camp or the doctors' tent ("the swamp"). Note that Burns does things that many of us as viewers might occasionally be guilty of doing in our own lives as well. He is deceitful, vain, cowardly, grasping, and incompetent; so are we from time to time, and it portends trouble for our hierarchies as well. So Frank Burns is a good "vessel" for the various guilts that viewers of the show might be experiencing.

Now, there seem to be two sorts of reactions to Burns. One is the reaction that is encouraged by the show, which is to laugh at Frank as his foolishness is shown for what it is, and to breathe a sigh of relief as happiness reigns over the camp once again at the end of the show. If you experience that reaction towards Frank Burns, then you are treating his guilty actions *comically*. A second reaction, however, is to want to beat Frank Burns with a tire iron. This reaction, which involves impatience with the forebearance and restraint with which Burns is treated and a longing to simply lob a grenade in his direction, treats his guilty actions *tragically*. These two reactions to Burns—as either a fool to be corrected or a tragic hero to be destroyed—illustrate how this text of popular culture can function as either a comedy or a tragedy, thereby providing us with equipment to live with our own guilts.

A similar choice between tragedy and comedy confronts viewers of the more recent comedy series, *Married With Children*. The peace of the Bundy family is constantly threatened by the machinations or stupidity of the father, yet the family order is generally restored at the end. But some viewers may prefer the more "tragic" solution of doing away with Al Bundy altogether.

The Pentad

Another major tenet of D/N criticism, particularly in Kenneth Burke's work, is called *pentadic analysis* (1969a). We noted previously that D/N criticism argues that people formulate their perceptions of the world through symbolic systems, especially through language. One important way in which the world is understood through language is through the explanations we make to ourselves for what caused a particular situation or experience to occur. This is an important aspect of how we understand the world because through these explanations we formulate our own motivations. If, for example, someone thinks that the world is the way it is because of money or economic circumstances, he or she will be motivated in a very different way than will a person who thinks that the world is the way it is because of God's will.

Burke argues that when people explain the world to themselves, and thus formulate motives for acting in the world, they do so by anchoring their explanation in one or a combination (a *ratio*) of five basic terms, called *the pentad*. The five terms of the pentad are

act (actions, things that are done, willed or intended undertakings)

agent (people, groups, beings with the power to choose and to act)

agency (the means, tools, or techniques with which something is done)

scene (the physical or social environment, or context, for action)

purpose (the guiding ideas, goals, or motives for choice and action)

Pentadic criticism operates on the assumption that texts, and authors of texts, will tend toward explaining the world consistently by using one or a simple combination, or *ratio*, of these five terms. Texts as a whole are studied for the ways in which they tend to suggest that the world is the way that it is because of a term or ratio between terms. The overall vocabulary of a text, the development of ideas or plot, the kinds of events that occur, key signs—are all studied to discover an underlying, and often not obvious, tendency to key an explanation of the world to a term or ratio.

For example, a concern for many people these days is that some children do not acquire skills in reading by the time they graduate from high school. The oft-repeated question "Why can't Johnny read?" is a question of why this aspect of the world (reading skills) is the way it is. But in answering that question people will also formulate motives for responding to the problem. One answer that people might give is that Johnny can't read because he is in a poor or underprivileged environment, surrounded by noise and squalor, exposed to few positive role models; this is a *scene* explanation. Another answer is that Johnny can't read because his kind of people just can't, that there is some sort of inbred genetic or dispositional deficit preventing his reading; this is an *agent* explanation. One might give an *agency* explanation, answering that Johnny can't read because he has not been given books that would interest him. One could give a *purpose* explanation, arguing that Johnny can't read because he is simply not motivated and has no inner drive or desire to read. Finally, perhaps Johnny can't read because he has never been taught, because nobody has ever done anything to instill in him an ability or desire to read; this would be an *act* explanation.

Burke argues that the great philosophies of the world are complex ways to explain experience and to formulate motivations by using the terms of the pentad. Charles Darwin's concept of survival of the fittest (which argues that the environment determines which creatures are fittest and therefore more likely to survive) is *scenic*, for instance. Mystic explanations of the world, including those of many religions, are *purpose*-centered, argues Burke. Because people construct such explanations of how the world operates for themselves, they respond favorably or unfavorably to similar explanations that are offered in discourse, including the texts of popular culture. A pentadic analysis can therefore be a useful explanation of the rhetoric of popular culture: The public may or may not respond to a text of popular culture because of their acceptance or rejection of its key pentadic term or terms.

Analysis and Examples

The Wizard of Oz is a text that can be analyzed through the methods of D/N criticism as well. Here, we will try out two of the methods suggested above. First, the movie offers a good illustration of how guilt is dealt with in both comic and tragic terms. Note that both the Wicked Witch and the Wizard are hierarchy breakers. The Witch is guilty in all particulars, acting against all the rules of the societies of Munchkinland and Oz. The Wizard is guilty in terms of the society of Oz and the pact that he makes with Dorothy and her companions. The Wizard is treated as a comic fool, however. His guilt is unmasked, literally unveiled, as Toto draws the curtain away from him while he works the controls of the machines of deception in his palace. It becomes clear that he is not who he claims to be, and cannot do what he claims to do. Once the error of his ways is revealed, however, he is restored to the community. In fact, he and Dorothy together plan to journey back to Kansas, but his incompetence gets the better of him in the end as the balloon takes off with him helplessly inside.

The Wicked Witch, on the other hand, is treated tragically and is destroyed in the end. It is inevitable that she does what she does, being a wicked kind of witch. But it is precisely her guilty acts that are her undoing; if she had never trapped the four companions in her castle, Dorothy would not have been there to throw water upon her, thus melting her.

Remember that in handling guilt comically or tragically, *The Wizard of Oz* was vicariously handling guilt for the audience through victimage. Consider the sorts of guilt that the Wicked Witch and the Wizard could represent for the audience. Perhaps one reason for this film's enduring popularity is that the guilts that are handled comically and tragically are really very ordinary and very common guilts. Many of us claim to be what we are not, and would like to hold power over others despite our failings. The temptation to strut and posture, and to impress others with empty phrases and bluster, is strong in many of us. These are the Wizard's failings, and we see our everyday selves in him. Similarly, few guilts are more common than a lust for power, for control over others, for getting our way, for having a castle full of possessions and an army to defend them. These are the crimes of the Wicked Witch, and these darker guilts are shared by many in the audience. In understanding how guilt is handled through the texts of popular culture, D/N critics must always ask how the audience for the text is being given equipment for living through their own particular guilts.

The Wizard of Oz can also be examined using pentadic analysis. One possible argument, for instance, is that the film is *agent*-centered. Let us examine several components of the movie to see why that may be so. Notice that between Kansas and Oz, each of several characters reappears in different disguise but as essentially the same person (and portrayed in the film by the same actor). It is as if the underlying person, the characteristics of the agent as agent, are strong enough to survive the transition from reality to fairyland and back: Professor Marvel and the Wizard are both genial humbugs; each of the farmhands seems to lack what the corresponding Scarecrow, Tin Man, and Lion lack; and Miss Gulch is as evil and grasping as is the Wicked Witch.

Another aspect of the agent-centered quality of the movie is the centering of the plot around ways in which the four companions are deceived about who they are and what powers they have, and how they overcome those deceptions. Dorothy is a person with the power to go back to Kansas immediately by tapping the heels of the ruby slippers three times, but she must discover that about herself. It is clear that each of her three companions already has the personal characteristic that he thinks he lacks. The Scarecrow thinks he needs brains, but it is he who invents a plan to get into the Witch's fortress. The Lion thinks he lacks courage, but he leads the charge in the ensuing battle. The Tin Man thinks he lacks a heart, but he has to be admonished not to cry for Dorothy, "or you'll rust yourself again, and we haven't got an oil can."

When they finally return to the Wizard, the Scarecrow, Tin Man, and Lion are each given what the audience knows to be a meaningless trinket; yet through that trinket, each suddenly "discovers" the thing he or she was "missing." It was there all along, as Dorothy discovers of her own heart's desire; what they have found is not brains, heart, courage, or home, but *themselves*. So the movie seems to advise the audience to look within themselves, to the kind of people (or agents) that they are, to discover the truth about the world.

D/N criticism, then, looks to the ways in which symbolic systems, and especially language, work. It assumes that motivations work the same way, insofar as they are derived from those symbol systems. The texts of popular culture are studied in order to determine how the signs that they are made of "work," interact with one another, and create motivations within themselves that are then available for audiences to use in confronting real life problems.

Media–centered Criticism

You will have noticed that, as predicted earlier in this chapter, strict lines of separation among the schools of thought studied here have not been possible. We discussed some feminist ideas when considering Marxism, for example. The fourth perspective we will discuss, that of *media-centered criticism*, has also been alluded to earlier in this chapter, within the discussion of feminist/psychoanalytic criticism. You may recall that we considered the ways in which experiencing a film duplicates the mirror stage of childhood, and the argument that this duplication of a pleasurable experience in childhood is one reason for the rhetorical effectiveness of film, for why it is so popular. That argument is a good illustration of media-centered criticism. Just as culture-centered criticism (which we will discuss later) argues that texts of popular culture should be analyzed using concepts taken from the culture in which they occur, media-centered criticism argues that texts of popular culture should be analyzed using concepts that take into consideration the *media* in which the component signs of the text appear.

Here we will focus specifically on the medium of television, in part because we have already looked briefly at some characteristics of film, but mainly because television is clearly the most important medium in the United States, Europe, and even most of the Third World today. Much of popular culture comes to us through the "tube," and that which does not is often obviously influenced by television. For instance, the newspaper *USA Today* (founded in 1982—well into the television age), is designed to be highly visual, with bright colors and many graphics, and it is sold on street corners in a box that looks like a television set. Media-centered criticism would therefore caution critics to consider the characteristics of television as a medium, and to show how those characteristics affect many other dimensions of how texts are created and received.

What Is a Medium?
We must first understand what is meant by *media*. A *medium* is sometimes defined as a channel of communication, a way to move signs from one person to another, or as the material in which the signs of communication are manifested.

The book you are holding is a medium through which some signs that your author has made have come to you. Sometimes medium is defined more narrowly as a *technology of communication*, such as television, radio, or film. A more inclusive definition, one that underlies media-centered criticism, sees a medium as a technology of communication in combination with its typical *social uses*. According to this definition, a medium is both (1) a means of producing and reproducing signs, and (2) the ways in which a given society or culture typically makes use of that means of production.

For instance, television in the United States is a medium that comprises not only a certain technology (the screen, broadcast or cable hookups, sometimes stereo sound, sometimes a video cassette recorder), but also a certain pattern of usage: Televisions are usually found in the home, and if not in the home, then in enclosed places of informal social gatherings (such as a bar). We are so familiar with that way of using television that we may lose sight of the fact that the same technology could have been paired with very different social uses. In the very early days of television, for instance, Adolf Hitler planned to place large sets on street corners and in other public places in Germany as a means of official propaganda; in this case there was no intention to have people keep televisions in the home. You can see how different television as a medium would be today were the technology with which we are familiar put to that different social use. To see a medium as both technology and social usage requires the critic to examine the ways in which technologies are used in culture and in the everyday lived experiences of people.

Media Logic

Media-centered criticism can take any medium as its focus, showing how the medium influences the texts that it carries and the audiences that it addresses. Many scholars are working on developing media-centered criticism, but two of the most interesting critics in this area are David Altheide (1985) and Robert Snow (1987; Altheide and Snow 1979). Altheide and Snow use the concept of *media logic* to explain what media-centered criticism is attempting to do. Underlying the idea of media logic is the assumption that as people become accustomed to a technology and to the social uses to which it is put, they internalize certain ways of thinking and perceiving.

For instance, suppose you spend most of a day recording music onto audiotapes on your stereo system. You will probably be making heavy use of the fast forward and rewind functions of the machine. Suppose that at the end of the day, you switch your stereo over to the radio, and you hear a song that you particularly like. You start to reach for the rewind button so you can hear it again, and you are caught up short, because of course radio does not have rewind as part of its "logic," as the tape recorder does. What has happened, say Altheide and Snow, is that you have internalized the tape recorder logic, so much so that you come to expect to find rewinds and fast forwards everywhere. If you really have internalized that logic completely, you may even start looking for fast forward buttons as you read boring textbooks!

Of course, we do not always "transfer" the logic of one medium to another. But one medium does tend to become dominant in any given society. In the nineteenth century in this country, the dominant medium was print (books, newspapers, letters, magazines, and so on). Today, television is the dominant medium, and it is affecting the ways that people habitually think about their everyday problems and experiences. Notice how media-centered criticism describes media as the fundamental factor in perceptions and motivations, just as Marxism identified the material and economic as fundamental, and feminist criticism identified sexual difference as fundamental.

Characteristics of Television as a Medium

Media-centered criticism is not restricted to television, but it is often concerned with it because of TV's importance to our culture. Media-centered television criticism therefore tries to explain some central characteristics of television as a medium (in terms of both technology and social use together). Let us briefly consider some of the characteristics of television that this approach has identified.

Commodification: One characteristic is *commodification.* A commodity is a good, something that is bought and sold, something with intrinsic value that can be traded economically. There are several reasons why television in the United States today has a logic that includes commodification. The first and most obvious reason is that television broadcasting is a commercial enterprise and is constantly selling commodities to the public. Television programming is saturated with advertisements. Often, advertisements blend into the regular programming, because (1) ads have production values that are as high as or higher than the shows themselves, so that the ads are interesting and eye-catching and therefore resemble the program; (2) the same actors will appear on both programs and advertisements, thus linking the two ("I'm not a doctor, but I play one on television"); (3) ads and programs often employ the same formats, such as that of music video, thus blurring any clear distinctions between the two; and (4) ads and shows are interspersed with each other with increasing frequency. The end result is that the selling of commodities becomes increasingly inseparable from what one sees in general in watching television.

Another reason why television is heavily involved in commodification is that the audience itself is a commodity. We do not often think of ourselves as commodities, but in a sense we are. Television as organized in our country depends on advertiser support, and advertisers are more interested in buying time during programs that have large audiences. So programmers are able to "sell" an audience to a commercial sponsor. We as that audience are, in a sense, sold to an advertiser for fifteen seconds at a time, on the expectation that we will be there in front of our television sets to watch a commercial at that time.

Television also commodifies because increasingly, the content of the shows themselves displays the "good life" as one that is rich in material goods (or commodities). Murder mystery shows will almost invariably involve the death of a rich and famous person. A story about the murder of an ordinary librarian living in an upstairs duplex in Cleveland is unlikely to become a TV episode because it does not give programmers a chance to show fine furniture, Waterford crystal, oil paintings on the walls, and a Rolls Royce in the garage. We have shows about the lifestyles of the rich and famous, not the middle class and obscure.

Finally, television commodifies because the set itself is an owned commodity. It is something that the viewer holds as personal property, and is thus a sign of one's economic status. It is interesting to note how all these forms of commodification interrelate. For instance, television sets were initially sold so as to provide an audience for commercials. In other words, ads came first, and people were encouraged to buy sets so as to become audiences (commodities) to be sold to advertisers themselves.

The impact of commodification is that it creates an intense concern for commodities in the minds of those who use television a great deal. Material goods come to be considered one of the most important things in life. People may come to think that having a lot of material goods (like the people they see on TV) is the natural way to live, and may therefore think that poverty is somehow unnatural or a moral defect. Media-centered critics would examine texts of popular culture, especially those on television, to trace the effects of commodification in the perceptions and motives those texts offer.

Realism: Another important characteristic of television is its *realism*. This characteristic has been well explained through George Gerbner's work with the concept of *cultivation* (1980). Cultivation refers, in this sense, to the ways in which television cultivates perspectives on what the world is like.

Television cultivates a sense of its own reality in viewers. It seems to be a window on reality for at least two reasons. First, it is a *visual* technology, and in our culture, seeing is believing. Television shows us pictures of things, and many Americans think that pictures cannot lie. So what we see on television, we assume to be real. We may know that a drama is staged and being presented by actors, but the distinction between drama and real life is increasingly blurred on television. News broadcasts, for instance, may present pictures of a prison hostage crisis that look exactly like the fictional drama on the same topic that you saw on a program the night before.

A second reason why television seems to be so realistic is that it is so much a part of our lives. We generally take it for granted, regarding it as a part of our homes, located in our everyday surroundings. We would never question the reality of what we see out our living room windows; in the same way, we take television to be a realistic window on the outside world. In fact, television has become a guarantee of reality. "How do you know," we might ask of a friend who has told us an unbelievable story. "I saw it last night on TV," she responds, thus clinching her argument. Much television *is* in fact about real life; we are used to live broadcasts and video journalism bringing actual happenings into our home, making these events much more present and alive than any newspaper article could.

Television is becoming increasingly intertwined with reality through shows like *Code 3, Unsolved Mysteries, Cops,* and *America's Most Wanted.* These are programs that merge dramatic reenactments with candid videos of live action. Because television seems so realistic, the perceptions and motivations portrayed in its programming cultivate a similar sense of reality in viewers. Gerbner and his colleagues have found, for instance, that people who are heavy viewers of police shows on television come to grossly overestimate the amount of violence that actually occurs in their communities (1980). The world looks more violent than it actually is to them because they think that they are seeing that real world on television. Media-centered critics would look at these and other perceptions and motives offered by television and identify ways in which they cultivate un-realistic or distorted views of reality. These critics would study the "world" that television creates and then judge the effects of that world on the larger society.

Intimacy: We will examine one more of television's central characteristics: *intimacy.* Television is highly concerned with that which is small, personal, and person-oriented. Furthermore, media-centered critics would argue that television serves to make these small, intimate concerns paramount in many aspects of our lives.

As we have noted, television is a technology that is interwoven with our personal lives because of its place in the home. Many people have more than one set, so that they can watch TV wherever they are in their homes, even in their bedrooms. The home setting of most television viewing would naturally make it an intimate medium. But of course we often read books and newspapers at home, also. To understand television as an intimate medium more fully, we need to think about what kind of programming tends to succeed on television.

Most television screens are rather small. There are, of course, large projection televisions available, but their price keeps them out of the range of affordability for most people. Most of us watch television on screens that are twenty or twenty-five inches across diagonally, or even smaller. For that reason, large and complex images do not work very well on television. What television does best is to show relatively simple scenes with only one or a few objects on which to focus. Thus, television does very well in showing people. The human face is a relatively uncomplicated thing to watch, and it does not require a large screen to be seen. In fact, some of the extreme closeups that we see on television would not work well on film: Nobody wants to see a face that is thirty feet across, pores and warts and all. But the human face and form do well on television, because the small screen keeps them human sized.

This suitability for portraying individual people helps to explain the specific ways in which television portrays events. Notice that some scenes that you would not ordinarily think of as involving shots of individual people often do just that. If a car chase scene is depicted, for example, television will keep returning to show the faces and bodies of people in the car as much as or more than it will show the cars themselves. Sports provide another example. Television actually does not do very well in showing two opposing lines in football as they break against each other. That is why the camera will focus on individuals as much as possible, following receivers as they run downfield or backs as they run with the ball. In between plays, the camera will zoom in for extreme closeups of players as they walk back to huddle or writhe in pain on the field. So when television is portraying panoramic action, it keeps pulling back from the broad view to show what it shows best: the people within the action.

Because of its location in the home, and because of what its size and technology can do best, television calls our attention to people. Furthermore, it focuses on people's concerns, experience, and problems. In this way, it is an extremely intimate medium. Joshua Meyrowitz has shown persuasively how television has robbed public figures of truly private lives (1985). Because TV demands a focus on the person and the personal, it is good at showing—or at pretending to show—the intimate facts of the lives of those whom it portrays. In an age of television, we know all about the president's colon and kidneys; such a state of affairs was unknown in the less intimate age of print.

Furthermore, television's intimacy tends to turn public attention toward the personal dimensions of any event of great public importance. Hostage crises do very well on television because they are about people; the larger political and social issues behind the hostage taking, however, are likely to go unexplored on television. The reasons why various factions in the Middle East are constantly at war with one another is difficult to explain on television; but if a U.S. citizen is taken hostage in the Middle East, the person's grieving family can be interviewed intimately, even in their homes. Thus, television will opt for the latter far more often than the former. To cite another example, changes in Eastern Europe and in Russia following the fall of Communist governments there are very complex and may be hard to portray or to understand on television. Therefore, a news special on those changes will likely focus on one or a few individuals, showing what their everyday lives are like and the problems that they face.

Media-centered critics argue that the American public increasingly tries to understand public problems by examining the experiences of individuals, and that this shift to the personal is a direct result of the dominance of television in our culture. Critics would examine texts of popular culture to show the ways in which complex political and social issues, especially when portrayed on television, are transformed into personal images. The problem of Mexican nationals crossing into the United States for work becomes the story of Raoul and his family; the problem of toxic wastes becomes the experience of Betty, who lives within a mile of a dumping site; and the problem of the homeless becomes the plight of Amos, a man who sleeps on hot air grates in the sidewalk. (Recall that in Chapter 3, we described this as a process of understanding complex problems through *metonymy*.)

Analysis and Examples

The Wizard of Oz, though originally a film, is actually a fruitful example for thinking about media-centered criticism, particularly criticism that addresses the effects of television. Interestingly, the movie did not do as well as a film as it has on television. It did not win any major Academy Awards, for instance, and was widely discounted as merely a children's movie by the critics of the late 1930s. Twenty-five years later, however, it was firmly established as a television institution, being broadcast once a year to enormous family audiences clustered around the set. Now it is broadcast even more often, and it is widely available on videotape. Although this is certainly not the only question that a media-centered critic would ask, it would be interesting to consider why *The Wizard of Oz* has done so much better on television than it did on film.

We might consider the characteristics of television in answering our question. First, the movie is visually lush and splashy, especially when the Oz scenes are contrasted with the dull black and white of Kansas. Of course, many movies that do well as movies are colorful and gaudy, but it could be that a television audience, attuned to commodities, will better understand how the commodity-rich Oz might be a place of wonder to Dorothy Gale from Kansas ("Can I even dye my eyes to match my gown?" "Yes." "Jolly old town!"). Good and bad in the movie seem to be aligned, respectively, with commodification and a lack thereof: The Wicked Witch's palace, although huge, is a bare and spartan place, while the "best place," the city of Oz, is encrusted with precious metals and jewels. In fact, the companions' first experience in Oz appears to be an enrichment with commodities, as the Scarecrow is restuffed with the finest straw, the Tin Man is waxed and polished, and the Lion and Dorothy have their hair and nails made beautiful.

Power is also signalled by commodities. The audience does not see where Glinda the Good Witch lives, but the other two most powerful figures—the Wicked Witch and the Wizard—have enormous palaces. The Witch's commodities are ugly, and not anything we would want, but it is clear from the sheer bulk of her castle that she is rich in commodities. And the (seemingly) powerful Wizard's palace has enormously high ceilings and halls that stretch for miles.

Can we say that *The Wizard of Oz* did better on television because of television's realism? Notice that "real life" in the movie—the scenes in Kansas—are in unrealistic black and white. The realism of living color does not appear until Dorothy gets to Oz. I can recall when color television sets began to replace black and white sets as standards in American homes. Like a slow tide, the acquisition of color sets spread across a neighborhood. And I can also recall the anticipation with which the first color viewing of *The Wizard of Oz* was awaited, because now the audience could participate in the Kansas-to-Oz transition (the move from black and white to color) with Dorothy. The family with the new color set had in fact gone from Kansas to Oz (no matter which programs they were watching) when they bought their new set.

But even for viewers who did not experience that transition from black and white to color, television's realism may in fact provide a more satisfactory answer for what is, after all, a central question in *The Wizard of Oz*: Was it real? Did Dorothy really go there, or was it all a dream? It is easy to imagine that Oz is a fictitious place as you leave the movie theater, because after all, you leave the movie behind. But the television stays right there in your home. It has been showing you realities all along, and so makes it easier for the young at heart to imagine that Oz was, in its turn, real.

Finally, consider the heavy emphasis in *The Wizard of Oz* on *characters*, on people and pseudo people. Practically all the action is portrayed through close-up shots of people and creatures. Furthermore, these characters are all extremely telegenic and interesting in close-ups. The mythical creatures, such as the Scarecrow, the Tin Man, and the Wicked Witch, need to be seen up close and personal, so that the realism of the makeup jobs can be appreciated. On the other hand, especially for children, a Wicked Witch the size of a movie screen might well be overwhelming. In sum, *The Wizard of Oz* found its right "size" on the television screen.

Media-centered critics study the texts of popular culture with an eye toward the media that present those texts to the public. In many cases, these critics would argue, the characteristics of a particular medium itself may be more important than are the texts displayed through that medium. Media-centered critics trace the effects of the medium that may be found in an audience's ways of thinking and processing information.

Culture-centered Criticism

The fifth and final approach to the rhetorical criticism of popular culture that we will examine is the newest, least unified, and least developed of the methods that we are considering in this chapter. It is still in the process of being formulated and clarified by critics and scholars. But by the same token, it is on the cutting edge of critical approaches, and a potentially exciting perspective to work from.

Cultures and Their Own Critical Methods

A major theme for us in this book has, of course, been the importance of *culture* as a source of perspectives, thoughts, values, feelings, ideas, and ideologies. Culture is comprised not only of artifacts, but also of ways of understanding artifacts. Since a way of understanding artifacts is essentially what a method of rhetorical criticism is, it makes sense to say that every culture contains its own methods for understanding artifacts. One rather extreme example illustrates this truth: During World War II, soldiers and sailors from the United States and its allies created temporary, makeshift bases on a number of islands in the Pacific, bringing with them a world of material goods that astonished and impressed the native people who were already living on those islands. With the end of the war, the military personnel abruptly departed, leaving behind odds and ends of military equipment. On some of those islands there arose "cargo cults," actual religions that centered around the expectation that the G.I.'s would return some day, bringing with them renewed prosperity. The castoff equipment that the military left became infused with religious meanings for the cultists.

Now, for the cultures that developed cargo cults, the leftover helmets, jeep parts, and so forth, that were left behind became part of the culture—but so did ways to understand them, ways to interpret them. Those ways of understanding all the castoff items were the religious systems that formed around them. Were a member of a cargo cult to come to the United States, see a helmet in a military relics store, and assume that the store was a religious shrine, we might think that he or she had misunderstood the helmet and what it means. But were one of us to go to a cargo cult island, we would be equally mistaken to identify a helmet placed in a hut as "just a piece of junk from World War II." Those of us living in the high-technology world of the United States today have our own "cargo cults" as well. We, too, have not only objects and actions that are peculiar to our culture, but particular ways of understanding and interpreting those artifacts, ways that might not be understood by people from another culture.

Every culture contains its own methods of critical analysis, its own questions and probes to be brought to bear on the artifact that is being examined. Such methods will be appropriate for understanding artifacts within, or peculiar to, that culture, particularly if we want to know what those artifacts mean for members of that specific culture. If we want to understand what a particular kind of Latvian hat means to Latvians, then we should look at it through Latvian eyes. Of course, this hypothetical Latvian hat will mean *something* to people from Japan, from Great Britain, and from New Jersey. But an awareness of cultures, and of the different methods of critical analysis that cultures give to us, should prevent anyone from assuming that a given artifact has only and always the meaning that one's own culture would give to it.

Ethnocentric criticism is this practice of looking at the artifacts of other cultures and judging them only from the perspective of one's own culture. Ethnocentrism has for centuries been a major tool of racism and imperialism. Soldiers, explorers, and imperialists from European countries would travel to places in Africa, Asia, and South America. Viewing the artifacts of the indigenous cultures of those lands from the perspective of their own cultures only, these European colonialists often labeled the indigenous cultures second-rate, primitive, or savage. Of course, viewing the artifacts of another culture as primitive and underdeveloped becomes a license for oppression. For centuries, people from European cultures used their own ethnocentric attitudes toward the artifacts of other cultures as an excuse to dominate and exploit people of those other cultures "for their own good."

Culture-centered criticism is not the same thing as ethnocentrism. Culture-centered criticism grows out of an awareness that cultures are best understood by using the methods of criticism and interpretation that arise from the cultures themselves. Culture-centered criticism understands that looking from one culture to another requires caution about the claims that one makes, and an awareness that the culture being observed might well see itself, and its own artifacts, differently.

Culture-centered criticism can, in fact, be an *antidote* to ethnocentrism. This is especially true when the criticism is applied to cultures that have been oppressed socially, politically, economically, or militarily. Such cultures have often been analyzed only through the methods of the very cultures that oppress them. Culture-centered criticism is therefore an important political strategy on the part of cultures that have been oppressed and exploited, to recover their own voices and eyes, both for understanding themselves or for understanding other cultures.

Afrocentricity

Culture-centered criticism is being developed on several fronts, as Asian, Hispanic, and other scholars discover and articulate methods of rhetorical criticism that grow out of their own cultures. An approach that is concerned with cultures of African origin is one of the best developed forms of culture-centered criticism so far. It may also be the most controversial version of culture-centered criticism.

We noted earlier that culture-centered criticism often serves as a political tool to counter oppression. People of African origin have historically suffered much oppression, culturally and personally, all over the world. An attempt to recapture a particularly African perspective is thus a method of empowerment for people of African heritage. It argues that those artifacts that are clearly part of the culture of African Americans—such as rap music, the traditional black church, jazz, rhythm and blues, and so on—cannot be adequately understood if analyzed from a European perspective (as they have often been). To understand what the call and response between a black preacher and congregation means, for instance, we must employ methods of critical understanding that arise from within African-American culture.

Here we will focus on efforts in the United States to understand the culture of black Americans as African-centered. We will turn to three primary sources by scholars who articulate critical principles that are grounded in the culture of black Americans. In his book *The Afrocentric Idea* (1987), Molefi Kete Asante explains methods of criticism that are fundamentally African in origin. His view is pan-African, looking to that which is common to people of African heritage wherever they may be found around the world. In *The Signifying Monkey: A Theory of African-American Literary Criticism* (1988), Henry Louis Gates, Jr. argues that many methods of criticism and understanding found in the culture of African Americans developed as defenses against slavery historically, and against racism more recently. Gates's concerns are more specifically American, and more directly political, than are Asante's. We will also examine the ideas of Jack L. Daniel and Geneva Smitherman in their article, "How I Got Over: Communication Dynamics in the Black Community" (1976). Daniel and Smitherman argue that methods of criticism in African-American culture are grounded in the institution of the Traditional Black Church.

All these scholars argue in favor of understanding the artifacts of black American culture using methods grounded in that culture. Although these four critics do not all use the term, we will borrow Asante's idea of *Afrocentricity* to refer to a culture-centered method that places "African ideals at the center of any analysis that involves African culture and behavior" (6). Through such a method, Asante hopes that African culture, including its manifestations among blacks in the United States, will become "subject and not object" (3), the perspective from which a thing is seen rather than the thing that is seen from some other perspective. Developing that critical perspective is, he argues, a political stance as well, in that it grounds people of African heritage, who have been dispersed all around the world, in an ancient and honorable tradition.

These authors, particularly Asante, are careful to note that they are discussing the ways in which African culture informs black American culture today. But they do not make the claim that all black people actively participate in that culture. They are making a cultural, not a racial, argument. They point out that there are also black Americans with a Eurocentric perspective. Furthermore, Afrocentric criticism is potentially something that people of *any* race can engage in, by remembering to apply Afrocentric standards when studying an Afrocentric culture. Afrocentricity is not an exclusive club; it is a perspective on how to understand a culture.

To develop any culture-centered critical method, we must ask what are the values, the ways of understanding and thinking, and the aesthetics that are most characteristic of a given culture. The Afrocentric method identifies a number of ideas, or *tenets*, that are especially important in African cultures, and that must therefore be incorporated into the methods used to study cultures grounded in an African heritage. One of the most important of these tenets of Afrocentricity is the value of *unity and harmony*.

Unity and Harmony: Unity and harmony comprise an overarching value that incorporates several component ideas. Daniel and Smitherman identify, among the tenets of what they term the "Traditional African World View," the cosmic values of "unity between spiritual and material" things and "harmony in nature and the universe" (29–30). Daniel and Smitherman also refer to the idea that human society is "patterned after natural rhythms" (31), by which they mean the cycle of social and environmental experiences that are shared by everyone within the culture (rather than individual or private events). The important event of the day, for instance, is not what happens to you personally, but what happens to your group as a whole (a town or family celebrating a wedding, bringing in a harvest together, and so forth).

Asante also notes the social value of harmony. Afrocentric rhetoric, he argues, is concerned with creating harmony and balance in the midst of disharmony and indecision (35). According to Asante, the Afrocentric mind is highly communal rather than individualistic, and has a distaste for individual achievement that is not related to collective advancement (105). Think of the rhetorical mistakes that a Eurocentric teacher might make, for instance, in encouraging a student from an Afrocentric culture to do well in school so that he or she could get ahead of all the others; that sort of Eurocentric individualism is the wrong rhetoric for the circumstances.

The value of social unity and harmony, of acting together, is an aspect of African culture that can be employed in rhetorical criticism to further understanding of cultures that are grounded in Africa. In the traditional black church, which Daniel and Smitherman take to be "an exemplary form of Black communication" (p. 27), a common pattern of interaction is the "call-response" in which the preacher and congregation will talk back and forth to one another in a way largely unknown among white congregations.

How can we understand this artifact of black culture? Observing it through Eurocentric eyes might lead us to see the congregation as disrespectful of the preacher, as too boisterous or ill-mannered. Such a perspective would misunderstand what call-response means in its original cultural context. Call-response serves to create a unity and harmony between preacher and congregation; instead of a series of interruptions of an individual sermon, it is part of an entire church service that is being created on the spot. Furthermore, Daniel and Smitherman point out that the call-response form can be found in patterns of communication among blacks outside the church as well, and in musical forms, such as jazz, created by blacks. Participating in these various forms of call-response creates a feeling of satisfaction within the individual as he or she participates with others in creating a unified harmony.

It is possible to overlook what is going on in call-response if we do not think about that cultural artifact with the African value of harmony and unity in mind. But with such a value in mind, we might then look at this and other artifacts of black American culture to see that value at work. For instance, basketball seems to be much more a part of the experience of black Americans than does golf; could that be, in part, because golf is such an individual, isolated game, while basketball requires the close cooperation of team members—harmony and unity—to set up shots, to maintain defense, and to move the ball down the court?

Orality: Another major tenet of Afrocentricity is that it is an oral culture, grounded in Asante's concept of *orature,* or the "total body of oral discourses, styles and traditions." Historically, African cultures have communicated through the spoken word, and knowledge has been encoded in spoken forms of literature. Orature thus depends on *nommo,* defined by Asante as the power of the spoken word, the belief that all power is ultimately that of oral communication (17).

This is an important concept for creating an Afrocentric understanding of popular culture. Eurocentric cultures, argues Asante, see power residing in a given text or artifact that is created by some source. To speak, perform, or present that text is merely to pass along the "substance" of the text that is already there. People of European heritage would, for instance, see a song as essentially and fundamentally the words and notes that are written down on paper; a performer is important, but only for passing the song along to a listening audience. But Afrocentricity regards the song, or any text, as created in its performance or presentation. It must not only be sung by the singer, but also heard and reacted to by the audience. Between them, both singer and audience create the text.

The importance of the spoken word is, of course, quite consistent with the importance, noted above, of unity and harmony. Only the spoken word creates an immediate bond between speaker and listener. The written word, in contrast, can be a communication even between one who is dead and an audience. But when a speaker speaks, a singer sings, or an athlete performs, and the audience is there to listen, remark, call encouragement, and make comments—in that moment the text is created according to the Afrocentric perspective.

The importance of understanding this idea as a principle of criticism is clear. The experience of a text within black American teen culture, for example, is most fully understood not by the critic simply listening to a Public Enemy or Salt-n-

Pepa tape, but by the critic seeing how that tape is received and reacted to by a specific audience of teenagers. The text of a gospel music service is not fully understood as the words and music on paper, nor even as the singer's voice alone, but rather as the singer's voice *together with* the ways in which the audience joins in verbally and nonverbally. Any text, from an Afrocentric perspective, is "the word revealed in life" (Asante 60). This concept is also described by Gates as the principle of "The Talking Book," which describes black American writing as often highly oral/aural, representing the "black vernacular" or speaking voice in writing and inviting itself to be read aloud.

Signifying: A third important tenet of Afrocentricity—*signifying*—is described at length, and with great complexity, in Gates's book. Gates points to the fact that historically, in much black American folklore, a figure known as The Signifying Monkey appears. The Signifying Monkey, and the practice of signifying itself, has a great deal of meaning within Afrocentricity, and cannot be fully explained here. But one interesting aspect of it is that it is a *strategy of indirection*. It is saying or doing one thing while meaning another, with the full knowledge that one's audience will understand the doubleness or two-facedness of what one says and does.

Gates gives as one example the practice of "toasting" or "the dozens," in which two people will try to outdo one another in heaping insults upon each other's parents and ancestry, economic prospects, physical appearance, and so forth. The words constitute actual insults on the one hand, but on the other hand are really only a game. Gates cites another example of one woman who observes another, obviously pregnant woman and remarks that the latter has been putting on weight. The pregnant woman merely responds that she has, indeed, been getting larger. To which the first woman replies, "Now look here, girl, we both standing here soaking wet and you still trying to tell me it ain't raining" (83). Rain, of course, has nothing to do with it; it is simply a way of taxing the woman with denying her pregnancy, but doing it *indirectly*. Indirection—saying one thing and meaning another—is thus an essential component of signifying (Gates 54).

Gates argues that signifying is a practice present in all African cultures and rooted in the mythic figure of "Esu," or the trickster. The trickster figure became especially important among black Americans, Gates claims, during the time of slavery, when resistance to oppression required an ability to say one thing but mean another. Slaves had to be able to sing "Steal Away to Jesus," which meant one thing to whites, while understanding among themselves that it meant something quite different, such as a call to a secret meeting. Signifying is thus a strategy for obscuring the apparent meaning, a way to colonize a white sign and make it have a meaning appropriate to one's own culture.

Again, the importance of understanding signifying as a rhetorical critic is clear. An artifact of black American culture will often be most fully understood by asking whether it has a double meaning, an "in-house" meaning among blacks that is specifically and intentionally in contrast to, or in defiance of, the meaning that it might have for white society. Eurocentric criticism tends not to value indirection as highly, and certainly not as a strategy of political survival against oppression. So, for instance, a Eurocentric critic might view the scenes in the film *Coming to America* in which Eddie Murphy portrays an African prince as straightforwardly funny. An Afrocentric perspective, on the other hand, might see these scenes as signifying, as having a double and indirect meaning. Perhaps, for instance, Murphy's portrayal is a burlesque of an African prince *as whites might see such a prince,* and thus is not only meant to be funny for all audiences of every color, but also *oppositional,* set up against whites' over simplified ideas about Third World people.

Other Tenets: Asante, Gates, and Daniel and Smitherman point to many other tenets of Afrocentricity, more than we can consider in detail here. But we will conclude by referring briefly to a few of them.

Oral cultures will trade components of various texts back and forth, because the boundaries between spoken texts are fluid (unlike printed texts, which have firmer physical barriers). Therefore, Afrocentric culture expects that texts will borrow from other texts freely, using a strategy called *intertextuality* (Gates 60). Critics should be on the lookout for that strategy, and note that it is culturally appropriate and expected. For example, much of the public speaking of Martin Luther King, Jr., was intertextual. He wove into a speech many brief passages from the Bible, proverbs, maxims, and his other speeches.

Asante points out that *rhythm* and its associated concepts, such as repetition and careful choice of word and gesture, are highly valued in the Afrocentric perspective (38–39). The phrasing of even a single word and the manipulation of pauses for precise effect are aesthetic choices that are not so highly prized in the Eurocentric tradition. In his famous "I Have A Dream" speech, for example, Martin Luther King, Jr., repeatedly uses a formal pattern of pausing for effect. Similarly, in one well-known passage of the speech, the phrase "I have a dream" is repeatedly appended to the end of the sentence before it. What is happening here is a manipulation of rhythm, in conjunction with a vivid style, that is very much in tune with the Afrocentric perspective.

Daniel and Smitherman argue that *religion* and its symbols hold a central place in the Afrocentric perspective (30). And Asante notes that *proverbs,* or repetition of the ancient wisdom of a people embodied in sayings, are important in black culture. He also refers to two scholars, Vernon Dixon and Badi Foster, who have suggested seven elements of Afrocentricity. Asante lists them as

> 1) the value of humanism, 2) the value of communalism, 3) the attribute of oppression/paranoia, 4) the value of empathetic understanding, 5) the value of rhythm, and 6) the principle of limited reward. There is, in addition, a seventh element: the principle of styling. (37)

Asante also offers as principles of Afrocentricity a focus on "1) human relations, 2) humans' relationship to the supernatural, and 3) humans' relationships to their own being" (168).

As we noted above, Afrocentricity is only one example of culture-centered criticism. We have focused on it here because it is one of the more self-aware and best developed forms of culture-centered criticism. But scholars are also exploring what it means to have an Hispanic, or a Chinese, or a Japanese way of understanding culture that is grounded in those cultures themselves. Culture-centered criticism is not negative; it is not a way to negate another's culture. Rather, it is a very positive attempt to show how all cultures contain within themselves the tools for their own analysis.

Summary and Review

We have studied five schools of thought, or approaches to criticism, in this chapter. It is important to realize, however, that in many ways the things you have learned in this chapter are less crucial than the things you learned in Chapter 3. By that we mean simply that the particulars of any given approach are not as important as is the act of criticism itself—the act of revealing, through any approach, that which is not obvious about texts.

In this chapter we have learned about different perspectives on what texts mean. In a sense, we have reviewed differing views on which meanings critics should look for as they study texts. We began with three "warnings" about the critical perspectives we would discuss: (1) There are differences of opinion within perspectives, (2) There is agreement among perspectives, and (3) Not all perspectives are covered here.

With those warnings in mind, we began by studying the critical perspective of *Marxism*. We learned that Marxism is based in the idea of *materialism*, that perceptions and motives are grounded in the base of material experience. Marxist critics look for ways in which texts reflect, or are symptoms of, those material conditions. Because of this concern with the material, a Marxist perspective often draws on *economic metaphors*, treating signs and texts as if they were commodities that could be traded. Marxism is also very much concerned with power. It shows how texts encourage *preferred readings* that support the *hegemony*, or dominance, of groups of people who are already empowered. But Marxism also reveals resources for *oppositional* readings, either *inflections* or outright *subversions* of preferred readings. We also learned that Marxists identify the *subject position* encouraged by texts, an idea we had encountered earlier.

The second perspective we examined was the *feminist/psychoanalytic*. This perspective is grounded in the psychoanalytic idea that a person's *desires* are always being *repressed* in socially acceptable ways, and that repressed desire accounts for much of our motivations at an unconscious level. Fundamental desires that are repressed in childhood account for especially strong motivations, and among these, the repression of sexuality has a particularly powerful impact. Feminist criticism takes up at this point, focusing on the ways in which fundamental differences between males and females are defined and ordered by different cultures, especially a *patriarchal* culture that oppresses women. Gender differences, we discovered, are encoded in signs, with *phallic* signs both expressing and perpetuating male dominance. We discussed some controversies over the extent to which those differences are natural and unavoidable, or created by cultures and thus manipulatable.

The third perspective reviewed was the *dramatistic/narrative* method. This wide-ranging school of thought is grounded in the idea that for humans, the use of signs is our fundamental reality and source of motives. Thus, the vocabularies, or *terministic screens*, by which we order our world are an especially important object of study for critics. The tendency of signs toward their perfection, or *teleology*, is one characteristic of signs that generates motives. We noted the importance of studying the type, or *genre*, that texts belong to. In particular, we learned about Kenneth Burke's theory of how hierarchy is maintained and guilt kept at bay through the related narrative structures of *comedy* and *tragedy*. We also reviewed Burke's *pentad*, and saw how texts may be studied as if they were keyed to act, agent, agency, scene, purpose, or some ratio among those terms.

We turned next to *media-centered* criticism. We noted that a *medium* must be understood as both a technology and the social uses to which that technology is put. The idea of a *media logic* calls the critic's attention to the inherent characteristics of a medium, and how habitual use of a given medium creates distinctive ways of thinking in an audience. Focusing particularly on the medium of *television*, we identified three characteristics of its media logic as *commodification*, *realism*, and *intimacy*. We saw that texts on television can be studied for the ways in which they reflect, or embody, those characteristics of the medium itself.

Finally, we turned to a new critical approach, *culture-centered* criticism. We learned that this perspective is opposed to ethnocentrism because it argues that the texts of a given culture should be studied using the critical methods and assumptions appropriate to that culture. We focused upon the specific perspective known as *Afrocentric* criticism, which studies the texts generated by African-centered cultures. When critics study texts of African cultures, they look for expression of certain themes or values, including *unity and harmony, orality, signifying, intertextuality, rhythm and style,* and others.

Looking Ahead

In the Looking Ahead sections of the first three chapters, we have formulated specific questions. Here, only one question really remains: How does the critic use these perspectives in actual critical practice? In Part II of this book, you will read some critical studies that apply the methods and techniques you have been learning to actual texts of popular culture. Thus, you will find several examples of how to "do" criticism. One thing that you should note as you read these studies is how they make use of the ideas held by the different approaches to criticism described in this chapter.

Remember that no one study is limited or restricted exclusively to only one approach. Your goal should be to explain the texts of popular culture, not to establish some sort of orthodox plan for following a prepackaged form of criticism. An approach to criticism that rigidly applies the terms of a single method or perspective to a text is sometimes referred to as a "cookie-cutter" approach. Always try to avoid an inflexible, "cookie-cutter" approach to rhetorical criticism. Instead, let the methods and techniques you have learned guide you in generating your own insights about a text. And as you read the following studies, note that while they are linked to the perspectives you have studied, they avoid a rigid application of the methods of any one perspective.

Part **II** Three Critical Studies

Chapter 5

Paradoxes of Personalization: Race Relations in Milwaukee

• •

One idea that you should have gained from reading Chapter 4 is that criticism is *not* meant to be a cut-and-dried, lockstep procedure. You do not conduct, say, Marxist criticism by slavishly following the "five easy steps to a Marxist analysis." In fact, the best critical studies will be those in which the critical machinery is not too obvious. You should use the concepts and categories that a theory or method offers, but you should not feel that you cannot bend those rules. You want your reader to learn about your subject matter and the insights that you bring to that subject. When criticism too obviously announces "Now I am doing the first thing you do for feminist criticism; now I am doing the second thing," and so on, its power to change people's perceptions is diminished. The real payoff of criticism is insight into what texts mean. Critical methods should serve that end.

Also, as we noted in Part I, schools of thought in criticism cross over into each other, borrow from each other, and often work well together. It can be unnecessarily limiting, therefore, to determine in advance that a criticism must be only dramatistic or only media-centered. On the other hand, some focus of attention is needed in criticism, too, so that the critic can help the reader to focus on certain issues.

In this chapter, the focus of the critical methodology will be largely *dramatistic/narrative*. We will be concerned with some motivations that arise out of some operations that public discourse performs. But, if the criticism is done well, insight into the subject matter overall will emerge from the analysis. Let us turn now to consider the general problem that the criticism addresses.

The Problem of Personalization

One of the most serious problems that democracies face today is a gap between the locations of democratic decision making and the problems about which such decisions are made. Increasingly, events that powerfully affect individuals are occurring at an international level. For example, today, decisions about world trade tariffs made in the U.S. Congress may very well have profound effects on shoe factory workers in both Italy and Massachusetts. And the good people of Anytown, U.S.A., may be asked to vote on the performance of their senator regarding arms treaties with Russia and humans rights in China.

The average citizen is required to make decisions about a wide range of issues today. Those decisions are either made directly, as in voting on referenda, or indirectly, as in voting on the performance of elected leaders. In either case, the citizen must find ways to understand problems that may be distant (possibly even international in scope), and that are likely to be extremely complex for that reason. Perhaps two hundred years ago, the citizens of Bent Whistle could concern themselves only with local politics and affairs. But those days are gone. A French conglomerate is thinking of building a factory in Bent Whistle, and if the citizens are to be certain about whether or not they want that factory, they must acquire an understanding of business and international commerce, environmental impact, and many other issues.

The challenge for the average citizen today, then, is to *personalize large and complex issues* in ways that make them understandable, without distorting those issues so much that good decisions cannot be made. We personalize issues when we translate vast and impersonal problems into smaller, more manageable images, stories, and texts. Personalization, in other words, is a *strategy of textualization or narrative*. We understand the problems of the Middle East by seeing them compressed into stories about specific hostages who have been kidnapped, or by making certain leaders the embodiment of good or evil (depending on our politics). The kind of textual strategy that is used in personalization is called *metonymy*, or *metonymization*. Metonymy occurs when something complex is reduced to a more manageable sign of that complex thing, as when the complexities of British government are reduced into the public figures of the Prime Minister, or of the reigning monarch.

Any public issue is in principle personalizable (or not); whether or not an issue becomes personalized is an entirely subjective, perceptual matter. I may know that environmental problems are important, but be unable to personalize that issue for myself; that is, I may be unable to imagine what ecological disaster would mean for me, what choices I might make now to undertake direct action (by stocking food or boycotting certain products, for example) or indirect action (by voting for Senators on the basis of their ecological records, for instance). So I may avoid personalizing that issue, and remain instead at the fringes of the issue, as a spectator.

On other issues, I may be motivated to personalize a public problem to a much higher degree. It would be possible to feel closer identification with war victims in El Salvador, for instance, if we shared the same religion. I might try to understand the conflict in Central America by personalizing it into images of its victims—by reading all I could about them and by forming my attitudes and opinions from stories about them. If we are able to personalize a distant and confusing issue, we are then in a better position to participate in decision making about that issue.

In the United States, people have often personalized race relations. Race relations are both a vast and complex issue *and* one on which every person is required to participate in decision making. Even whites who actually encounter blacks in the flesh no more than once a week may still entertain the most passionate and vocal opinions about them, while blacks and other nonwhites are understandably sensitive to the ways in which public issues near and far might affect their personal abilities to get and keep jobs, live comfortably and with dignity, and so on. Ours is a very race-conscious society. The issue of race relations therefore provides particularly good examples of the ways in which large public issues are personalized or brought to more manageable size.

The personalization of race relations must be done textually, through discourse or narrative, by way of metonymy. Someone who wants to understand their place in any large public problem cannot have immediate access to the whole of that problem. Instead, that person looks for ways in which the problem is expressed in texts and narratives. Someone who wants to understand the problem of pollution cannot examine all pollution; that person must turn to texts that personalize pollution and express it in a manageable way. In this chapter we will see that the strategy of personalization generates two troubling paradoxes. These paradoxes arise from the very act of personalizing vast, abstract problems; they arise as those problems are textualized and dramatized in metonymy.

The vehicle for our exploration of race relations in this chapter will itself be some personalization, based on the author's experience. We will focus our attention on race relations in the greater Milwaukee area, and on the relative economic, social, and political status of blacks and whites living there. I am a white resident of the Milwaukee area. I live in a largely white western suburb close to the center of the city, and I drive to work at a university on the other (eastern) side of town, situated next to another suburb. My route to and from work takes me through that part of town in which most black residents of Milwaukee live (some 97.5 percent of blacks in the greater metropolitan area live in the inner city). I have no close personal friends or colleagues who are black, although several of my students are. My situation therefore parallels that of many white Milwaukeeans; I am placed in a good position for understanding how many people in this city (or in other similar cities) might use texts to understand the large, confusing issue of race relations. Therefore, I will self-consciously assume the position of a white exposed to an average mix of texts in the city of Milwaukee, and I will attempt to show how whites might personalize race relations there.

In considering both the theory and the ethics of personalization, I will explore some paradoxes of personalization that arise specifically in the area of race relations (though I think these paradoxes may be generalizable to other public issues that entail personal involvements). I will focus specifically on the ways in which the complexities of race relations in Milwaukee were metonymized in the public discourse revolving around two disastrous, fatal house fires within the black community. One of these fires killed twelve people on the night of September 30–October 1, 1987; the second killed six people on the night of October 14–15, 1987.

I began gathering public discourse from the press concerning these two events, and for a period of about two months kept track of stories with any mention of the fires, blacks, and race relations in general in Milwaukee. My research led me to take note of a great many texts, not all of them explicitly about racial issues, but all of them "fuel" for metonymizing complex racial issues. Most of my material is taken from the print media, especially newspapers. Although some television broadcasts are included in the texts that I examined, logistical problems involved in obtaining ephemeral news broadcasts kept those texts to a minimum. I believe, however, that the printed material that I gathered is representative of material found in other media as well.

Finally, I want to be very clear that the personalization—the metonymies— that I construct are from my assumed position as being representative of other whites; I do not attempt to say how October and November of 1987 looked to blacks in Milwaukee. Therefore, what follows is a reconstruction of how race relations probably look to most whites in Milwaukee; the reader may take nearly every sentence as preceded by, "In one likely white perception of events. . . ." The conclusions I reach will be directed at how whites might re-evaluate some of the ways in which we understand personal roles in race relations through metonymy and personalization. Let me now don the persona of the Average White Observer and begin.

The Scene and Focal Events

The context of race relations in Milwaukee is a particularly rich one, drawn from vivid memories and much public discussion of problems between blacks and whites. One does not have to live in Milwaukee very long to get a sense that blacks here are in economic and political trouble, and that racial strife is a decades-old context for present woes. Long-time residents will remember the racial discord of the 1960s, in which actual armed tanks rumbled through the suburban streets and Father James Groppi led blacks on protest marches into predominantly white (and violently outraged) residential areas. Within the recent memory of residents is the controversial tenure of a "law-and-order" police chief who was notorious for organizing squads to investigate political activists and dissidents, especially civil rights activists. Within the past two years have come indictments of numerous real estate agents for practicing racial discrimination by attempting to protect traditional racial boundaries between neighborhoods.

Problems in the Black Community

Milwaukee's sizable black community was lured to this town of Germans and Eastern Europeans by the growth in industry in the 1940s and 1950s. Unlike blacks in other Northern industrial cities like Chicago, blacks in Milwaukee have no long-standing political base. Furthermore, the construction of Interstate 94 in the early 1950s destroyed the core of what had been a vital black business and residential area. Consequently, the failure of Rust Belt industry in the 1970s and 1980s has had exceptionally severe consequences for the black community. A Milwaukee Urban League study released during the period under study here details the resulting unhappy statistics: 77.6 percent of blacks born in Milwaukee in 1986 were born to single mothers, and 29.9 percent of the black population lives below the poverty line, with an unemployment rate of 25.9 percent (McCallister, Nov. 12; Cole, Nov. 5).[1] Furthermore, these figures do not reflect the widespread *underemployment* and inadequate compensation of those blacks who *are* employed.

In addition, residents of Milwaukee have available to them countless press reports of crime from the black community that seem to outweigh stories of disturbances anywhere else in the city. It is the policy of the major newspapers, the *Journal* and the *Sentinel*, not to specify race in any news stories unless that is relevant to the issue. But race is often implicated by other information provided in stories. Milwaukee is a "city of neighborhoods," a euphemistic way of saying that it is highly segregated. Therefore, any address from or reference to the north, near north, or northwest side of the city may be read as likely to involve blacks, while references to the south side (except for the near south, which is heavily Hispanic) and suburbs will suggest conservative, blue-collar whites, and references to the east side will hint at more liberal, white-collar whites.

Also, Milwaukee's ethnic makeup is such that some names are highly identifiable as white names; Hyrniewicki, Czysz, Kuemmerlein, and Anagnastopoulos, for example, are names that prompt readers to view their owners as Central, Eastern, or Southeastern European in origin. In general, of course, no such marker exists for blacks, except for those few names which seem to be associated somewhat more frequently with blacks than with whites in recent years (Jefferson and Washington, for instance, were two family names of persons killed in the fires) or names which seem to be chosen strategically as alternatives to traditional European names (Shanika, Shavonda, and Sharinda were names of children killed in the fires). Therefore, the seemingly "innocent" texts provided in crime stories are often racially marked or at least racially suspect, and thus guide the ways in which people personalize the environment of race relations. If Anton Drabowicz runs amok with a meat axe on the south side, one is likely to read that as a story about a white. James Jones murdering his mother downtown is hard to peg, but Chavarte Jefferson assaulting his wife on the near north side will quite probably be read (correctly or not) as a black crime.

In sum, then, the media feature many crime stories that point—by way of location or, less often, by way of name—to the black community, thus facilitating the perception of blacks as living in a violent context. So it was around the time of the two fires in the fall of 1987. For instance, one story depicts a struggling family on the near north side, in which the mother was found by the father shot to death; according to the father, "it was like walking into a nightmare, only worse" (Sykes, Nov. 17). A picture some weeks later confirmed the race of the

---

[1] I have observed a special convention for references in this chapter. All of the references to telecasts or articles here are from 1987, so I have not included that year in the citations within the text. And all the articles are so short as to be no more than one or two pages; therefore, I have not included page numbers in the citations within the text. (Page citations for all print references do appear in the bibliographic listings at the end of the book.)

family as black. The continuation of this story on an inside page accompanies another story, with a picture, of a black woman who was slain at home ("Funeral set," Nov. 11).

News reports on the day of the second fire include a story about black suspects arrested for killing a white ice cream delivery man (Gribble, Oct. 15), and another about Milwaukee Brewers' player Gary Sheffield, a black, who was arrested for drunkenness and violence in New York (Faust, Oct. 15). Other prominent news reports around this time included renewed interest in a recent killing of a black child by black children in nearby Beloit (Ward, Nov. 15), another story of a stabbing in the black community (Cuprisin and Lisheron, Oct. 25), and the tale of a mother in the same neighborhood who was so incapable of caring for her children that she did not understand how to flush a toilet (Knoche, Nov. 15). In short, the picture painted by the press about life among blacks is grim and unflattering. Thus, the social context for the period under analysis here is likely to be perceived as one of poverty, violence, and failure for blacks.

Violence against Blacks

Black crime and hopelessness did not make up the only ongoing story at this time. Violence and discrimination against blacks and other minorities by whites was also a prominent story. On the Madison campus of the University of Wisconsin, recent racial incidents had prompted a march by 300 protestors (Esposito, Oct. 16). The issue was not resolved, and doubts persisted about the ability of the University administration to control racist fraternities and to curb individual acts of racial violence (Jones, Nov. 9b). Other press reports (Jones, Nov. 1a, Nov. 1b) cited long lists of insults and attacks—both verbal and physical—upon blacks and Jews in Madison, a town and campus that had always prided itself on its liberal atmosphere. One black parent was prompted to wonder in print, "Is my child even safe at that place?" and called the incidents in Madison an "unconscionable blight" on the state (Short, Nov. 15). Also prominent in the news at this time was an ongoing attempt in the United States Congress to allocate reparations to Japanese Americans who had been stripped of property while in internment camps during World War II (Cunibert, Oct. 11), which added to the context of racial tension and white guilt.

The School System

Another important part of the racial context was concern over the quality of the Milwaukee public school system, which was widely perceived to be failing, especially in its work with minority students (Bednarek, Oct. 25). A long-standing and costly lawsuit among several parties had raged for months over the issue of how to arrange court-ordered busing for integration. The suit was settled amidst mistrust and suspicion on all sides during the two month period studied, further intensifying the focus on racial issues (Bednarek, Oct. 22).

White Political Attitudes

A final factor in constructing the context for the fires is the taxation and social service mix in the city and state. Milwaukee and Wisconsin have traditionally been high-tax, high-service, liberal Northern polities. But an election the year before the fires had replaced a liberal Democratic administration at the state level with a moderate Republican one. This change was based largely on the mood reflected in a letter to the editor of *The Milwaukee Journal,* complaining that middle class people "haven't received raises in years and some of us have taken huge cuts in pay. . . . Without our hard work there would not be money for welfare, food stamps, or heat assistance" (Dlugi, Nov 15). Another disheartened taxpayer complained that "it just is very disturbing to me and my husband, as taxpayers who have worked continually for 32 years, to read in the newspaper about a 38-year-old woman who has 13 children and five grandchildren. . . . I am really getting fed up with going to work every day, paying my federal and state income taxes, and for what?" (Conrad, Oct. 25).

This resentment of welfare recipients and the poor—specifically, resentment at having to support them in the midst of a faltering Rust Belt economy—led to such measures as Republican Governor Tommy Thompson's "learnfare" proposal, which would have tied welfare payments to regular attendance by schoolchildren (Schultze, Oct. 25). Although the plan was defeated by the legislature during this time (Bergquist, Nov. 5), it highlighted the issue of public support for social services and an attitude toward the poor that was frequently expressed at the time. (A revised version of the plan was later passed.)

Tragedy and Metonymy

Into this scene of texts featuring images of black oppression, failure, violence, disadvantage, and plain hard luck came two events which could serve as centers around which a text of race relations in Milwaukee could be written. The first was the worst house fire in Milwaukee's recorded history: Twelve people, ten of them children, died during the night of September 30–October 1 (Romell, Oct. 1). Most of the victims were members of an extended family living in the house, though some were merely guests for the night. A little more than two weeks later, six children in a family were killed in another house fire less than a mile from the first ("Six children," Oct. 15). In this fire, the oldest victim was a teenage sitter who was caring for the other five children while their mother was in the hospital giving birth to another child. The fact that all victims were *identified* as black (actually, five of the second set of victims were biracial; more on this in a moment), the close proximity of the houses, and the long-term economic problems of both sets of victims allowed the two fires to become a metonymy for the problems of black Milwaukeeans in general.

Metonymizing the Tragedies

It was clear from the start, even before the second fire, that the potential for metonymizing complex social problems through the image of this disaster was great. A newspaper report of the first fire clearly linked the *general* state of blacks in Milwaukee with these *particular* victims: "The pre-dawn fire Wednesday that killed 12 people, 10 of them children, is tragic evidence of Milwaukee's need to do something about decaying Inner-City housing and hard-core unemployment, officials said Wednesday" (Romell, Oct. 1). A newspaper headline following the second fire further signaled a clear pattern of metonymy: "Diverse social ills had role in tragedy" (Gill and Romell, Nov. 5).

Soon articles discussing the trend among the poor people of doubling up on housing, with resultant dangerous overcrowding, began to appear (Hajewski, Oct. 16). Noting that "the similarities are chilling" between the fires—among them that "the families in both fires were on welfare"—another article referred to the deteriorated condition of inner city housing (Kissinger, Oct. 16). Some letters to the editor used the two sets of victims as symbols for the effects of Governor Thompson's cuts in welfare (Deshotels, Oct. 25). Although it was apparently not the case that playing with fire caused either blaze, an article discussing pyromania in children also appeared, explicitly linking the two fires with a larger social issue in its statement that "many of these [pyromaniac] children come from chaotic families or single-parent homes" (Wilkerson, Oct. 25).

Even articles not directly linked to the fires could nonetheless be incorporated into a metonymy insofar as they bolstered the image of blacks as poor, wretched, violent, or victimized. One article reviewed the centrality of "suffering" in the lives of Malcom X and Martin Luther King, Jr. (Krenn, Oct. 15). Another article described a group home for delinquent teenage boys, and the accompanying pictures showed only blacks (Norris, Oct. 8). According to this article, these unfortunate youngsters seemed not to have much going for them: "Bill . . . is struggling with deep psychological hurt. Jerome uses joking to cover immaturity and insecurity. Robert angers quickly and is given to lying."

Telecasts concerning the second fire followed that story with one segment after another depicting failures and heartbreaks that could be read as hardships specific to the black community. Channel 12's story (Ten o'clock, Oct. 15) was on a "scared straight" program at a local jail, featuring footage of (predominantly) black inmates bemoaning their wasted lives. Channel 4 emphasized that the fires were within the same neighborhood, thus implicating the black community directly as a site of tragedy (News 4, Oct. 15). Channel 6 (News at 6, Oct. 15) covered the failure of the National Football League strike, with footage of its unsuccessful (and black) leader, Gene Upshaw. In short, it was apparent that the fatherless family configuration and economic suffering of the victims of these two fires were being used to symbolize widespread concern over illegitimate births, high crime, and welfare dependency within the black community.

Metonymy and Paradox

Let us consider metonymy itself a little more closely. Metonymy can be either positive or negative. For instance, a single person can be made to stand for whatever is good or bad about an entire group of people. Thus metonymy is clearly a rhetorical strategy; indeed, it is one of Kenneth Burke's "four master tropes" explained in *A Grammar of Motives* 1969a. When metonymy moves broad public issues into images of and about people, the metonymy has the effect of personalizing. When metonymy motivates individual actions and attitudes, it also serves to personalize. And when metonymy turns people into icons toward whom one may act, that is personalizing as well.

In short, the issue of race relations in Milwaukee became symbolized in the image of these particular fire victims, who became a set of signs around which all the other discursive texts of violence, economics, and so on revolved. Milwaukeeans participated in that metonymy by reading press reports or viewing telecasts, and then formulating actions and attitudes for their own lives in response to what they saw and read; in this way, race relations became personalized for many white Milwaukeeans in the fall of 1987.

What happens when personalization occurs through narratives of metonymy? Some paradoxes are inevitably entailed when such metonymy takes place—paradoxes with ethical implications.

The Paradox of Identification

Public problems often involve large groups of people, and to the individual person those groups can easily remain faceless. A nuclear accident in the Ukraine or a chemical accident in India is a terrible thing, but the individual American can easily remain aloof from such a problem that confronts people who are foreign and anonymous. The same is true of problems that the ordinary white person will perceive as afflicting blacks in Milwaukee. In the absence of close personal contact with an entire demographic group, the response to stories of hardship and crime is likely to be along the lines of either (a) "what's the matter with those people," or (b) "these people are in serious trouble." Neither response, however, is likely to call up much personal involvement or action, or any real understanding of the complex issues involved (though it may motivate calls for collective action; more on this in a moment). For the average white person, formulating some sort of response to the perceived problems of blacks is much like formulating a response to the problems of nuclear power, the destruction of the rain forest, or acid rain. Many such problems remain beyond the ken of individuals; that is, they seem too bewildering or complex for us to understand.

The complexities of drought and political oppression in Ethiopia remain beyond the understanding of most people, too. But television footage of starving Ethiopian children in the 1980s galvanized public response, motivating personal and individual action in response to a public issue. One of the most important ways in which contemporary public discourse metonymizes complex issues is by presenting them in images with which the public can *identify*. In *A Rhetoric of Motives* (1969b), Burke argues that identification fuels all motivation; showing the public the ways that they as individuals can connect to broad social issues is, therefore, a primary way of mobilizing motivation for individual action. When people identify, they make a link between the self and the other. That link also calls forward a political stance towards such larger issues as nuclear power, discriminatory practices in South Africa, or environmental destruction, for example.

Identification and Race
So it is with the issue of race relations. To the extent that whites can identify with the travails of blacks, then whites will be motivated to overcome their own racism. Clearly, then, identification is also a strategy with ethical implications,

insofar as it enables or discourages moral choices. As Burke reminds us, identification will occur if people see that they are like other people, that their interests are joined.

Resources for identification were present within the wider context surrounding the Milwaukee house fires in 1987. For example, much of the discussion over the racial incidents on the Madison campus of the University of Wisconsin at the same time offered the possibility of motivation through identification; a number of images of blacks and of their motives that enabled white identification emerged from that discussion. A black writer of a letter to the editor noted that the heartache of racism

> . . . comes from your child's description of the knife held to his throat by a white bully in grade school. It comes from watching your baby struggle proudly to pronounce the "big words" someone painted on the front of your house during the night: filthy epithets! It comes from watching that person you love dearer than life get passed over and put down and treated as if her skin were the only part of her that matters. And even *with* these realities, your child still earns a 3.0 and he still makes the football team and he still beats out the others to play first chair in the high school orchestra. (Short, Nov. 15)

It would take an alienated heart indeed not to identify with the universally relevant anguish and pride in that letter writer's powerful sentences. The racial problems in Madison were similarly metonymized in the plaint of Geneva Brown, a first-year student at the university: "To have someone physically threaten me just because I'm black is something I've never [before] encountered" (Jones, Nov. 9a); most whites have also probably never before been threatened on the basis of their race. Racial problems are represented in Charles Holley's statement that racism "hurts down deep, because I'm a human being" (Esposito, Nov. 9); it would, presumably, hurt whites as well. Similarly, the pain of racism is evident in this excerpt from an interview with California Congressman Norman Mineta, a Japanese American, who recalls being separated from his family during the World War II internment camps:

> "I didn't want to be separated from my parents," Mineta said, faltering. He had been recounting the story over lunch in the House members' dining room, but stopped altogether as he started to cry. Listening in, one of his young congressional aides also started to cry. The congressman composed himself. "We should have done this in the office," he said. (Cunibert, Oct. 11)

These examples from the period under study illustrate the ways in which complex issues, such as racism on college campuses or reactions against Japanese Americans in World War II, are metonymized into issues—the anguished parent, the frightened child, the shock of unexpected indignities—with which whites can identify.

But the particular issues which the victims of the two house fires stood for highlighted certain problems for identification through metonymy, which become clear as we move from context to more focused texts relating to the two disasters. Metonymizing a complex problem into a concrete symbol can give the public something with which to identify; but if the metonymy involves the strange, foreign, or frightening, it may also give the public concrete images which *threaten* identification. The first fire victims were presented in terms which placed them exactly on the knife's edge of this paradox of identification. Enough facts about the victims were provided to allow a middle class white audience to identify with them to an extent, yet enough difference (especially difference based in race) was still evident to forestall a complete identification.

Enabling Identification

Let us consider the texts that served as resources that *enabled* identification first. The victims of the first fire were portrayed positively and along many dimensions with which whites could identify. Morvay (Oct. 1) writes of one victim, " 'Thomas was a church-going man,' his niece said." We are told that Thomas worked for the city, and a picture of a loving extended family is painted. We learn that the family spoke by telephone every evening with a grandmother in Miami. This same grandmother is quoted as piously avowing, " 'I know God took my grandchildren and my daughter right on back to heaven. The Lord is too wise to make a mistake.' " And the distraught mother of two other young victims is quoted as saying what any parent would say under such circumstances: " 'Let me go see my babies . . . just let me go. I've got to see them.' " Christopulos (Oct. 1) quotes another grandmother in mourning: " 'Why couldn't it have been me instead of my poor little baby? . . . When I got there, I kept praying Anthony would be all right.' " A white audience can sympathize with such grief, and with the rudeness of a funeral home representative who interrupted the interview to force a card on the bereaved woman. We can also sympathize with the heroic efforts of neighbors to rescue the children, which were foiled by the intense flames (Romell, Oct. 1).

Reports of the second fire also contained material encouraging identification by way of the children who died in the fire. All three evening news telecasts interviewed teachers and principals of the children, who gave sincere and positive praise for them; and printed news reports typically gave brief, upbeat biographies of each child (Ahlgren, Oct. 15). Channel 12 focused mainly on the impact of the children's deaths on their neighbors (The ten o'clock news, Oct. 15). One neighbor was quoted as saying, " 'They need to do something for these kids, these people, or there're gonna be a whole lot more bodies to come get.' " This was the only station to report that neighbors could hear cries for help coming from the house, a horrible fact which must surely have drawn universal sympathy. Channel 4 (News 4, Oct. 15) described the human face of "people who are stunned, who want to do something"—as the white audience surely would.

The metonymy of human misfortune into heartbreaking images of children was the best chance for identification offered by coverage of the second fire. An older brother of the victims is quoted as saying at the funeral, "Each of them was going to be somebody. They were just beginning. Not a one of them had a chance for nothing" (Mitchard, Oct. 23), displaying a kind of pride and sense of loss that people of all races could understand. Mitchard (Oct. 15) quotes a Sunday school teacher of the children who had seen them only that evening: " 'The big kids were on the porch last night with the babies at 9 p.m.,' she said reasonably, 'and so they can't take them . . . you can't spare . . . you just can't. . . .' " The collapse of this woman's narrative into anguish speaks eloquently of the pain of losing children. Mitchard quotes another neighbor who showed the kind of shock with which many could identify when she said, " 'It's a strange thing when children perish and you cannot cry. I would dearly love to cry, but I can't.' "

Other stories focused on the predominantly white firefighters who had dealt with both blazes, and the effects the fires had on them are forceably presented to a white audience as the reactions they themselves might have had (Kissinger and Rumler, Oct. 15): They quote one firefighter: "All I could think of was 'not again.' It's harder this time, when it happens so close together," and "The first thing I did was that I went out and bought four more smoke alarms," said Gleisner, who has a 9-month-old son at home. And finally, a photo essay (A time, Oct. 22) showed pictures of the funeral, of the lost children, and of weeping family members.

Forestalling Identification

But consider how fine is the knife's edge of identification, for texts that allow identification may quickly turn into texts that discourage it. Gilbert's story (Oct. 11) of the funeral for ten of the victims, held in Miami, begins on a theme inviting universal identification: "A mother and nine young cousins killed last month in Milwaukee's worst house fire were laid to rest. . . ." But the story then moves on to a description of the funeral service that marks it as appropriate for a traditional black church service—and therefore unlike anything that most staid whites (and Milwaukee *is* heavily staid Lutheran and Catholic) observe on Sunday morning. Gilbert describes the funeral as "a searing service marked by raw grief and uncontrolled outburst" and "a roller-coaster, gospel gathering, elevated by passionate displays of faith and family togetherness." Whites are further reminded of the difference, or otherness, of these metonymized people by their nontraditional, non-Anglo names, such as Shanika, Shavonda, and Sharinda (Romell, Oct. 1).

Many reports of the second fire also provided ample symbolic resources for tilting the paradox of identification in the direction of difference. Although there was much to spark white identification with the victims of the second fire through a metonymy of tragedy and loss, such positive texts were countered and overwhelmed by the spectacle of the victims' unfortunate mother, who was giving birth to her thirteenth child at the time of the fire. This poor woman and the family's general circumstances became a metonymy for white resentment of what is perceived as black welfare dependency, high illegitimacy rates, and other problems noted earlier. The family is depicted by Romell and Gill (Nov. 4) as "plagued by poverty"; their article chronicles a dreary history of the father of most of the children as an unemployed alcoholic and child abuser. The mother, Diane Washington, was a thirteen-year-old runaway when she first came to live with this man, and since divorcing him she had become attached to the father of the rest of the children, a man from Chicago who had been arrested on felony firearms charges. One child described the quality of life in the Washington family as "baloney and crackers. . . . It wasn't all the time, but sometimes we ran short of food, you know." The family is described as moving at least once every year because of their inability to meet the rent. The mother is said to have no intention of marrying again. Her desperate circumstances lead her to describe her life in ways with which no middle class white person could identify. " 'I live the life I want to live,' " she is quoted as saying, " 'and go and come like I want to.' "

This mother in particular became a symbolic lightning rod for white frustration stemming from the context of the fires, a metonymy for allegedly self-inflicted problems that befall many poor blacks. Ahlgren (Nov. 15) depicts Mrs. Washington as producing one child after another with reckless abandon, and declares at one point, " 'Now I guess I'll quit. I have my football team and my basketball team.' " News reports noted that the family was eligible for government aid that could have paid their gas bill, but that for some reason this help had not been requested. Payment would have allowed the gas company to resume service, thus doing away with the need for the space heater that had caused the fire. Clearly, the implication was that the mother was not even capable of obtaining the welfare to which she was entitled (Kissinger, Oct. 16; The ten o'clock news, Oct. 15).

Press reports concerning Mrs. Washington were riddled with seemingly unintended irony. The child born just before the fire was named Passion'ate Love (Mitchard, Oct. 23), and Gill and Romell (Nov. 5) quote her as saying, in all innocence, "Like my mother told me one time, I made my bed, I have to lie in it." The temptation in both cases, for any reader not inclined toward identification with her, is to say in exasperation, "Yes, that's just the trouble."

As a metonymy for poor and helpless people, Mrs. Washington clearly encouraged reactions that were the opposite of identification. As one letter complained,

"... she loved children and wanted her own football team. I find my senses reeling! . . . The problems of poverty that embrace so many of our neighbors are certainly not helped by increasing the numbers of a family. (Richfield, Oct. 25)

Another letter similarly noted,

Diane Washington "loves" children and so do I. But how, in all justice to the children, can she keep producing while her children are at the public's mercy? Her 16-year-old pregnant daughter, with a 9-month-old baby, is following her mother's example. When will this end? (Tessler, Oct. 25)

Resentment was also expressed in this landlord's complaint:

There is absolutely no justification for 13 or 14 people living in a two-or-three bedroom home, using a penny for a fuse. You can rest assured that the landlord did not know they all lived there. (Thomas, Oct. 25)

Mr. Thomas's letter is clearly metonymizing general problems into the images of the fire victims, for the actions he describes match neither set of fire victims; yet he is explicitly writing about the fires.

The Persistence of Race

An important dimension of the texts of race relations is the role of race itself as a fundamental category for classifying humankind. It must be said that in most of the United States, and perhaps in Milwaukee particularly, race is a factor that will always interfere with identification on the part of some people, no matter how much material there is to foster identification. Race is a marker of a difference that will make *all* the difference, and for these people, the racial category into which a person falls will color, so to speak, any and all of their judgments about that person.

At precisely the time of the second fire, unrestrained identification occurred with another child in dire straits, young Jessica McClure of Texas, who was being rescued from a well over the course of two or three days (News at 6, Oct. 15). Although she was farther away, concern for this white child among white Milwaukeeans was undiluted. But as noted above, sympathy was not so unreserved for those involved in the two fatal fires. Thus, racial prejudice led to a judgment structured by the rhetoric of racial categories, illustrating the fact that in the United States today, *any* discourse with racial components is a discourse that will divide people.

Another interesting dimension of the texts of racial categories is that for many whites, and perhaps for blacks as well, an individual falls into the category of *black* for possessing any detectable amount of black racial makeup at all, sometimes for merely associating with blacks. In this case, the work of the texts of racial divisions is also extended to those who are white but who have very close connections with blacks.

In the case of the Milwaukee fires, there were two instances in which the public was allowed, perhaps even encouraged, to think of individuals as black because of their involvement with people of that racial category rather than on the basis of their own physical appearance or heritage. It turns out that Diane Washington, mother of the second victims, is identified (in only two instances) as actually being white (Romell and Gill, Nov. 4; A time, Oct. 22). And Jill Schreck, mother of some of the first fire victims, bears a name which sounds German (in this town of German heritage); she also looks Caucasian in a picture of her published in the newspaper (Survivor, Oct. 7). Yet the overwhelming sense created by press reports about the fires was that everyone involved was black— despite the presence of whites, and despite the fact that the children in the second fire were as white as they were black. Diane Washington's own identification with blacks puts her on that "side of the fence;" she is able to stand in for irresponsible blacks even though she is white. Blackness seems to be a difference that cannot be overcome by similarities.

The peculiar rhetorical insistence in the available texts upon the importance of the category of blackness is also echoed in other news stories that were linked to the fires. On the very day of the second fire, a white Milwaukee alderman was convicted of accepting a bribe from a black attorney, a story carried immediately after coverage of the fire on all three television stations. And a newspaper article about the alderman's downfall at the hands of the black attorney (Bargren, Oct. 15) appeared on the same page as (1) an article about blacks who had slain an ice cream delivery man, and (2) a story about the firefighters involved in both disastrous fires. All three stories were continued together on the same inner page. In short, the introduction of blackness into a mix of texts such as this turns it into a category which, for many whites, will be an insurmountable barrier to identification.

In sum, the identification engendered by images of dying children might easily have been outweighed by the persistent accumulation of press reports depicting Mrs. Washington as an irresponsible bearer of children at the taxpayers' expense—as the very epitome of the hopeless and incorrigible welfare mother. In the case of the second fire, metonymy may have countered, rather than furthered, identification. Metonymy is thus a risky strategy for motivating personal involvement in public issues. If you make what is abstract, or far away, more concrete through images of a child, a fire, or a welfare mother, you either court identification with the image or you risk the confirmation of your audience's worst fears about "those *other* people."

The person attempting to metonymize complex issues into an understandable text is therefore faced with a choice about how to see "those people" and how to place ourself in relation to them. This is an ethical choice insofar as it concerns how we treat and define others. When we metonymize, we are responsible for the outcome. Identification is therefore not a passive occurrence but a chosen action, and management of the paradox of identification is an ethical choice.

The Paradox of Action:
The Public and the Personal

We have been considering connections between broad public problems and personal implication in those problems. To move from the public to the personal requires a risky metonymization that may, in the end, scare the personalizing individual back to considering problems impersonally; the person might then see problems as interesting but not personally relevant, just as we might know, for example, that election results in France will affect us in *some* way but not in a way that will motivate us to see any kind of personal involvement in the matter. Another route of movement from the public to the personal can be seen in the distinction between public initiatives or legislation and individual perceptions or action. It is one thing to think to oneself that "there ought to be a law," another thing to go out and actually do what one thinks needs to be done, or to alter one's deep-seated opinions and prejudices. You might think that the state should finance soup kitchens, for example, but simply *thinking* that is different from volunteering to work in a soup kitchen. The latter is a form of personalization.

The two fires in Milwaukee often called forth the first, nonpersonalizing kind of response in the form of demands for legislative action to address a particular problem. The city council quickly passed a law requiring landlords to maintain smoke detectors in rental property, and U.S. Senator Robert Kasten fired off a letter to the newspaper announcing legislation to help the poor heat their homes in winter (Kasten, Oct. 25). And around the same time, in response to the racial incidents on the Madison campus, a plan to grant free or reduced tuition to minorities was introduced (Deger, Nov. 12).

But the disasters also called forth texts that enabled personalization, urging specific personal action and a change in attitudes. One writer of a letter to the editor, who was from an almost entirely white suburb and bore an Eastern European name (Jankowski, Oct. 25), described her own experience as a volunteer at the second funeral; she also called for individual involvement in the long term, writing, "We as a community should experience the grief and work toward improving Inner City life so this need not happen again."

Personal Action and Loss of Vision

The paradox of action lies in the fact that the shift from public policy to individual action can sometimes be accompanied by a loss of the political vision, available at a broad and public level, that should guide individual action. To think in terms of broad sweeps of history, of the relations of large groups of people, and of economic and political trends, is to think in terms of underlying *causes* for misfortune and oppression. Institutionalized racism, for instance, is not something that can be grasped by looking just at this or that specific example, isolated instances that can almost always be rationalized on a case-by-case basis. Institutional racism is grasped by thinking at precisely the level of broad, public issues, to see how thousands of acts of oppression (by the police, by the class system, by the schools, by other institutions) cumulatively take their toll in shaping broad patterns of social relations. That is a kind of understanding that simply cannot be grasped if I restrict my vision to a particular African-American woman, no matter how many insults and slurs she may suffer; one cannot understand her experiences as embedded in broad patterns of oppression unless one backs off to connect her experience with that of millions of others.

The paradox at the broad, public level is that political action and involvement can then take the form of simply "letting Congress do it," thus refusing individual responsibility and involvement. The paradox at the level of personal decision and action is that such involvement may proceed in ignorance of the broader forces that have caused problems to occur in the first place. And the risk of that kind of ignorance is that it can turn political action and involvement into patronization. Action directed toward those less fortunate than ourselves, if uninformed by the *causes* of those misfortunes, can turn into a kind of "almsgiving" that soothes our consciences but blinds us to our implication in those causes for misfortune. The paradox of action, then, can threaten to paralyze us, preventing the ethical choices involved in metonymizing complex issues into the personal.

The Paradox in Milwaukee

One can see this paradox occurring at the level of individual action and attitudes in Milwaukee. A representative anecdote of such a paradox is the story of a white woman who was going to buy some cigarettes with two dollars and heard of the second fire (Gill and Romell, Nov. 5). This woman went directly to the neighborhood of both fires, knocked on the door of a complete stranger, and gave the two dollars to the black woman who answered the door as a token of her concern. One can sympathize with the motive for personal, individual action in response to this tragedy, not as an isolated instance (in which case the donation would be irrelevant) but as a metonymy of long-term racial problems. Evidently it was the metonymization of social problems into particular people living in a specific neighborhood that gave the cigarette smoker a place in which to act. But one can also read in this story (though I found no direct acknowledgement of it in the newspaper article) how patronizing the woman's action was—how little it cost her, how proud she may have felt about her "gift," and how that gift may have served to blind her to her own involvement in the broader forces that led to the fire in the first place.

Of more concern, however, is the implication of blacks themselves in such patronization. For it turns out that the black woman favored with the two dollars is touched by the gesture: "That $2 meant more than the smoke alarm legislation," she said (Gill and Romell, Nov. 5). The paradox is that on the one hand, the public policy action of the smoke alarm legislation stands a good chance of saving lives, yet it invites no personal action to overcome problems; on the other hand, the personal action of giving two dollars may seem more involved, but it is also too easy and leads to an avoidance of uncomfortable questions.

A similar example reported at about the same time described a white man who sought to do something to help untrained and jobless black teenagers. He hired a skilled black carpenter to remodel inner-city houses while simultaneously teaching his skills to those teenagers. On the surface it seems like a worthwhile, concrete action on the part of the white man. Yet it was reported that "Wigdale [the white man] believes that young black men don't have enough role models and recognized one in Coleman [the black carpenter]" (Lynch, Oct. 22). Disturbing questions arise in response to such a statement: How can Wigdale know what it's like to be a "young black man"? Who is he to judge that Coleman would make a good role model for the young men? Will Wigdale then hire those young men once they are trained? What responsibilities for black joblessness must be borne by the construction industry in general, and how might Wigdale's actions allow him, and others, to overlook those responsibilities?

Blacks "in need of help"

The paradox of action at the personal level is intensified by news reports of blacks "in need of help," particularly reports that portray such help as coming *not* from blacks themselves or from within black culture, but from the white community. One telecast concerning the second fire (News 4, Oct. 15) featured an older brother of the victims who turned directly to the camera and instructed the viewing audience to avoid space heaters at any cost. He claimed personal responsibility for having turned off one of the smoke alarms and absolved the white landlord from any blame in the fire. Such claims, even if true, hide the broader forces, such as unemployment and substandard housing, that led to this family's problems in the first place.

Even more pointed was an interview during this time period with a group of black students who were attending a predominantly white school on the south side of the city, far from their homes. One student described her previous, neighborhood school as "too roguish. It's bad." Another said that teachers in predominantly white schools "are more educated," while another claimed that predominantly black schools are "a lot of trouble" (Gilbert, Nov. 9). The message of this interview was that blacks are *in need of* whites, an attitude that intensifies the patronizing stance of some who would become personally involved in racial issues. Within such a context, even those arguments for self-help made by blacks themselves become fodder for those who would focus more on the idea that help is needed. As one black leader is quoted as saying about his own culture's statistically lower performance on tests of academic achievement, "It has nothing to do with ability. It has to do with work. We watch more television than anyone else in America" (Mulvey, Nov. 5).

The specter of African Americans "in need of help" extended beyond Milwaukee in the discourse available at the time of the fires. During this same time period, Michael Jackson's album *Bad* was released, as were numerous publicity photos depicting the startling changes that had been wrought in him by cosmetic surgery. In short, Jackson's appearance had taken, since his early days with the Jackson Five, a marked turn for the Caucasian. Guensburg (Oct. 6) reported the shocked reaction of black teenagers in Milwaukee: "He looks like a ghost. He looks like the bogeyman," and "He's lost some of his soul." Famous African Americans such as baseball player Ozzie Smith were quoted as saying, "I don't mind a guy trying to look different, but Lord, there's got to be a limit." Black psychologist Diane Pollard noted, "I find it psychologically interesting. It's really eccentric behavior. It does send a negative message about being black." An accompanying article described Mr. Jackson's eccentricities, including sleeping in a hyperbaric oxygen chamber and attempting to buy the bones of the "Elephant Man" (De Atley, Oct. 6).

Stories about Michael Jackson, like the story about the black teenagers attending a white school, portray blacks "in need of help"; such stories also suggest that blacks get that help not from themselves or their culture, but from whites and white culture. Such an undercurrent supports a stance of condescension and patronization by whites who might become personally involved in racial issues; in turn, any action taken by these whites becomes a missionary involvement—a stooping to conquer, a "giving of alms" to those who have no other resources. Such is the stance created for those who would metonymize racial problems into images of desperate, incompetent, or eccentric blacks who seem incapable of succeeding without white help.

Some Solutions

The problems of identification and action, and the paradoxes one encounters when attempting to personalize broad public issues, are complex. Such problems are closely connected to the ways in which people order the world for themselves. Certainly, other people may be constructed as like or unlike me, thus aiding or hindering my identification with them. But because people are complex sources of texts, the ways we construct others as like or unlike ourselves includes how we construct stances, or roles, for others and for ourselves.

Let us now consider how the paradoxes of identification and action may be minimized through a conscious awareness of how people, whites in particular, understand the general public problem of racial issues and construct a personal role for themselves within those issues. I believe that with this set of problems, as with any others, an awareness of how we use the texts of popular culture—and of *other* ways in which we might order our experience—is liberating and subversive. And as argued in Chapter 3, that is the highest calling for the critic and teacher of rhetoric: to make people aware of both how we now, and how we might in the future, understand complex problems (in this case those revolving around race relations).

Reciprocal Personalization

Racial issues tend to be reciprocal. That is to say, what one says about blacks can and should imply actions or attitudes appropriate for whites. But that reciprocity does not always occur *explicitly, consciously, strategically.* What happens in the readings of the fires offered above is that the *fire victims* are metonymized as certain images, but those doing the metonymizing are not. Whites construct explicit positions for blacks as victims—as helpless, violent, and irresponsible— yet they construct no explicit positions for themselves. Whites are implicitly constructed, then, as patrons or superiors, as those who can give alms or advice, like benevolent aunts and uncles. Whites construct Michael Jackson as a dancing bear, but they do not consciously see that they must reciprocally define themselves as bear baiters.

It is this willingness to metonymize others, combined with a failure to see oneself as a metonymy (a symbol of larger forces and issues), that contributes to the paradoxes of identification and action. In regard to the paradox of identification, for example, when others become metonymized images that are strange and different, the strangeness is always in relation to an idealized vision of the self that is very likely an unexamined one. To look to my own side of the equation or inequality requires me to "unpack" that vision of myself—to confront it and make decisions about whether I wish to retain it or not. The ethics of creating one stance or subject position or another are in that way brought to my attention, and I am able, then, to make a conscious ethical choice.

Metonymizing Yourself

In regard to the paradox of action, individual action is divorced from larger social issues if I refuse to see myself acting as a metonymy, a metonymy in relation to the metonymy that I construct for blacks. For to see myself as a metonymy would require me to ask, "A metonymy of what?" With the particular issue of race relations, constructing a position for myself within a metonymy might lead me to see that I too am implicated in the social conditions that I metonymize into concrete images of blacks. Since those are the images that will guide and motivate my action, an awareness of my implication in them could preserve a useful tension between my own individual action and my social awareness.

Such an awareness, and such a tension, might lead me to realize that I benefit from reduced competition for adequate housing, for example. I also benefit from inadequate wages paid to produce the products I buy and the stores that I shop in. I benefit from the excess profits made at the expense of workers and the poor by companies, the stocks of which support my universities and retirement funds. I benefit from a pool of cheap, even desperate labor willing to do jobs that I would not do under any circumstances. Among some of the people I identify as family and friends are people whose racism contributes directly to the oppression of people of color. I have received the benefits of a disproportionate allocation of public school resources to the schools I attended and to the almost exclusively white college preparatory courses in which I was enrolled within those schools.

None of these reflections need lead to guilt on my part, since I did not cause or initiate the system which brought them about. These reflections should, however, spark a crisis of ethical decision about the extent to which I participate in reproducing such a system. I did not invent racist oppression, but I can become aware that I lie safely cradled in its benefits to whites. To see myself as having something to do with the death of more than a dozen people crowded into a house that burned in the inner city, and to see myself as implicated in some of the reasons why Diane Washington could not pay her gas bill and had to rely on a faulty space heater, can lead to a change in my ability to identify with the people involved in the fire. And it can also change the role of my personal political action from something designed solely to help *them* into something designed to help *me* as well.

Metonymizing Others

A second strategy for minimizing the paradoxes of identification and action is to metonymize more strategically, more carefully, and with more awareness. One of the prime ways to do so is to find images that correspond to smaller and more carefully differentiated groups. Very few of the press reports I studied during the period under analysis attempted to differentiate among blacks either explicitly or implicitly. Heightened public awareness of the problems befalling blacks in the inner city focused on poor, inner-city blacks as stand-ins for a whole race, an entire demographic category. The overcrowded household in the first fire and the large and seemingly irresponsible Washington family in the second fire came to represent not just the limited category of impoverished blacks, but blacks in general.

When one over-metonymizes in response to the two fires, such over-metonymizing exacerbates the paradoxes of identification and action. It is difficult to identify with entire social groups. If an entire group is metonymized with a negative image, the public is left with few symbolic resources for localizing the damage—that is, for understanding that the group is actually complex and that only one aspect of it is represented by the present image. Recognizing that such an image is limited can mean that failure to identify with the image will then not be read as failure to identify with an entire group; in this case, hope for future identification with other parts of the group may be kept alive. Action directed toward specific images or situations may be less likely to be turned into patronization if people remain aware that the action is directed toward a limited goal, and that other people who are like the target of this action in some ways may *not* be in need of help, may indeed be in a position to give help as well. If my actions are no longer perceived as "helping blacks," but instead are understood as helping a specific group of people, then I am less likely to see my actions in a grandiose light. But I am also aware, then, that there remains a large group of other blacks, and the resources of black culture itself, that my actions do *not* affect. And those other resources may then be seen as vaster and more meaningful than my own efforts in this one isolated case.

Resources for Careful Metonymy

Some articles available to the public at the time of the fires did provide the potential for reminding readers of such differentiation among blacks, and consequently, of the potential for self-help and resourcefulness within the black community. A historical article by Donald Jackson (Oct. 22) describes a black dean at Boston University, representing a more restricted group of well-educated urban blacks, moving into an area of Beacon Hill (a neighborhood in Boston) that was populated by blacks in the eighteenth century. The move is a reclamation of black history, by blacks. Closer to home, St. Mark's African Methodist Episcopal Church in Milwaukee is portrayed as a strong, financially secure institution that serves the community and is a bastion of self-help and self-reliance within the inner city (Breyfogle, Oct. 22).

As construction of images moves toward smaller and more differentiated categories, metonymy moves toward synecdoche—that is to say, from reduction toward representation. Synecdoche is a trope of representation rather than reduction. The Washington family as a metonymy of all blacks must always remain just that, a metonymy. But it may very well work as a synecdoche for poor, divorced, biracial families in the inner city, if that kind of representation is the only symbolic task to which it is put. Synecdoche gives way to metonymy when our images stand for issues or problems that, in their entirety, are too large to comprehend from any perspective. Breaking up those issues into manageable categories which can then be represented through synecdoche may be the best symbolic strategy to pursue.

Stepping Back from the Critique

Let me now step back and become critically self-conscious for a moment: What good has this criticism done? If these reflections on the paradoxes of identification and action seem sensible to you, then your ability to see how some texts work in popular culture has been expanded.

Students want relevance in their education, though they may not often have an explicit desire to be *changed* by relevant education. From the perspective of rhetorical criticism, relevance in education has to do with showing students how they are constrained culturally in the ways they experience the texts that surround them. Relevance means showing students alternative ways to remake the world into something fairer, more just, and more equitable. Ancient rhetoricians trained their students to manipulate meaning in the forums of the day. Today, meaning is managed on many fronts besides that of the public speaking platform.

Meaning is managed by the people of Milwaukee as they read their newspapers and watch their televisions. How that meaning is managed will affect, I think, whether we sit passively and allow our experience to be shaped for us, whether we rouse ourselves to give two dollars to black strangers in the inner city, or whether we see the real possibilities for change in ourselves, in how we experience, and in the worlds we make together. The equipment for living that you as students have is not neutral machinery. It is morally and ethically loaded, and critics who study how the rhetorical dimensions of popular culture work as that equipment serve as symbolic engineers.

We might also think of how the criticism in this chapter has used the dramatistic/narrative critical perspective. You will recall that the key idea to that approach is that discourse itself will generate certain motives as a result of how language or other signs work within the discourse. In other words, the dances and moves that words go through are actually what motivate the users and receivers of the words. In this chapter we have noted that to personalize public issues requires turning those issues into discourse, or "textualizing" the issues. We have to talk or write about complex issues such as race relations in order to get a handle on them. But what happens in the talking or writing? When we squeeze real life into metonymies, what do the metonymies do to how we think about and react to the real life situation? This chapter has shown how paradoxes arise, not just from "real life" experience but from that textual, discursive act of metonymizing itself.

Chapter 6

Twin Peeks: Using Theory in Two Analyses of Visual Pleasures

••••••••••••••••••••••••••••••••••

Barry Brummett
Margaret Carlisle Duncan

Earlier in this book, we learned that criticism is often inspired and guided by theory. Theory, you will recall, is a generalized statement about the patterns in experience. Theory offers a description of how texts work or why they come to be. A set of principles or concepts suggested by a theory to explain some kind of experience is often borrowed by a critic. Those principles then call the critic's attention to certain dimensions of meaning in texts, and they provide the conceptual and organizational structure for the resulting critical analysis.

In this chapter, we look more closely into the question of how critical analysis interacts with theory. This chapter actually contains two analyses of very different subjects: televised sports and shopping malls. In writing your own analyses, it is a good idea to be more focused than that. But here, we give you two analyses for the price of one so as to help you think about how theory works with criticism. In this chapter, you should look for how theory is used to guide and develop the critical analysis. But you should also look for the ways in which criticism helps to improve our understanding of theory. We will see that criticism can bring together more than one theory so as to show how, in understanding particular kinds of texts, a particular theory needs to be merged with or changed by other theory. We will see how critical analysis can "talk back" to a theory and suggest that its scope of application be narrowed or expanded.

We will begin with a theory of *visual pleasure*, grounded in feminist and psychoanalytic theory. That theory has, as we will see, been borrowed by several media critics, especially in studying film. Our first critical analysis will argue that the feminist/psychoanalytic theory of visual pleasures needs to be supplemented with another, media-based theory if it is going to be applied fruitfully to television, specifically to televised sports. We will also borrow from some Marxist theory to help make that application of the theory of visual pleasures to televised sports work.

Our second critical analysis will begin with the same theory of visual pleasures, but will argue that it can be usefully applied beyond the range of just the visual. Here we will make heavier use of Marxist theory to show that the original theory can be expanded and enlarged through critical application. We will show that a wider application of the theory can help us understand the ways in which people experience shopping malls.

The Basic Theory of Visual Pleasures: Voyeurism, Fetishism, Narcissism

What pleasures do people find in looking at things? Looking is, of course, a very common experience for most people. It may be so common that we do not really notice that there are different kinds of looking at the things of this world, and different kinds of pleasures involved in those ways of looking. By calling our attention to things that are "right in front of our face" but that we do not often think about, criticism can alert us to meanings that are important to us on a subconscious level.

As you might expect, theories of looking have been particularly important to scholars interested in studying the visual media of film and television. These scholars originally turned to some psychoanalytic and feminist theories to explain what the different kinds of looks are, and how some texts of film and television encourage certain kinds of looks so as to influence their audiences. Let us begin by examining the basic theory of visual pleasures, called by the technical name of *specularity*, and how it was developed by scholars interested in film.

Most specularity theorists have written about the cinema. They use the term *scopophilia* to describe pleasurable looking, and they attempt to explain "scopophilia . . . [and the] circumstances in which looking itself is a source of pleasure" (Mulvey 1975, 8). Cinema theorists have drawn heavily from the work of the French psychoanalyst Jacques Lacan (1977) in studying viewing pleasure.

Although Lacan writes widely of psychoanalytic matters, specularity theory mainly uses his explication of the "mirror stage," to which we referred in Chapter 4 (Lacan 1977, 1–7; Hall 1988, 49–50; Nichols 1981; Kuhn 1982). Lacan argues that at an early stage in the development of the infant, the child discovers its reflection in the mirror. Several things happen in that moment. The child begins to perceive itself as a unified whole. The child's self-concept becomes connected with *images* of itself; that is, the child begins to develop a sense of self by examining external images, as seen in the mirror. The child rejoices in discovering a perfect unity between self and image: when the child moves, the mirror image moves. This discovery will never again be equalled, for the child soon learns more important ways to represent things, through signs such as language, in which signifier and signified are never wholly unified.

Theorists of cinematic looking argue that movies are popular in part because they put viewers in a state of "artificial regression" to this mirror stage (Baudry 1980a). These theorists stress the relative immobility of the filmgoer (Baudry

1980a, 45, 1980b, 33; Metz 1980, 385), which duplicates the immobility of the infant. They argue that the "varied" and "dense" spectacle which is film *feels* similar to the child's delighted discovery of its mirror reflection (Augst 1980, 429). And these theorists hold that the tendency of viewers to "lose themselves" in film duplicates that mirror stage's first episode in "the long love affair/despair between image and self image" (Mulvey 1975, 10).

Theorists further explain the kinds of pleasurable looking offered in mainstream cinema. Here we must introduce some terms that will be very handy later on though they may seem technical, or even strange, right now. Mulvey argues that pleasurable looking in cinema is either *scopophilic* (meaning the pleasure is found in another object of the look, rather than the self) or *narcissistic* (meaning the looker finds delight in identifying with his or her own image) (1975, 10).

Voyeurism

Scopophilia can be further subdivided into two categories. Sometimes, scopophilic cinematic looking takes the form of *voyeurism*. A voyeur is someone who looks at something illicitly, without being invited to look and without being noticed. Theorists observe that a movie theater is dark, allowing the spectator to become wrapped in furtive solitude (Barthes 1980, 1–2; Augst 1980, 429–30). The people on the screen can be seen but they cannot see the viewer; therefore, realist cinema "proposes for the viewer a position at the keyhole, seeing but not seen, like the psychopathic voyeur" (Nichols 1981, 79). The actors must not consent to being watched, or the voyeuristic spell will be broken (Augst 1980, 429).

Fetishism

The second scopophilic pleasure of cinema that theorists describe is *fetishism*, which differs from voyeurism because the pleasure is obtained not from secret looking but from openly looking at an object that is "satisfying in itself" (Mulvey 1975, 14). Fetishism is seen most clearly when people are fascinated with some spectacle. Fetishistic pleasure might be derived from breathtaking scenery in the film *Dances with Wolves*, for example, or from the long vistas of wealth and material possessions in the halls of the final scenes of Orson Welles's film *Citizen Kane*.

Narcissism

Theorists argue that a third, nonscopophilic pleasure of cinematic looking is *narcissism*: "In looking at representations of the human body, or parts of it, the spectator identifies with himself [sic]. . . ." (Kuhn 1982, 59). In fact, French theorist Roland Barthes calls the whole of cinematic looking narcissistic (1980, 3). This kind of looking is pleasurable because we recognize our own likenesses in the images on the screen. The little child who imagines that he or she is the castaway in *The Black Stallion* or the boy defending himself in *Home Alone* experiences narcissistic pleasure.

"Cookie-cutter Criticism"

This three-part theory of visual pleasure has proven useful to the scholars just cited in explaining how film appeals to an audience. But every critic needs to apply theoretical ideas carefully so as to avoid pitfalls. One problem that you should watch out for is that of "cookie-cutter criticism." This kind of criticism occurs when the analyst applies the concepts and categories of a theory rigidly and uncritically. Such uncritical criticism sometimes results from not thinking carefully enough about whether a theory really "fits" the experience being analyzed without any alterations whatsoever.

Cookie-cutter criticism sometimes ignores important dimensions of a text so as to force the text to fit the theory, whereas better criticism results from revising theory as needed to help us better understand texts. Even professional scholars are sometimes guilty of cookie-cutter criticism. Some of these scholars have attempted to apply the theory of visual pleasures to *television*. They have concluded that those three categories do not fit television, and that therefore television cannot be as pleasurable and interesting as are movies. Let's examine their arguments first, before assessing them.

Cookie-Cutting and Television Criticism

Many theorists argue against the relevance of the three types of visual pleasure for understanding television (Flitterman-Lewis 1987, 172, 187). These critics deny that television can offer the voyeuristic, fetishistic, or narcissistic pleasures of film.

For example, some theorists argue that since most television is seen in the familiar, well-lighted, and busy surroundings of the home, it cannot offer the voyeuristic pleasure of film. Barthes notes that for television, in contrast to film, "the darkness is dissolved, the anonymity repressed, the space is familiar, organized, . . . tamed" (1980, 2; also see Flitterman-Lewis 1987, 188), thus destroying some conditions required for voyeurism. Several theorists argue that the physical nearness of, and our control over, the television set remove the distance needed for voyeurism (see Ellis 1982, 138–39). Ellis argues that television's small image makes it rely on personal close-up shots, which decrease distance as they render the characters more attainable and intimate (1982, 131). Scholars point to television's reliance on the "three camera" system, to which we referred in Chapter 4 (page 123); this system, which places the viewer outside the physical space of the picture, is a technical factor that works against both voyeurism and narcissism. According to Flitterman-Lewis,

> Television breaks down the voyeuristic structure of primary identification—there is no camera position to be occupied in this way. . . . Television's fractured viewing situation explodes [cinema's] coherent [subject], offering in the place of the "transcendental subject" of cinematic viewing, numerous partial identifications, not with characters but with "views." (1987, 190, 197).

Finally, some scholars argue that television cannot be voyeuristic because, they claim, the experience of watching television is entirely spectacular, invited looking. Fiske explicitly argues that when on television, Madonna "turns herself into a spectacle and thus denies the spectator the empowered position of the voyeur. . . . There can be no voyeurs in spectacle" (1987, 253).

Other critics argue that the fetishistic pleasures of cinema are greatly reduced (although not eliminated) in television. Television, they argue, is not much of a spectacle when compared to a sixty-foot movie screen. A concern with the distracting conditions of television's placement in the home leads a number of scholars to argue that television is not looked at with the "gaze," the kind of concentrated look used for film. Instead, television is looked at with a "glance," and this reliance on the "glance" especially reduces fetishism (Ellis 1982, 137, 143; Flitterman-Lewis 1987, 187; Fiske 1987, 57). Altman reviews some interesting research which shows that television is rarely looked at attentively, and that "intermittent attention is in fact the dominant mode of television viewing" (1986, 41–42).

Finally, some theorists deny the possibility of narcissistic pleasure when they note that television discourse is so fragmented and changing that it does not give viewers stable images with which they can identify. Theorists point to television's segmentation in half-hour blocks (Ellis 1982, 126) and to constant commercial interruptions of the discourse. They argue that narcissism requires time for people to imagine themselves in certain images, and that television's images change so quickly that narcissism is impossible.

Now please stop and think about these arguments, using your own common sense. Something is wrong here. We have all experienced moments of great pleasure, even of the specific visual pleasures outlined above, from watching television. People do find television pleasurable from time to time. It seems that in denying its relevance to television, the scholars we have just reviewed are taking a "cookie-cutter" approach in their application of the theory of visual pleasures.

Three Dimensions of Media

While the scholars we have just cited have worked up an interesting theory of what visual pleasures are, they have not paid equal attention to what *television* is. Therefore, their "cookie-cutter" attempts to apply that theory to texts have missed the obvious truth that at least some kinds of television are visually pleasurable. The problem here is that they write as if television were all one thing. They refer to television singularly, as if sitcoms, news, MTV, shopping networks, and soap operas were all the same. If we want to understand television's visual pleasure, we need to balance the theory of visual pleasure with a media-based theory.

We have developed a theory elsewhere (in Duncan and Brummett 1989) that can help us out here. We have argued that to understand how any medium (such as film, television, newspapers, and so forth) works, we need to think about three dimensions of media. One dimension is *discourse*: the verbal and nonverbal images, the talk and the pictures, that are usually conveyed by a medium. A second dimension is *social practices:* what people do with, and how they use and behave around, a medium. For instance, custom dictates that people do not talk loudly in movie theaters but that they *can* converse while watching television in this country. A third dimension is *technology:* what any particular medium can do because of its technical characteristics. Television and radio, for example, can offer live broadcasts and instant replay, while movies can offer high quality visual images.

When we think about a medium by examining the three dimensions of discourse, social practices, and technology, we discover that important differences begin to emerge *within* media. If you think about television in terms of discourse, you soon realize that there are very different discourses conveyed by that medium. The talk and images of a charity telethon are very different from those of a news documentary, for example. If you think about television in terms of social practices, you soon realize that different kinds of programs call forth very different behaviors, from reverent silence for religious broadcasts to practically ignoring many sitcom broadcasts while one reads the paper, does homework, or washes dishes. If you think about television in terms of technology, you soon realize that only certain kinds of programs make use of live broadcast and replay capabilities, while other kinds of programs, such as nature specials, might make more use of television's high mobility. When we think about television using the three dimensions of media, then, we realize that television is not a single, isolated thing. Therefore, if we are going to analyze visual pleasures on television, we need also to be aware that the media theory we have been discussing will call our attention to some kinds of television but not others, because pleasures will likely vary from one type of television to another.

Analyzing Televised Sports

In the critical analysis that follows, we are going to show that televised sports do offer all three of the pleasures suggested in the theory of specularity. This can be most clearly seen by considering televised sports in terms of the three dimensions of discourse, social practices, and technology. So that is how we will proceed with our analysis, showing that televised sports do offer each of the three pleasures by way of those three dimensions.

We choose televised sports as a subject for three reasons. First, televised sports are a good example of why one should not overgeneralize about a medium, since it clearly does offer the three visual pleasures that so many television critics claim cannot be found in viewing TV. The kinds of looking involved in spectator sports challenge the usual tendency to generalize about how looking at television works. Second, televised sport is obviously an enormously popular and influential experience in the United States, central to and reflective of our culture (Novak 1976). As we shall show, the theory of visual pleasures works best for those for whom sports are influential—for committed fans, as opposed to the casual viewer who may turn on sports for want of better entertainment. For social and political reasons, it is worthwhile to theorize about *how* spectating works for them. Third, televised sports are especially dependent on the visual. You can follow most soap operas by listening to them, but you lose a lot if you turn your back on a football game. Therefore, televised sports provide a good illustration of visual pleasures.

We will examine the ways in which televised sports create the visual pleasures of fetishism, voyeurism, and narcissism in complex and interlocking ways. We will organize our discussion of each category of visual pleasure around the dimensions of discourse, social practice and context, and technology. Our goal is to consider these three dimensions together insofar as they contribute to each pleasure under discussion; this approach will best allow us to make that integrated argument.

Spectator Sports and Fetishism

Discourse and Narrative: We noted earlier the observations of some theorists that television cannot offer the pleasures of fetishism because it involves the glance, or quick looking, much more than the concentrated gaze. The same might appear to be true with spectator sports. The visual image of televised sports is constantly shifting; this is one of the most distracted, active kinds of programming (Morse 1983; Fiske 1987). But the visual and aural discourse of televised sports creates a story that integrates and unifies those separate images into a coherent spectacle, allowing for fetishism in the form of fascination with the image and a desire for more looking. Sports viewing unifies glances into a gaze of continuous visual pleasure. The audience is specifically invited by commentators to look intently upon the spectacle.

Furthermore, the ongoing banter of the commentators' discourse takes the form of a narrative; one of the most common strategies of sportscasting is to lay a "story" over the visual images of action on the field (Duncan and Brummett 1987, 169–172). This imposed narrative helps the fan unify glances at hundreds of brief images into a rapt gaze at a coherent spectacle. Although "coverage is kaleidoscopic and visually dynamic, . . . the telecast has its own unity . . ." (Williams 1977, 136). Morris and Nydahl note that televised sports narrative is "rhythmic and intended to intensify experience" because "from the point of view of the networks, the sports spectacle is spectacle first and sports second . . ." (1983, 202).

The narrative unifies glances into a gaze of desire by turning athletes into fetishes, or objects of desire and fascination. Marxist theory reminds us that under capitalism, all objects that are desired become commodities with specific, measurable properties that define their value. This happens in the spectacle of sports. Fans look at athletes and their motions appraisingly, longingly, just as they might look at new cars on the showroom floor. To encourage such an attitude, commentators' discourse features detailed analyses of the preceding plays, and recitations of the athletes' heights and weights, of their times in the 100-meter dash, their batting averages, or their free throw percentages. This narrative invites us to examine and visually fondle the commodities we are watching. We are looking at bodies in motion, but the discourse treats them as objects with specific values.

For example, about a gymnast competing in the U.S. Gymnastics Championship in 1988, an NBC commentator remarks, "Seventeen-year-old Rhonda Faehn on the vault, 9.75 on her first vault; remember she scored a 10 in last year's Nationals in this event. She's currently tied for seventh place after the compulsories. And the judges score a perfect 10 for Rhonda Faehn." Any gymnast who receives a perfect score, a 10, becomes a particularly valuable commodity, as regular viewers of gymnastics learn. Sewart argues that sport is becoming increasingly commodified, and complains that "what we are witnessing is the reduction of athletic skill, competition, and contest to commodified spectacle sold in the market for mass entertainment" (1986, 181–85).

The narratives of televised sports sustain the fans' desire for continued looking through "suspenseful references by the commentators" and "manipulations of time and space" which create a story "that no spectator would experience in the arena while watching the actual event" (Morris and Nydahl 1983, 200). Televised sports commentary alternates between play-by-play reporting and colorful descriptions that we will refer to as *color commentary*. The play-by-play commentary names and interprets the action, and the color commentary fills in the dead (nonaction) time with evaluations of the athlete's performance, analysis of instant replays, and bits of statistical and biographical information. The function of both kinds of discourse is to rivet the audience's attention to the athlete and contest by making them commodified objects, much as the function of a salesperson's pitch is to rivet the audience's attention to the goods he or she is selling.

As we watch the shifting visuals of the 1988 U.S. Gymnastics Championship (including close-ups of the gymnasts' faces, instant replays in slow motion, wide-angle views of The Summit, and bird's-eye views of floor exercises), a commodifying narrative like the following helps us to knit these various scenes into a unity:

> And after the compulsories here are the leaders: Hope Spivey and Phoebe Mills tied for first, Garrison-Steves third, Yamashiro is fourth, a tie for fifth between Gunthorpe and Brandy Johnson; Kristie Phillips, the defending champion is tenth. . . . Forty percent of today's activities will count toward the total score and the National Championship.

The commentator functions as a cheerleader, demanding our attention through the liberal use of scores and rankings, exclaiming over the leaders and front-runners, lamenting the fate of athletes who have slipped from first place to tenth—in short, neatly unifying the many visuals through commodification.

Social Practices: The fetishistic structure of the glance within the gaze is also enabled by the social practices which typically surround televised spectator sports. Here, we turn to how the committed fans themselves behave, and how they use the television when it is tuned to sports. Unlike casual viewers who watch soap operas, situation comedies, or police dramas because that is what happens to be on, fans look at sports on television quite intentionally. Gantz's research reported that for fans, "a TV sportscast is an anticipated activity that is read about, talked about, and waited for" before the event (1981, 270), and that for these enthusiasts, "viewing rarely is the default option, selected when there is nothing to do" (273). Once the game begins, trips to the bathroom or refrigerator are delayed until time-outs; the action cannot be missed.

This high level of involvement in the game is intensified by the fact that people typically watch sports with others. Dorr, for example, suggests that one major function of television is relational; it is frequently a shared, social activity within a family or group of friends (1986, 114). Prisuta found that this is especially true for sports telecasts:

> The data also indicate that sports is a family affair, with interest and involvement. . . . [T]hey counter the popular stereotype of the father, or other male family member, absorbed in television sports and oblivious to the family around him. Interest in sports, manifested via television viewing . . . , is likely to be consistent throughout the family. (1979, 99)

Gantz also found this to be true: "For the TV sports fan . . . TV sports was something to do with friends, talk about with friends, and enjoy/participate in while watching" (1981, 267).

It is clear that televised sports viewing is anything but casual for committed fans. Prisuta found that over half the respondents in his study reported intense, emotionally involving viewing (1977, 97). Gantz (1981) agrees that sports telecasts are far from functioning just as electric wallpaper for fans; his subjects reported shouting, disputing calls, and discussing the game among themselves excitedly. Gantz's conclusion supports our argument against overgeneralizing conclusions about television in general: "The extensiveness of communicative behaviors while viewing may be accounted for by viewer involvement; viewers may be more involved in sports programs than other entertainment programming" (274). The communal nature of how sports are actually watched intensifies the commodifying, fetishistic nature of how people watch the screen: "Viewers also appear to be far more vocal and interactive with others while watching" (Gantz 1981, 273–74).

Technology: Finally, the technological characteristics of how sports are televised encourage a fetishistic look. The succession of glances required to take in the quickly changing image is unified into a gaze by the devices of instant replays, close-ups, and slow-motion coverage. Morris and Nydahl argue that "the single device most central to the manipulation of live events in order to create drama in televised sports seems to be the slow-motion replay" (1983, 201). Such devices enhance our ability to look at spectacle. What was a flashing array of quick glances is slowed down and seen in close detail through an electronically contrived gaze; televised sports make use of such technology to an extent unknown in other televised genres, such as soap operas.

Williams argues that sports telecasts focus on the individual even when depicting team sports, and that this is a function of both narratives that feature heroes and villains "within a larger biographical and personalized perspective" *and* close-up shots of individual athletes (1977, pp. 137–38). A mosaic of visually appealing charts, graphs, close-ups, and slow-motion replays appears on screen to command the audience's attention. Morse describes the ways in which the technology of televised sports wields a powerfully fetishistic appeal:

> Throughout the game, graphics in . . . bright contrasts are superimposed on the [ongoing] image of the game, keeping the viewer abreast of the record of an athlete or team. Sometimes a framed insert of a player's face or even of a part of the body is superimposed over the game, at times replacing the [game's image] entirely. During the game, elaborate advancing and receding frames may set apart the instant replays; they may also appear unmarked. These colorful graphics and moving frames exert a visual fascination. (1983, 50)

Spectator Sports and Voyeurism

In televised sports, the possibility for voyeuristic pleasure does arise from time to time, though not as the major pleasure. Voyeuristic pleasure comes from seeing what we know we have not been invited to look at. Thus it cannot be planned, and it comes as a break in the main business of the activity. But it is a visual pleasure all the same. Some scholars have argued that "sports events are the principal subject matter for *live* broadcasts" (Morris and Nydahl 1983, 195), which makes such telecasts considerably different from other types of programming (Gantz 1981, 263–64). As a "live" program, sports offers unplanned opportunities for uninvited looks. The sports viewer knows that there is the possibility for accident, injury, grief, violence, and even comedy at any sporting event.

Discourse: The discourse of televised sports signals the opportunity for voyeuristic looking, the chance to view without invitation, by a rupture in the flow of fetishism. The discourse calls attention to itself through its absence, when the flow of narrative suddenly stops, even if for only a moment. An athlete writhing in pain or an enraged coach throwing chairs onto a basketball court have not invited us to watch at that moment; they have probably forgotten that we *are* watching. It is in that sudden moment that the possibility for uninvited watching (with its voyeuristic pleasures) is realized.

The broadcast of the 1988 U.S. Gymnastic Championships on NBC offered viewers several voyeuristic moments, signaled by the commentators' silence: a view of a young child in the stands who had fallen asleep with his mouth gaping open; a close-up of Kelly Garrison-Steves gnawing on a stick of gum, then laughing and covering her face with her hand as she became aware of the camera's presence; a close-up of Kristie Phillips's convulsive breathing and her furtive wiping of a tear after a disappointing score. In each of these voyeuristic moments the smooth, effortless patter that we have come to expect from sports commentators suddenly stopped, as though they themselves were thrown off balance by each unexpected event. By their silence commentators seem to feign ignorance of such voyeuristic moments. But that very silence—so rare in American sports broadcasts—tells us that something out of the ordinary has happened, and a chance for voyeurism is at hand.

Social Practices: Because theorists argue that solitude is necessary for voyeurism, the communal nature of watching sports might seem to disqualify it for that pleasure; in this case, other people know you are watching. But the social practices of watching sports in groups, as noted earlier, create, paradoxically, a kind of "communal voyeurism." There is a tacit agreement among those who watch that it is acceptable to see the unplanned, uninvited image. For the purposes of the sportscast, fans become a kind of communal person who may together watch unplanned images without shame. No group of viewers watching an injured football player lying on the field will consult among themselves as to whether it is okay to keep watching. This practice of communal voyeurism counterbalances the shared, public nature of watching that would ordinarily prohibit voyeurism.

Technology: The technological capabilities of televised sports also enhance its occasional voyeuristic pleasures. Meyrowitz (1985) argues that television, especially through its capacity to broadcast realistic visual images live, has collapsed the ability of public figures to keep "front-stage" and "back-stage" activities separate. This can certainly be seen in the use of long lenses and remote, directional antennae microphones; a beet-red coach can be seen and heard chewing out a sweating player face to face on the other side of a field house, with no awareness that the exchange is being observed. And the occasional furtive foul in basketball, not meant by its perpetrator to be seen, can be shown again and again in close-up detail through instant replay and slow motion. In this way the illicit image of voyeurism can be captured and held, intensifying its pleasure.

It is important to note that the moments of voyeurism we have described are not sexually explicit. Certainly, sexually interested looking is rarely, if ever, invited in television sports. But it is possible nevertheless. In the context of spectator sports, any look based on sexual desire will be voyeuristic. When looking becomes sexually motivated for the individual, he or she takes on an illicit, outlaw role. Such an outlaw viewer is taking pleasure from a voyeuristic look.

Spectator Sports and Narcissism

Fetishism slides easily into narcissism: We see ourselves using or linked with the goods we admire. From a desire to see and admire them we move to a desire to identify with them. Narcissism is pleasure derived from seeing or imagining the self in what it is that we look at.

Televised sports offers its viewers the possibility to identify with and to imagine themselves as certain kinds of athletes. At the simplest level, little children might wish to grow up to be Evander Holyfield or Michael Jordan, and so derive narcissistic pleasure from looking at these athletes. Weekend tennis players might take their cues from looking at Steffi Graf, then go out to the local courts to try to do as she does. As Gantz reports, "Being a fan serves fantasy and escape functions and can be a pleasurable experience, particularly when one's player or team performs well. Fans can vicariously experience the struggles and successes of the athletes" (1981, 264).

Discourse: Commentators follow discursive patterns that increase fans' narcissistic identification with the athletes. Often color commentators, former athletes themselves, speak from the point of view of the competitor, thus enabling us to imagine ourselves in his or her place. In the 1986 Wimbledon Men's Doubles Finals (broadcast on NBC) the color commentator frequently spoke from the athlete's perspective, thus encouraging the audience's narcissism:

> *You* get some funny bounces, and *you're* really embarrassed out there sometimes. *You* just can't help it, but *you* get jammed, *you're* off-balance. . . . Wilander forced the opening; *you* have to do that in a tiebreaker—*you* have to force the shots (emphasis added throughout).

During the 1986 Wimbledon Women's Doubles Semi-final (also on NBC), a different color commentator again spoke from the athlete's perspective:

> That's the idea of team work. *Your* partner hits a great serve, and *you* should be there to poach and hit the other girl. She doesn't want to move in front of the ball if *you're* gonna hit her. . . . Pam Shriver has a real height advantage. She's the tallest one on the court. I think she's six feet two and on her serve that gives her an advantage because the higher *you* are, the easier it is—*you're* able to serve and hit down into the court (emphasis added throughout).

But the discourse of televised sports encourages another kind of identification. Commentators tell stories about the games and their players, filling in the identities of individuals and teams. Dick Enberg discussed Rhonda Faehn's spoon collection and Kelly Garrison-Steve's marital status during the 1988 U.S. Gymnastics Championship coverage on NBC, for instance. Commentators will even create imaginary conversations and attribute them to the athletes and coaches during the competition (Duncan and Brummett 1987). During a 1985 broadcast of a Purdue University-University of Arizona basketball game, for example, the color commentator said, "Mickey Crowley and Lute [Olson are] having a little conversation, Crowley from out of the East; he says, "I don't understand all that far West talk anyway. I don't know what you're talking about. I'm from the streets of New York' " (ESPN 1985).

Such color commentary works to further the audience's identification. More and varied information about an athlete or game means more images with which the viewer can identify. Thus, the discourse of televised sports provides viewers with the pieces needed to assemble fantasies about themselves. Sports discourse allows, indeed encourages, readings that people can construct in varied ways to remake the televised image into their own image.

Social Practices: The social practices surrounding televised sports in this country strongly encourage male over female narcissism. In the United States, men are statistically the larger audience for televised sports (Nielsen Company 1988). And it is certainly the case that males constitute the majority of televised athletes (Coakley 1986, 104–5). Gantz has reported that females are more likely to watch sportscasts as a last-resort option (1981, 267). These facts tend to restrict the pleasures of narcissism available in televised sports to men.

The narcissistic appeal of sports is shaped by the popularity of televised sports among men. Fiske argues that our society has created a masculine ideal of strength, control, and autonomy that can rarely be realized in men's main arena of endeavor: work (1987, 201). For this reason, many men have "developed a masculine style for their leisure and social activities that consists of excessive signs of masculinity in an exaggerated and compensatory display" (201). While some men are able to attain the masculine ideal through participation in sports, many more must attain it only in their fantasies as they watch the very best athletes on television. Televised sports allow men to narcissistically identify with images of exaggerated strength and control, heroes and heroic efforts in football, basketball, weight-lifting, and Olympic events like the decathlon, the marathon, and so on. Gantz found that "to thrill in victory" was the *most* important motive for watching sportscasts reported by his (predominantly male) subjects (1981, 267).

Technology: The technological capabilities of television also further narcissistic pleasure. Videotape allows the insertion of prerecorded interviews into ongoing programs, and such interviews allow intimate glimpses into the lives and thoughts of players and coaches. Such insertion of the personal into ongoing action allows viewers to construct images with which they may narcissistically identify. Coverage of both the 1984 and 1988 Olympic Games featured the "Up Close and Personal" series of prerecorded interviews with selected athletes. One memorable "Up Close and Personal" focused on Olympic decathlon competitor Jurgen Hingsen and revealed that he liked his wife to iron his underwear (ABC 1984). The live coverage of the 1988 Gymnastic Competition (NBC) included several previously taped interviews. In one, highly ranked Kristie Phillips explained to us why she changed coaches; in another, Bela Karolyi, gymnastic coach extraordinaire, told us why he would not be going to Seoul with the U.S. gymnastic team.

Female narcissism in response to televised sports is infrequent. Women and girls turning on ESPN or NBC Sports World have relatively few opportunities to view female athletes. The most common sports image by far is the male body.

Stepping Back From the Critique of Televised Sports

The three-part theory of visual pleasure provides an interesting and manageable set of concepts for guiding the critic's analysis of texts. That is just what a theory should do for criticism. But sometimes the simple pairing up of theory with text will not do, because such a pairing results in "cookie-cutter" criticism—an overly simplistic application of a set of concepts to a text. To avoid that problem (which befalls even professional rhetorical scholars of television), we complemented the theory of visual pleasures with a media-based theory. Media should be analyzed in terms of its three dimensions of discourse, social practices, and technology. Understanding television through those three dimensions has led us to see that there are actually different kinds of television; it has also helped us to see that televised sports is a kind of television that *does* offer the three visual pleasures of fetishism, voyeurism, and narcissism.

You will have noticed the heavy use of scholarly references in this chapter so far. In explaining theory, we often quoted other scholars or referred to their work. That practice is common among professional critics; its purpose is to provide background information concerning the theory, as well as to bolster the "credentials" of the criticism itself. On your own or with others in your class, you might think about why theoretical concepts need that kind of backing; what purpose do all those references serve?

This critical analysis has, we hope, taught you, the reader, something about televised sports. You should now be able to enjoy a game more fully, being able to note more carefully how it offers visual pleasures. But we hope this analysis has also encouraged you, the critic, to be careful in applying theory to texts in your analyses. Theories sometimes need to be supplemented, or helped out, with other theories, to avoid overgeneralizations and simplifications.

Beyond Visual Pleasures:
Analyzing the Shopping Mall

We have learned that the three-part theory of fetishism, voyeurism, and narcissism began as an account of pleasurable looking in general. It was adopted as a way to explain the pleasure of looking at film or at television. But in the second critical analysis in this chapter, which we begin now, we are going to extend that theory beyond the visual.

In this criticism we will make heavier use of Marxist theory to argue that those three visual pleasures can be used to identify pleasures across all the senses, pleasures that the capitalist economic system uses to maintain itself. We will treat fetishism, voyeurism, and narcissism as three pleasurable ways to act, to function, even to *be* under capitalism. In that way, we will stretch the original theory beyond the visual, even beyond media application. This stretching is encouraged by the object of the criticism itself: shopping malls.

When we first set out to analyze shopping malls, it seemed clear to us that the three categories of visual pleasure were relevant to understanding why people like to go to shopping malls, and how the malls influence people once they are there. But the experience of the malls is more than just visual, and only part of it has anything to do with media. The object of criticism itself, the mall, called for a stretching of the theory, which is not uncommon when people apply theory to objects of criticism. Stretching of the original theory is also a very good way to avoid lapsing into cookie-cutter complacency, as it requires the critic to think of how theory needs to be changed to account for experience, rather than simply slapping a theory on top of experience whether it fits or not.

Our goal in this criticism, then, will be to show some of the ways that malls attract people and keep them coming back. We will also consider malls as rhetorical instruments of the whole capitalist economy, as gigantic rhetorical texts that are designed to turn people into the kinds of consumers that keep capitalism going strong. We will focus on no single mall, but will instead draw examples from a lifetime of mall-going, from malls in the greater Milwaukee area to the nation's largest mall, the Mall of America in Bloomington, Minnesota. Before getting into specific analyses, we need to review one important concept from Marxist theory that will be useful here.

Reviewing the Notion of Subject Positions

You may recall our discussion of the *subject position* in Chapters 3 and 4 (pages 98–100, 119–20). We learned that any text (from a speech to a mall) "calls" to those who experience the text to assume a certain role or persona in relationship to the text; this role or persona is called a subject position (Althusser 1971; Hall 1985; Silverman 1983). To derive pleasure from any experience, one must assume a certain subject position in response to the text of that experience. In other words, you need to "become" a certain kind of role or persona in order to understand the meanings of texts. In the first criticism of this chapter for example, the role of the *sports fan* was a distinctive subject position assumed in response to the text of televised sports.

In the section that follows, we will show how the theoretical categories of fetishism, voyeurism, and narcissism may usefully be seen as pleasures that define the subject position of *the shopper*. Malls are enormous texts that "call" people to become shoppers. In fact, malls make little sense to people shopping in them unless those people surrender themselves to the three pleasures by taking on the subject position of shopper. We will argue for that claim by examining each pleasure in turn.

We will also look at the political implications of the shopping mall as text. The subject position that one assumes in relationship to a text is politically implicated. In response to an old Western film, one can root for the cowboys or for the Indians, but either option involves assuming a certain subject position in regard to the text that also entails a certain political position. In what follows, we will consider the ways in which people are turned into shoppers by malls. But we will also look at the political work that this transformation accomplishes: It perpetuates the capitalist system itself. You may also recall that we discussed the Marxist idea of *reproducing the conditions of production*—the idea that any system, such as the capitalist economic system, takes steps to ensure its own continuation (page 114). We will therefore be on the lookout in this criticism for how malls reproduce their own conditions of production by creating the subject position of shopper, even if the shopper buys nothing in any given trip.

Fetishism in the Mall

If a friend invites you to go shopping in the mall, think about the kind of invitation that is. Is it necessarily a request to spend money? Could you go along and "shop" even if you were completely broke? Of course you could, and perhaps you often do. It is clear that "going shopping" refers only partially to the actual exchange of money and goods. Shopping is something to do, it is a recreation, much more than it is simply buying and selling. That is especially true in malls. One might go shopping at a grocery store or a plumbing supply store, for instance, with the intention to buy a specific product. Your friend would be very unlikely to ask you to go shopping, with no specific purchase in mind, in a hardware store. But malls are different.

As long as there have been markets to which people would go for the fun of looking, moving through the crowd, and touching and smelling new goods, societies have set aside special places for those pleasures. The old, pre-mall idea of "window shopping," of looking at spectacle from the outside, has been enhanced and replaced by the more enveloping and inclusive experience of the mall as a totally encompassing site, an arena, a giant play pen. The mall is the cathedral of late capitalism: It is a place to be in, to walk around in, to be immersed in (Featherstone 1991; Fiske 1989a, 1989b; Pressdee 1986; Rojek 1985; Shields 1989; Urry 1990). Spectacle is available to be experienced visually, but also through the other senses and through motion and placement of the body.

The truth of such observations can be seen especially vividly in the largest mall in the United States, the Mall of America, in Bloomington, Minnesota. If you go to this mall with the intention of buying a specific item, such as a hat or a toothbrush, you will be frustrated. The number and the layout of stores make any intention to go to a particular store futile. The endless corridors of the mall curve and branch away at angles from one another. As you walk down a corridor, new corridors open up to the left and right. Escalators invite you to walk through the same tangle above or below you. Soon it becomes difficult to remember where you are, but it also seems unimportant, for new and more interesting stores are just ahead in each corridor. The four stories of the mall do not seem to be uniformly stacked one upon another; you catch inviting glimpses of stores on other levels, but getting there may be confusing and is likely to make you forget where you were before. The Mall of America wants its customers to simply wander through the spectacle; its confusing layout will frustrate any shopper's attempt to march right to any specific store for a specific purchase.

Fetishism is obviously an experience available through the dense spectacle of stores and their displays. Racks of shoes on sale cluster out into the doorways of Florsheim and Famous Footwear. The floor-to-ceiling glass walls of Dunham's Sporting Goods display athletic gear and equipment. The open construction of most malls enables an appreciation of spectacle on all sides, as stores are viewed across the chasm of a central open area. Fetishism is experienced aurally as theme songs from familiar childhood movies issue forth from the Disney store; it is experienced olfactorily as the Cinnabon shop deliberately emits its buttery fumes out the front of the store rather than up an exhaust pipe. Fetishism becomes tactile, or experienced through touch, as shoppers stroke clothing hanging on the racks in Bachrach's or flip through rows of CDs at Musicland, and children fondle demonstration models stocked in the doorways of Kay-Bee Toys.

Fetishism also occurs in the large, open public areas of malls, as shoppers gather to rest or simply to savor being inside in an atrium rising hundreds of feet to an all-glass ceiling, filled with full-sized palms and bamboo trees. At the center of the Mall of America is Camp Snoopy, an amusement park filled with full-sized attractions like roller coasters and log rides. The frantic twirling of rides fills your field of vision as the roller coaster swoops around just over the heads of shoppers. Upbeat music accompanies a fashion show being held in one corner of the central atrium, while the perky rhythms from a nearby Bradford organ store fill the open area in front of the Marshall Fields anchoring one extreme end of the mall.

The swirl of noise and music fills the public spaces in all malls. The shopper is invited to see, hear, smell, and walk through this teeming confusion of spectacle. Purchases are obviously the "bottom line" for the mall and its management, but towards that end the stuff of spectacle is provided as text for the person walking in out of the bleakness of everyday life. Just as the medieval cathedral called forth the subject position of worshipper within the context of religion, so the mall calls forth the subject position of the shopper in the context of capitalism. Creation of that subject position is of more long-term importance than is any single purchase. The mall therefore works to reproduce the conditions of production by creating shoppers, as much as it functions to sell a compact disc or a new set of dishes on any given day. In other words, the long-term desire of the capitalist system is to create consumers of goods. People must come to love goods, and part of doing that is coming to find the places where those goods are sold pleasurably. Goods are good, the message goes, even if you buy none today. In this way, the pleasure of fetishism serves the needs of capitalism by *delighting* shoppers, making the mall itself a source of pleasure that will bring them back, to buy tomorrow if not today.

Voyeurism in the Mall

The text of the mall offers opportunities for voyeurism that very clearly go beyond the visual, even for this most visual of terms. Part of the social context of every mall in every city of the United States, perhaps of the world, is the estrangement of classes, races, and ages from one another. In the everyday world, social rules separate those categories of people from one another. The mall, however, is one of the few sites in which different groups of people are exposed to each other under conditions in which voyeurism can occur (large, public sporting events are another such site). Few people go to the mall with the sole expressed purpose of "people watching." Nor is such an activity invited, especially when it crosses the demographic boundaries that divide estranged groups. Nevertheless, at the mall the shopper enters a site in which one can overhear, peep at, smell, brush against, and be near people whom one would not ordinarily encounter.

The homeless seem to follow an unwritten understanding that they may come into the Grand Avenue Mall in downtown Milwaukee, to sit on its many benches or walk through its three blocks of corridors, as long as they do not harass or solicit money from regular shoppers. This arrangement, which provides the street people with respite from the northern winter for a time, provides a site of voyeurism for the shoppers. The shabby man slumped in a corner of a bench and staring off into the middle distance may be surreptitiously examined, even sat next to, with no fear of incident or retaliation, just as the compulsive mutterings of the bag lady striding up and down the aisles may be overheard as she passes. Of course, the other end of the economic scale is available for voyeuristic inspection as well, as the fashionable denizens of wealthy Milwaukee neighborhoods like Fox Point or River Hills stroll through the Bayview Mall. What these people buy in Benetton, Craig's, Madison's, or Marshall Field's—even the snacks they purchase in the food courts—can all be examined by those from the other side of the tracks.

The large food courts that are found in most malls allow wonderful opportunities for voyeuristic people watching. One can sit and eat or drink while watching people go by. If the food court is situated at the top floor of an enormous open, central area, as at the Grand Avenue Mall, one can watch people on floors below who are almost certain not to know they are being observed. With a little more care, one can watch, overhear, and be physically close to those seated at nearby tables.

Some malls, such as Mayfair Mall in the suburb of Wauwatosa, actually sponsor walking clubs for older citizens who go there to get exercise, especially in winter. Thus nuclear families that do not include, and possibly seldom see, senior citizens can go to the mall and be with, see, or even walk with (voyeuristically, of course) both vigorous and arthritic older people. Other malls, such as Northridge, are geographically situated to draw a highly racially mixed clientele, pulling people of all ethnic groups from both the suburbs and the mall-less inner city. Malls are a place to hear what people of other races or economic groups sound like, to see what they buy, to see how they move as they walk from store to store, to hear them admonish their children or socialize with one another. The idea that the mall is a place where it is acceptable to get close enough to a person so as to illicitly "check them out" may strike some as outrageous; but that is precisely what makes the experience one of voyeurism. The "checking out" happens without being invited to happen.

Voyeurism, regardless of which sense facilitates it, is a kind of enablement, even an empowerment of sorts. The shopper can see or be with or walk near people who cannot be experienced in those ways under any other circumstances. The mall gives people a kind of empowerment to do certain things. The economic system itself depends on a certain kind of empowerment as well, the empowerment of *currency*. You are probably used to thinking of currency as money. But it is more than that. If you have money, you have a currency that empowers you to do certain things—to purchase goods and services.

Similarly, being at the mall gives one a kind of *currency*, a medium, that enables the voyeuristic sensation of different others. At the mall, you are allowed to be near people who might not even let you into their neighborhood. The experience of voyeurism therefore duplicates at a formal level the capitalistic mechanism of currency as that which enables purchasing and enrichment through goods. The mall becomes a site in which a subject position of shopper is created, a subject position that is empowered (1) to experience, to be with, those who are ordinarily kept at a distance, but also (2) to buy if one has the currency. But of course, one does not always have the currency of *money*. Voyeurism keeps people coming back to the mall by giving them the *sensual* currency of a license to peep, to touch, to smell, and so on. In times of economic recession, voyeurism empowers the shopper by facilitating a pleasure, even at a time when the *other* pleasure of purchasing is denied. In this way shopping also reproduces conditions of production for the mall itself. People find the mall a place to experience the pleasure of voyeurism in all its modes, visual and beyond. Thus, people become conditioned to return to the mall for that pleasure, and ultimately to support the economic system that underlies the mall.

Narcissism in the Mall

The pleasures of narcissism are intertwined with those of fetishism and voyeurism, given the density of the experience of shopping. Mixed in with the spectacles of the mall and the opportunities for people watching is a frank and deliberate invitation to narcissism. The subject position of the shopper is invited to invent itself in different ways by using the resources of available commodities. It is important to recognize that what gives you narcissistic pleasure may not give the same pleasure to your friend if he or she has different styles, desires, and expectations. Therefore, the mall must be thought of as a large smorgasbord of signs, from which people take what they need to construct the image of themselves they desire.

Shoppers wander through, look at, feel, and smell clothing and accessories, which give them the opportunity to construct for themselves different personae. Eddie Bauer offers one set of subtexts in which the shoppers can picture themselves as rugged outdoor types. Redwood and Ross presents a different set of subtexts for the construction of an executive look. The process is playful in the obvious, childhood game sense of playing "dress-up." Adults play dress-up at the mall, appropriating its constituent signs for their own images.

The experience of the shopping mall is, in short, the experience of a series of signs that can be turned into mirrors. For shoppers, subject positions are constructed that take pleasure in imagining, literally constructing images of the self in this guise or that. Malls offer themselves as this sort of mutable, adaptable text, as raw materials for the work of narcissism, because of the commercial possibilities that follow from that work. As people imagine themselves in one way or another, they eventually buy goods that facilitate that kind of construction of images and of subject positions. Narcissism at the mall fuels the sort of desire that is the condition of reproduction of both the mall itself and the economic system on which it depends.

We have suggested that shopping malls work as engines of fetishistic, voyeuristic, and narcissistic pleasure. You can test this idea for yourself the next time you go shopping, or as we have been saying, the next time you take on the subject position of the shopper. But criticism should not leave its audience unchanged, and we would hope that you would experience shopping and malls with more awareness and discernment after reading this analysis. Good criticism can mean the "end of innocence" for its readers: If the criticism works, you may never again be able to enjoy a favorite movie or hear a favorite song without a deeper, and even perhaps disturbing, understanding of what that text is doing to influence you and others.

Perhaps this critique will have had that same effect. If our analysis is correct, there is no such thing as an innocent trip to a shopping mall. That which is "just for fun" is also in support of a particular system of economics—precisely because it *is* fun. We will neither indict nor praise that system here; our point is to make you aware of the ways in which, as a shopper, you reproduce the conditions of production for the mall and its sales. A good consumer is exactly what the mall wants you to become; instead, we would urge you to become a self-aware subject as you go shopping.

Stepping Back From the Critique of the Shopping Mall

Our focus in this analysis has been on using a theory of three pleasures to help you understand better the experience of shopping. As has already been noted, the ultimate test of this or any other criticism is whether you are now equipped to experience life more richly through understanding better how meanings are created.

We did not use as many scholarly references in this critique as in the first (of televised sports) because the basic theory had already been explained. But sections addressing new theory, such as that of the subject position, did have many references. Again, please consider, on your own and in discussions, the purpose that such citations serve in criticism.

Note that in applying the theory of the three pleasures to the shopping mall, we had to stretch and extend the original theory beyond the merely visual in shaping our discussion of the idea of pleasures and of how a subject position can be created around those pleasures. But you as a reader of the criticism in this chapter should now be empowered to extend the theory even further. With that structure of three pleasures in mind, and having now had it illustrated for you with regard to both televised sports and shopping malls, what other far-flung experiences do you think it can help you to understand more fully? Criticism generates new insights as it pushes the theoretical "help" that it borrows, and those insights can empower you to understand other experiences in a more meaningful way as well.

Chapter 7

Afrocentrism and
Do the Right Thing
●●●●●●●●●●●●●●●●●●
Detine L. Bowers

To say that a text is rhetorical is to say that it responds to some real life concerns or problems of an audience. For many African Americans, *Do the Right Thing* was a response to racial violence.

Racial Violence in New York

On Saturday, December 20, 1986, those African Americans living in the Bedford-Stuyvesant section of Brooklyn who were tuned into their local radio stations heard the routine rap of Brooklyn deejays. But in addition to the rap, there was especially alarming news for the African-American community. A story had broken during the early morning hours that one of their youth was dead and two others had been injured in beatings with baseball bats by a gang of white youths outside a pizzeria in the Howard Beach section of Queens.

The event brought an overwhelming rhetorical response from many in New York City. The responses were motivated by ever-increasing tensions among ethnic groups, a renewed black nationalism, and what seemed an alarming increase in police brutality toward African Americans during the 1980s. Many government officials and institutions, including the police, had come to be seen as racist agencies of a power structure that aimed to destroy the African-American community. That power structure was perceived as Eurocentric: grounded in European ways of thinking, feeling, and acting. Opposition to that Eurocentric power structure took a variety of forms including public debates, letters to the editor, protest march speeches, and film. Spike Lee's *Do the Right Thing* (1989) was one of many rhetorical responses to the violence against African Americans; this is the specific rhetorical text we will examine in this chapter.

This chapter is an exercise in Afrocentric interpretation. Afrocentric criticism is one variety of culture-centered criticism, which, as we discussed in Chapter 3, attempts to understand artifacts and texts through methods of interpretation that arise from the cultures generating the artifacts. We will borrow heavily from Molefi Kete Asante's ideas about Afrocentrism (also discussed in Chapter 3) in our examination of *Do the Right Thing*, on the premise that although Spike Lee is an American citizen, he draws on and expresses many of the cultural resources of his African heritage in the creation of his texts. "Afrocentrism," as Asante writes, places "African ideals at the center of any analysis that involves African culture and behavior" (6). To draw on Afrocentrism is not to assume that all African Americans are Afrocentric. There are Eurocentric African Americans just as there are Afrocentric Europeans. In our use of Afrocentrism we are referring to world view, not race. We must also acknowledge that some traditional Afrocentric concepts have been assimilated into Eurocentric life and vice versa. This chapter simply provides one example of culture-centered criticism, an approach that could be grounded in *any* other culture.

The rhetoric in response to the racial violence in New York showed a clash between the language and values of Eurocentricity and those of Afrocentricity. Spike Lee captures this clash, in part, in *Do the Right Thing*. Of course, *Do the Right Thing* can be read at many different levels and from many different perspectives, but our purpose in this chapter is to show how reading the film from an Afrocentric perspective allows it to be understood as a response to a dominant, Eurocentric power structure that maintains itself through hierarchy, prediction, and control. This criticism is limited to explaining how such a reading works. But such a reading is an important one. In this work, we aim to show how an Afrocentric reading is actually a useful strategy for survival for those in black communities.

African-American communities throughout the United States have historically used a variety of discourse forms to respond to Eurocentric oppression, forms such as public speaking, preaching, and poetry. While Spike Lee uses a traditional American communication medium, film, his text is part of a larger body of Afrocentric rhetoric. In adding his film to the body of social and political commentary on racial tensions in New York, Lee's work incorporates other community rhetorical responses, such as those of rap artists. His film uses what the community *knows* to fashion a response to violence. In other words, from an Afrocentric stance, the film "depends for its decoding upon shared knowledge of the participants" (Mitchell-Kernan, 325). Through his work, Lee "talks back" to the American community about experiences and shared knowledge and values among urban African Americans. To do this, he recreates twenty-four hours in the life of the neighborhood of Bedford-Stuyvesant in a metonymization of the black experience in urban America. For these reasons, *Do the Right Thing* is an appropriate text to study from an Afrocentric perspective.

First we will briefly compare Afrocentric and Eurocentric orientations and criticism. We will study different attitudes toward time as one example of how Eurocentricity and Afrocentricity clash. Then we will turn specifically to *Do the Right Thing*, to see how it uses five related dimensions of Afrocentricity to fashion its rhetorical response to racial violence.

The Afrocentric Rhetorical Condition:
Structure and Resistance

Every act of rhetorical criticism is evaluative, and grows out of a particular orientation to the world. The critical act is especially fruitful when we recognize that the interpretation of what we see and hear as rhetorical critics stems from certain psychological and social orientations that we derive from our cultures. Criticism is an activity born from social definitions of what constitutes permissible message content, structure, and form. Indeed, the very act of criticism makes certain cultural assumptions about who is a credible critic within a society. Americans hear "criticism" from those who hold high positions of rank within society. One example is the political "spin doctors" who have become the American social hierarchy's political critics and experts. These "spin doctors" speak the language of a particular culture: the established social hierarchy.

Spike Lee understood the cultural nature of criticism, specifying that features and interviews be written by African-Americans for his film, *Malcolm X,* because he felt that the questions they asked would be especially relevant to the film. Lee saw that Afrocentricism provides a cultural understanding of his project that Eurocentricism does not. His concern that the mainstream media would ask questions that he considered irrelevant was related to cultural orientation rather than to race or a desire to avoid rigorous criticism, especially since he clearly wanted all of America to see his film. After all, Afrocentric questions about other texts have often been discounted in Eurocentric discussions because they were not perceived to be relevant to the Eurocentric mindset. Concerns about paternalism in *Webster* and *Diff'rent Strokes* were sometimes dismissed by Eurocentric television producers, for instance. Lee requested a certain understanding of his project that shared his Afrocentric orientation.

Whether an orientation is primarily European, African, Latino, Asian, or based in a subculture of any of these groups, each orientation carries with it a set of assumptions about how the world is structured and how people of various races or cultures fit within their structure of beliefs. Those assumptions are the basic points of disagreement between Eurocentric and Afrocentric orientations to life, discourse, and criticism.

We will argue in this chapter that Eurocentricity is based upon hierarchy and power, and the Eurocentric discourse aims to gain control over the audience. Such discourse operates from a hierarchy of authority, thereby stifling oppositional discourse. When we say that Eurocentricity is *hierarchical,* we mean that it assumes that some people should be in control of others. Eurocentric discourse assumes that a person will try to attain a high rank in society, and that success depends on winning control over others. Central to Eurocentricity is the idea of prediction and control—the idea that with the correct conditions or manipulations, a persuader will (and should) win over a persuadee. Asante argues that an orientation that privileges such prediction and control in language naturally confers power (and credibility) to those who already control those same rules of discourse, and thus creates a stacked deck:

> For example, it does not matter if the language of the imperative is polite and gentle, so long as the imperative structure endures; a social environment has been created where one, for instance, gives orders and the other is expected to obey. Sometimes this occurs in social situations where political and economic power resides in one class or one race and powerlessness in another class or race, for example, South African whites and blacks. Such a rhetorical condition seldom allows reciprocity, despite the illusion, within the framework of a unidirectional perspective. (Asante, 4)

Asante's definition of a rhetorical condition is "the structure and power pattern, assumed or imposed, during a rhetorical situation by society" (22). The "rhetorical condition" is created by the set of rules implicit in the dominant discourse. The rhetorical condition in the United States today is one of Eurocentric domination. The rules of that discourse are assumed to be the natural way to speak. Those rules are what we call rhetorical *structure*. In the Eurocentric tradition, the structure of acceptable discourse is static, or unchanging—an ongoing, human-imposed model that governs our actions. Eurocentricity assumes that the way things are is simply natural and unchanging.

But Afrocentrism recognizes that rhetorical structures are variable, not static; structure is negotiable. According to Asante, "structure becomes a form of discourse, apart from its character, in the words of a discourse" (22). This means that a way of speaking, a structure, is not viewed as simply a frame for reality. Instead, structures are seen as tools that can be manipulated. There is a difference between simply following a grammatical rule and seeing the rule itself as negotiable and open for flexibility in its form. In sum, an Afrocentric understanding of structure "explains how one can disidentify from controlling structures, because it is so easy for structure to take over from content and manipulate the message, orchestrate it, at will" (26). The Eurocentric structure of discourse is resisted by Afrocentric ideas of discursive structure on many points. We can see how Eurocentricity and Afrocentricity differ by examining one central point of conflict: attitudes toward time.

Afrocentric Orientations to Time and Improvisation

Time

One dimension of the conflict between the Eurocentric controlling structure and Afrocentric alternatives to that structure manifests itself in different orientations to *time*. Eurocentric and Afrocentric orientations to time differ considerably. Traditional African cultures have historically emphasized experience in daily life as the criteria for when, or at what time, activity occurs. Things happen when the flow of everyday life leads them to happen. In contrast, Eurocentric culture structures time according to standard, predictable units of hours and minutes.

Life is expected to adapt itself to that structure: There is a "right" time to go to work, to speak, to arrange an activity, to show up for an event, and so forth. These adaptations illustrate the Eurocentric importance of human prediction of, and control over, what happens in life. Eurocentric cultures are often preoccupied with discussions of when or what time people go to work, what time they must eat, and when they must go to sleep.

Control and Prediction of Time

Instruments of measurement, such as clocks and calendars, aid people in creating a common time to perform an act. But creating a precise time to perform an act is emphasized less in Afrocentric cultures. Precise time is not perceived as being as important as the natural events or experiences that occur in daily activity. For example, in African-American sermons, the minister may ask the congregation to ignore watches or clocks, as the divine word should not be time-bound and divine inspiration should not be subject to temporal measurement, a human creation. The congregation is encouraged to appreciate the *meaning* of the event. Because Eurocentric cultures are generally preoccupied with the exact time an activity begins or ends (prediction and control), imprecise (or spiritually-inspired) times to perform an act—such as "someday," "soon," or "by and by"—are often considered unclear, vague, even "primitive" by Eurocentric peoples. But such "imprecise" descriptors are appropriate from an Afrocentric view that emphasizes things like the influence of nature in our lives.

From an Afrocentric perspective, participation defines time. In other words, what matters is *how* people respond to, or participate in, the events of their lives, not the date or hour when the response or participation occurred. For example, the act of participating in a public speech during a march on Washington, of recalling the experience, of participating in meetings attended, of participating in the ritual of going to work and of recollecting what happened along the way, or of participating in a party are all more important than when they occurred. The event, not the date, is how Afrocentric time is reckoned.

A Eurocentrist might view this orientation as ambiguous and unstructured, because a Eurocentrist mindset values prediction and control over the activity— the ability to control workers so that they predictably arrive for work at eight A.M. sharp, for instance. An Afrocentric view means that prediction and control, though understood, are less important. The issue here is the difference in *emphasis* between the two orientations, not in the ability to understand or even practice the one or the other concept of time. An Afrocentric view believes in and values mystical elements of the universe, believing further that we should live in spiritual harmony and unity with that universe. Those mystic elements include constant action and reaction in spontaneous, spiritually-driven rhythms. The rhythms of the universe are not fixed and static, but instead permit *improvisation*, or creatively changing the timing of an action to adapt to certain situations. The Afrocentric view of time undergirds its appreciation for *improvisation*, as opposed to prediction and control.

Improvisation

Black nationalist leader Malcolm X noted the Eurocentric and Afrocentric orientations to time as they relate to improvisation when he recalled his first attempt to dance:

> The white people danced as though somebody had trained them—left, one, two; right, three, four—the same steps and patterns over and over, as though somebody had wound them up. But those Negroes—nobody in the world could have choreographed the way they did whatever they felt—just grabbing partners, even the white chicks who came to the Negro dances. . . . Anyway, some couples were so abandoned and wide, improvising steps and movements—that you couldn't believe it. I could feel the beat in my bones, even though I had never danced. (Haley, 51)

Here is an example of Afrocentric emphasis upon improvising actions as they relate to the unfolding of nature, versus Eurocentric emphasis on prediction and control of when the dancer should move to the beat. Malcolm X understood Eurocentric-structured dancing, but he chose rhythmic dance—dance as natural as the rhythm of the heartbeat. Asante writes that "in a transpersonal sense, the more I recognize and develop my powers, the more human I become. I am in tune with the rhythm of the universe" (185).

The Afrocentric orientation emerges in rap and hip-hop (and their ancestor, jazz)—art forms that permit improvisation and ambiguity and resist an emphasis on prediction and control. Timing in hip-hop is more spontaneous and complex than in much other popular music of the 1980s. According to Asante,

> One of the most interesting facts about [the Afrocentric] search for transcendence is that although it is not calculated, but rhythmic, the rhythms change, move, flow towards harmony. . . . It is the same with athletes, who can "switch up" in terms of their movements but still be right in time with the rhythm. The way we learn to do that is to provide for the time what is not necessarily there; this is the essence of scatting, syncopation, possession. (195)

Because of the stress upon improvisation, Afrocentric discourse is not based upon a predictable flow of ideas, but upon a continuous cycle of action and reaction, and therefore constant activity. This view of discourse leads to certain ambiguities. Two does not necessarily follow one in the universe of Afrocentric discourse. Three may follow one and four may follow two if such an arrangement functions to meet the goal of harmony and unity within a spontaneous universe driven by give-and-take forces. This means that Afrocentric thought requires the participation, or reaction, of another person in the presentation of a text. This view, as it applies to rhetoric, also means that Eurocentric ideas of beginnings and endings are not emphasized. When and how the discourse begins or ends are not as important as the interrelationships within the discourse and the participation of agents who are creating the event. For instance, during a sermon, a black preacher might provide the black congregation with many reasons why God is good, then suddenly ask a specific member of the congregation to testify about how good God has been to her. Including a member of the congregation in the process of creating the sermon's message would not be expected in a Eurocentric church since such an act does not follow Eurocentric Protestant sermonic structure and form.

The audience's "affirmation" (or reaction) is a crucial part of Afrocentric discourse that is governed by a belief in communion between the audience and the message sender. This affirmation is viewed as an interruption in Eurocentric thought, because a response from the audience is considered untimely, something that breaks the linear flow of ideas of the speaker. How often do we see the congregation in a predominantly white Protestant church speak to the minister during a sermon? How often do such ministers elicit responses from the congregation during sermons? Eurocentrists might view this kind of behavior as undisciplined and unstructured. However, the Afrocentric purpose of the work is achieved through improvisation and participation, because the audience is as important to the process as the speaker. Since both the minister and the audience occupy the same time and space, responses from both create a natural balance. The minister might incorporate proverbs, rhythmic vocal sounds, figurative tropes, declarative statements, or stories; and any or all of these devices may be used by members of the congregation as well to achieve collective harmony and unity, not just persuasion. To ignore the audience is to destroy the unity of minister and audience acting together. In the world of African-derived discourse, this kind of improvisational interaction with the audience is referred to as *call-and-response*. Call-and-response is important to African-derived discourses such as sermons and storytelling, essential discourse forms that are aimed at educating and revitalizing communities.

We have seen how in just this one point of contention—views of time— Eurocentricity and Afrocentricity differ in perception of the surrounding world and arrangement of ideas and actions. It is important to realize that Eurocentric structure is dominant in our present rhetorical condition. Afrocentric views of time, or of other dimensions of experience, are rhetorical responses to, even struggles against, that dominant structure. African people use Afrocentric readings of the texts of experience so as to resist oppression.

Let us turn now to a consideration of how an Afrocentric reading of Spike Lee's *Do the Right Thing* might have helped shape an audience response to racial violence. We will consider specifically how two different cultures can interpret messages, forms, and style in strikingly dissimilar ways, as evidenced in reactions to this film.

Approaching *Do the Right Thing:* An Afrocentric Rhetorical Interpretation

Many factors contribute to a culture-centered orientation to life and language. So far, we have explored timing as an example of structural orientation from Afrocentric and Eurocentric perspectives. At the core of an Afrocentric orientation to life and structure are many other fundamental beliefs and values, including humanism, communalism, oppression/paranoia, empathetic understanding (as demonstrated by Spike Lee's call for responses to *Malcolm X* from Afrocentric writers and critics), rhythm, the principle of limited reward, and styling (Asante, 37). These beliefs and values are interrelated, not separate and distinct. In Afrocentric thought, "one must understand that to become human, to realize the promise of becoming human, is the only important task of the person. One becomes human only in the midst of others" (Asante, 185). These and other dimensions of Afrocentricity define what it means to be African people. It is a collective, not individual, vision.

Do the Right Thing can be read using many components of Afrocentric theory. It is a rich work, but the space constraints will limit our interpretation to some of the important moments of the film. We will focus our reading on the film's presentation of the conflict between Eurocentric structure and Afrocentric resistance to that structure's values of prediction, control, and hierarchy. This resistance to Eurocentric discourse is organized around an Afrocentric idea of five components of the communication process: (1) harmony and unity, (2) call (and caller), (3) response (and responder), (4) spiritual agents, and (5) *nommo*, including signifying, or indirection (see Knowles-Borishade).

These components of communication gain power from their interrelatedness. For instance, the caller must work toward harmony and unity through both spiritual agents (responders who fulfill the communication act) and *nommo*—the power of the spoken word. Thus, each component implies the other. Since the five components of the communicative process are interrelated and interactive, lines of demarcation are not always clear. And the interrelationships among harmony and unity, caller, spiritual agents, *nommo* and response are essential to how they function. As Asante writes, "We become seekers of the type of connections, interactions, and meetings that lead to harmony (p. 185)". These interrelationships allow the audience to participate by completing the circle or filling in the blanks—and by reaching a conclusion if they wish. The audience is as active as is the caller.

Do the Right Thing can be read Afrocentrically as presenting a picture of African communication patterns. More importantly, the film portrays those African patterns as preferred alternatives to Eurocentric communication patterns. An Afrocentric reading of the film sees Eurocentric assumptions about communication as a major source of the problem of racial oppression. Thus, African people can use an Afrocentric reading of the communication patterns shown in the film to *resist* that Eurocentric dominance. We will see how each of the five elements of Afrocentric communication can be used to ground that resistant reading.

Harmony and Unity

The notion of harmony and unity is the first and most crucial principle of Afrocentric rhetoric because it pervades all other parts of the communication process—callers, responders, spiritual agents, and *nommo*. Why are harmony and unity at the center of an Afrocentric communication model? Human life in traditional African societies is spiritually based, and the power of the divine spirit is evident in both sacred and secular rituals. Divine spirit is first and foremost in the activities of life within these societies, and that spirit can be seen in people and objects. There is a communal relationship between the divine spirit and the worshippers. Everyone is united by this divine power, which allows for the emergence of communal values.

Harmony and unity overcome divisions based upon structure and categorization. The ideas of right and wrong, good and bad, and love and hate are Eurocentric divisions or categories that have led to disharmony and confusion. Asante writes that "opposed to the bias of categorization is the wholistic view found in the traditional African world view" (184).

From an Afrocentric perspective, the characters and the action in *Do the Right Thing* show how communal harmony and unity resist the Eurocentric hierarchical power that requires structure and control and lacks a communal spirit. The white characters in the film—Sal, Pino, Vito, Clifton, Charlie, and the two police officers—are all there to control or dictate behavior within the African-American community. Rarely do these characters interact with the African-American cultures in anything other than a patronizing (or worse) way. They are there to step on African-American feet—to collect their money, to force them to turn off water, to regulate their cultural language, or to kill a member of the community; they are essentially there to control behavior and make it predictable. Despite this control, the idea of harmony and unity is the pervasive value in the actions of characters who resist the Eurocentric controllers. Mookie, Buggin' Out, Mother Sister, Da Mayor, Radio Raheem, Mister Señor Love Daddy, and the three Corner Men (Sweet Dick Willie, M. L., and Coconut Sid) attempt to foster understanding among themselves as well as with those whites who enter the predominantly black community. They search for answers to their immediate problems and assert their identities, using an Afrocentric style that the Eurocentric culture rejects.

It is the day-to-day experiences shown in the film—the sharing of both positive and negative experiences and the harmony and unity achieved through these experiences—that rings true for Afrocentric audiences. A Eurocentric perspective will see contradictions in the film: Mookie is sympathetic but "lazy," Buggin' Out is a leader yet is ignored, and so forth. But an Afrocentric reading will see the unity or harmony that transcends those contradictions. Afrocentric thought seeks out commonalities rather than differences.

The film's setting is a few blocks of the Bedford-Stuyvesant neighborhood in Brooklyn over a hot summer twenty-four-hour period, and the action takes place in the Italian-owned Sal's Famous Pizzeria, a black-operated radio station (WE LOVE 108 FM), Mookie's sister's apartment, and Mookie's girlfriend's mother's apartment, along with the sidewalks and streets of the neighborhood.

Mookie, a central character, lives with his sister, Jade, and works as a delivery boy at Sal's. Sal, an Italian-American, and his two sons, Pino and Vito, operate the local pizzeria in this African-American community. Mookie has a relationship with a Puerto Rican woman, Rosie, with whom he has a son. He assumes no responsibility for them. Sal and Pino are blatant racists, but Sal patronizes, while Pino antagonizes, African Americans. The film climaxes when tensions among Sal and two of Mookie's friends, Buggin' Out and Radio Raheem, result in Sal's destroying Radio Raheem's boombox and a fight between Sal and Raheem ensues. When apprehended, Radio Raheem suffers a brutal death at the hands of the New York City police officers. Mookie then leads his community in destroying Sal's Famous Pizzeria by breaking in and burning the place.

Though Mookie does burn down Sal's place at the end of the film, little about the African-American characters' actions throughout the film is violent. Buggin' Out, the self-styled political spokesperson who challenges the Eurocentric hierarchy, strives for community harmony and unity. Though Buggin' Out is a shallow character in some ways, he upholds the traditional community value of communal love that the community radio station, WE LOVE, symbolizes. In a scene in which the white yuppie Clifton rudely shoves him with his bike and dirties his new Air Jordan shoe, Buggin' Out asserts an ethic of righteousness and foregoes revenge. Buggin' Out's refusal to beat up the white neighbor, even though he gets peer pressure to fight back, tells us that though this man may be viewed as irritating by both black and white characters in the film, his ultimate choice is for harmony.

Buggin' Out asserts his cultural ethic during the confrontation: "Yo! Yo! You almost knocked me down man; the word is 'excuse me' . . . You lucky a black man has a loving heart." Beyond the materialism of a dirtied shoe is the fundamental issue of respect. Buggin' Out questions what he deems Clifton's lack of respect for his person (as evidenced in his pushing him without an apology); but Buggin' Out also questions Clifton's community values, since he lives in the black community but does not abide by the tenets of African-American culture. Nonetheless, harmony and unity generally govern the discourse of the African-American community in response to the Eurocentric structure during the confrontations in this film.

Harmony and unity also serve to resist the Eurocentric power structure when regulators visit to monitor and control community behavior. The most notorious regulators are the police. One scene in particular epitomizes the clash between Eurocentric and Afrocentric orientations to structure. Two white police officers are shown driving past the three "Corner Men," M. L., Sweet Dick Willie, and Coconut Sid, who sit on the street corner and reflect upon the experiences of everyday life with little concern for time. Coconut Sid ironically refers to the cops as "New York's finest." The scene of the police car's slow drive past the corner concludes with a statement by the officer driving the car, in reference to the Corner Men: "What a waste." Coconut Sid, from his corner, likewise says, "What a waste." Sid's underlying contention is that money is being spent for these regulators to patrol this quiet corner, these men's private place in which they have been "rudely interrupted."

Though Sid and the policeman use the same words, the meaning differs totally. The structural hierarchy the regulators represent is the opposite of Sid's. Sid views the structure as expendable; prediction and control of human behavior just for the sake of it is a waste of society's resources. But from the police officers' Eurocentric perspective, the Corner Men are unproductive citizens, useless to society in their dwelling on the street corner, their backs against the wall. But the film shows that the Corner Men subscribe to harmony and unity; we do not see them physically fighting the system, nor do they use the language of control to fight back.

The Corner Men complement other characters and their actions in the film. Mookie is another unassertive character, but he is the force behind the film's title and theme, "Do the right thing." The phrase embodies the ideal values of the black community in the film: humanism and empathetic understanding. But in the end, these values seem to dissolve. Thus, the film itself does not live up to the Eurocentric ideal of a happy ending or a tidy resolution. It places human weaknesses and flaws alongside the moral ideal; it exposes rather than resolves. These are ambiguities, and the film constantly reminds us of these ambiguities in life, people, and language. The theme of the film, from a Eurocentric view, is ambiguous, seeming to call for "right" while some actions of characters continue to do "wrong."

Harmony and unity (the pervasive value among good people) are not created in extensive dialogues about what constitutes the "right" thing to do, as might be expected in Eurocentric cultures, but in passing references, the acts of agents, and recurring symbols. The phrase, "Do the right thing," explicitly identifies the theme and is embodied in the advice of Da Mayor (a community sage) to Mookie: "Always do the right thing." Though Mookie is irresponsible as a father and boyfriend, he is also the agent for the community message. Da Mayor, Buggin' Out, and even Sal, urge Mookie to "do the right thing." Buggin' Out tells Mookie to "stay back." Mookie feels pressure to maintain allegiance to both the community and to his employer, Sal. His actions become ambiguous and the audience is not clear where he stands until the culminating act of the film, his throwing of the garbage can through the window of Sal's Famous Pizzeria after the police kill Radio Raheem. In the end, Mookie must make a real choice between his community and the hierarchy he unenthusiastically serves as delivery boy, where "orders" are taken regularly. Mookie's act stresses community unity over individual identity, and collective harmony over disharmony.

In another scene, Mookie communicates harmony and unity when he attempts to persuade Pino that there is an African origin of civilization and to educate him concerning the important contributions of famous African Americans. He includes Pino, Sal's son and an employee of Sal's Famous Pizzeria, in a dialogue about the community, knowing that Pino is generally angry toward blacks (though he idolizes a few token celebrities like Prince and Eddie Murphy). Despite Pino's blatantly racist language, Mookie refuses to engage in a confrontational exchange during this scene or any other where Pino insults African Americans; he opts instead for harmonious discourse. Conflict lurks at the corner of every action, keeping the audience in suspense. But until the end, moments of tension in the film result in only benign—and unresolved—confrontations. Problems are rarely resolved on the screen, leaving the audience to answer the question, or complete the form, on its own.

Harmony and unity are also illustrated in a scene suggesting a purification ritual. It is an extraordinarily hot summer day and the community gathers on the street near a fire hydrant. Two youths turn the hydrant on, and everyone plays in the water. Even the mentally impaired character, Smiley, participates. This can be read as a moment in which the community achieves harmony with nature. The full blast of the fire hydrant awakens the many community agents to participate in the moment of cooling off. Radio Raheem, accompanied by his boombox, does not physically participate in the water purification act and is granted respect and right of way. It is Raheem's transcendent spiritual status as a young sage that allows him to step outside this social ritual. The communal nature of this activity is further reinforced when a Eurocentric intruder, an Italian-American man, disrupts the purification ritual with his material concerns about his car and is not granted the right of way. This man is another rude intruder who has little patience for or understanding of the actions of this community, and eventually namecalling begins and conflict erupts. Beyond the issue of the car getting wet, the film shows direct confrontation with a man who prejudges the community response and antagonizes the community's members with his dictatorial tone.

The ever ready hierarchical controllers, the police, appear on the scene moments later. Da Mayor's response to police questioning about the incident shows that he is faithful to his community. When the police arrive, the intruder, Charlie, points to Da Mayor as a witness to what happened when he attempted to pass through the neighborhood. When the police ask Da Mayor to corroborate the outsider's story, he says, "Those that'll tell don't know; those that know won't tell." This proverb, words of wisdom commonly used in African-derived cultures, speaks for the community as an agent in resistance against the agencies of the hierarchy. With worn-out patience and a hostile attitude toward Da Mayor (the scene's spiritual agent), Charlie overtly links the proverb to Africa when he responds with, "What the fuck is that, voodoo shit?" This moment is especially important because it demonstrates a failure in communication between Charlie and Da Mayor. The audience can see that Charlie misunderstands Da Mayor; but here that misunderstanding is shown to be explicitly verbal, a matter of Charlie's being unable to "speak the language" of the community. A proverb just won't do for him; he seeks straight talk. But this community's orientation to language privileges indirection. Again, there is a rhetorical clash between an agent of the hierarchical power structure and an agent of community-based power.

Another important scene is Buggin' Out's criticism of the Wall of Fame at Sal's place. Unlike the Corner Men, Buggin' Out overtly challenges the Eurocentric structure when he questions Sal about the exclusion of African Americans on the Wall. Buggin' Out's request for the inclusion of African Americans on the Wall of Fame is a request for balance. The Wall of Fame exists within the larger black sphere of the Bedford-Stuyvesant community and is subsidized by that community. Buggin' Out seeks acknowledgment of community support for Sal's business in his request for African-American representation on Sal's Wall of Fame. He wants to include Sal in harmony and unity.

A love-hate theme is prominent in the film, and that theme has to do with harmony and unity and orientations to structure. First we must understand that in Eurocentric thought, structural and conceptual opposites are emphasized. But, from an Afrocentric view, structure and categories are less important when it comes to human relations. Asante writes that, in Eurocentricity, there is a *"bias of categorization,"* which divides people into teachers and those taught, sinners and saved, black and white, superior and inferior. Opposed to the bias of categorization is the wholistic view found in the traditional African world view" (184). The result of emphasizing commonalities rather than differences in views is ambiguity. Radio Raheem's "boxing match" between love and hate illustrates this ambiguity quite effectively. Raheem enacts a "boxing" scene between the right hand of love, "the soul of man," and the left hand of hate, "death and destruction." From an Afrocentric stance, Raheem does not depict love and hate as distinct, opposed categories. What he emphasizes instead is that the two forces coexist, knuckle to knuckle. Hatred and love are inseparable. In this scene we are given the most telling glimpse of Raheem's fundamental character—his own ethical sense. His character demonstrates his own coexistent feelings of hatred against the oppressor and love for his community. But, most importantly, he is faithful to brotherhood and to the community he loves. For instance, Raheem makes clear his love for Mookie during the storytelling. In the confrontation scene with Sal in the pizzeria, Raheem stands beside Buggin' Out and the community while he explodes in anger and hatred when Sal destroys the boombox, which is representative of the community voice, with a baseball bat. Hatred and love are coexistent forces from an Afrocentric point of view. But from a Eurocentric view, which divides or dichotomizes concepts, they are perceived as polar opposites.

Jade, Mookie's sister, communicates explicitly the value of community harmony and unity despite her individual differences with others about worthwhile means of empowering the community. When Buggin' Out discusses boycotting Sal's Pizzeria, Jade has little tolerance for Buggin' Out's militance. She declines participation in the boycott: "If you really tried hard, Buggin' Out, you could direct your energies in a more useful way. . . . Put me down for doing something positive." Though the scene reveals internal conflict within the community over the means to empowerment, harmony and unity transcend the conflict at the closing of the dialogue when Buggin' Out tells Jade, "I still love you, anyway" and Jade responds, "I still love you, Buggin' Out." Love of community supersedes individual differences. This affirmation of character despite disagreements operates throughout most of the film.

Finally, images of the Reverend Martin Luther King, Jr., and Malcolm X as symbols of black empowerment also serve to perpetuate harmony and unity. The spiritual presence of these leaders within the community is reinforced as Smiley attempts to sell copies of a rare photograph of the two leaders together. This photo is a mere image, from an Afrocentric view. The voice of the past ancestors remains alive as Smiley emphasizes that both the memory of these men and the hatred they resisted live on together. Therefore, a sale of the photo is not merely a capitalistic exchange but a renewal and affirmation of community. After a sale to Mookie, Smiley says in his slow stutter, "Thaaannnk you, blaaack man." Smiley serves as the reminder of community responsibility as he carries images of the past. In a sense, he appears to be an "interruption" in the film. But his existence as the bearer of this photo actually affirms the community's vitality by constantly reminding its members of the best they can be, and of the condition in which they now find themselves. Again, what Eurocentrists might consider a dichotomy—Smiley's silent voice set up against the politically inspiring voices of King and Malcolm X—is shown to be a unity.

The King-Malcolm X photograph surfaces again after the fire at Sal's, when Smiley places it on the wall, and again at the conclusion of the film, when a large, poster-size image of the two leaders is displayed on the screen following quotations from their respective philosophies. Neither of the leaders is presented individually. These images and quotations remind the audience of the ambiguity of love and hate because from an Afrocentric view, the ideas of these two leaders—though superficially incongruous—are not dichotomous, but an interactive unity.

The Call(er) and the Chorus

Eurocentric communication processes have traditionally been more linear and unidirectional than Afrocentric models of communication. In Eurocentric models, a sender conveys a message to a receiver, and though they share in the communicative process, the receiver does not participate in creating the message and its meaning. An Afrocentric model begins with a caller who initiates the rhetorical act in anticipation of a response from a community member or the community at large. The caller, while a major part of the communication process, differs from the Eurocentric speaker because the caller is not "in charge"; his or her intention does not delimit or legislate the meaning of what is said (Asante, 192–93).

The caller activates spiritual force through a direct relationship with God, spirits, nature, or higher truths—a spiritual force that creates unity between caller and listener(s). First among the many callers in Do the Right Thing are the two divinely inspired callers and spiritual agents who are deceased but whose voice, or nommo, continues to be heard in the community: Martin Luther King, Jr., and Malcolm X. Though they are dead, these community ancestors coexist with the Bedford-Stuyvesant community in the sphere of the living. Their voices as callers are heard through the words of Smiley and Buggin' Out, as well as through the quotations that appear on the screen at the conclusion of the film.

In addition to King and Malcolm X, there is a special group of spiritual callers made up of remembered and revered community role models. The film recalls these role models to the community through the voice of the radio announcer, Mister Señor Love Daddy. At one point Love Daddy calls out a roll call nearly fifty historical and contemporary black musicians from a dazzling variety of African-American musical styles. These community "voices"—Mahalia Jackson, Run-DMC, Stevie Wonder, Ella Fitzgerald, Prince, and others—are musical artists, but they also become participants in a "we," in the collective community, when Love Daddy announces their names on the radio and thanks them for making the Bedford-Stuyvesant community's "lives just a little brighter."

Closer to home, many of the people in the film's Bedford-Stuyvesant neighborhood function in the role of caller during various points of the film. The role of caller in Afrocentric theory is not static; anyone who awakens the community to new truths about themselves and their identities is a caller. The most consistent of these various callers in the film is Mister Señor Love Daddy. Love Daddy is the arbitrator. He encourages harmony and unity in the community. In the opening and closing morning scenes (separated by only 24 hours), Love Daddy literally calls to wake up the community with his playful, energetic language on WE LOVE Radio. The power of the spoken word rings through his vocal style and his frequent wordplay.

In another scene, Love Daddy calls both the theater audience's and the film community's attention to their actions. He calls a halt to a sequence of racial name-calling by Pino, Mookie, a Korean grocer, a Puerto Rican teenager, and a New York City police officer by addressing the camera directly and announcing, "This shit has got to stop right now!" Love Daddy is most frequently shown during transitions between scenes. From his storefront radio station, he links community calls with community responses through his empowered voice located in the center of the community.

Buggin' Out is the most notorious caller in the film. He is the community instigator. His goal is to awaken the people to the hierarchy that oppresses them. He calls for community support in boycotting Sal's Famous Pizzeria until Sal's Wall of Fame acknowledges the community that he serves. Buggin' Out's line, "Since we [blacks] spend so much money here, we do have some say," drives his campaign against Sal's. His message can be read as an attempt to achieve harmony and unity among white merchants like Sal and the black community. Buggin' Out gives a call to include Sal in this "We love" family that supports Sal's Famous Pizzeria and that loves his pizza. But Sal wants no part of it.

Sal's emphatic negative response to Buggin' Out's idea to include African Americans on the Wall of Fame constitutes a clash between the hierarchical controlling power and the spiritual power of the black community. He explicitly refers to the pizzeria as his own place, stressing the importance of individuality, not community: "This is my pizzeria. Only American Italians on the wall." Sal is a regulator who is most comfortable with his position as an overseer or a boss, not as a participant in the community. The irony of this aspect of the film is that Buggin' Out, as caller and instigator, asserts community dissatisfaction with the Wall of Fame. Yet most of the community disagrees with his plan to boycott Sal's. Though the values of the black community clash with Sal's, Da Mayor, Jade, and Mookie do not agree with Buggin' Out's approach. But a harmonious strategy for living transcends that disagreement. Harmony and unity remain the fundamental ideal that motivates the African-American characters in the film. All lines lead back to establishing a harmonious, collective "we."

Mookie functions as a community caller in the most controversial scene of the film when he throws a garbage can through the window of Sal's Famous Pizzeria. Until this scene in the film, Mookie has maintained a noncommittal stance, leaving the audience unsure of how he will respond at a moment of crisis. But the reverberations of Da Mayor's "Always do the right thing," Sal's "Do what you gotta do," and Buggin' Out's "Stay black," are hints at what will be Mookie's final, definitive stance. Mookie becomes the leader after the scene of police brutality, in which several of "New York's finest" kill Radio Raheem. For the first time, Mookie is given an important choice. He is shown, hand over face, during the agonizing moment that requires him to search for a higher truth, a truth from within. The moment of truth comes when Mookie takes on the role of caller, steering the community away from violence against people—action that defies harmony and unity. Instead, he guides the community toward venting their anger in action toward property, an action that is in closer keeping with community beliefs in nonviolence.

Finally, we must consider the role of the "chorus" in the film. A chorus of community members often accompanies the caller, and this chorus bears witness to the truth of the spoken word. The chorus is not necessarily comprised of spiritual agents who function as sages or "wise ones," but chorus members do act as witnesses who attest to the truth or validity of what is spoken. It is not the individual caller's voice, as agent, that invokes power. It is the collective interaction among the caller, the chorus if it exists, and responders who use *nommo* to lead the community collective to higher spiritual truths. The collective action of all these agents generates the power of *nommo*.

The film's teenagers—Punchy, Ahmad, Cee, and Ella—participate as a chorus when they attest to the truth of the word the caller espouses in several scenes. When the yuppie character Clifton steps on Buggin' Out's sneaker while walking his bike to his house in the neighborhood, the teenagers support and encourage the caller (Buggin' Out) as leader. They egg Buggin' Out on to confront the outsider who has intruded upon his private sphere and property. The chorus of teenagers is also vital to the scene that culminates in the climax of the film. This group's desire to order pizza after the official closing of the restaurant opens the door for confrontation between the hierarchy and community-based spiritual power. Though the teenagers unite behind Buggin' Out, Radio Raheem, and Smiley when they confront Sal about the Wall of Fame, they shun violence. In fact, Ella screams and yells during the fight between Sal and Radio Raheem as the confrontation moves toward violence.

Spiritual Agents

Through folklore passed down from slavery days, African-American culture has retained certain West African religious customs and rituals. These customs originated in the belief that spiritual powers govern an individual's action. Spiritual agents hold these powers and function as enablers of divine authority. They have special insight about ancestors (both living and dead) and deities. The spiritual forces give power and wisdom to people of the community so they may further the unity of the group. Spiritual agents, or sages, speak as judges and witnesses to foster harmony and unity. They are knowledgeable about the community's past and its present. These wise ones both describe and prescribe patterns of discourse (Asante, 103–8).

A trace of this spiritual agency is particularly evident in two characters in the film: Radio Raheem and Da Mayor. These two agents possess *spiritual* power, not controlling, or hegemonic, power. Their spiritual power affirms respect and self-esteem.

One of the best examples of this spiritual agency is Radio Raheem, a radio-blasting, tough-looking, and seemingly fierce character. Raheem commands respect for both himself and his community. Empowered by a near-mystical spirit, Raheem, armed with a blasting boombox, is a power symbol for the black community in the film. Raheem resists hierarchical power. He is granted the respect of the teenage "chorus" because of his authoritative presence. He seldom speaks, but his status in the community is affirmed in several scenes. The first is when Radio Raheem greets the teenage chorus with, "Peace y'all." The teenagers Ahmad and Punchy bow in praise of Raheem's spiritual force, toughness, and place in the community, saying things like "Peace, Radio Raheem; peace, man. You the man, I'm just visiting, it's your world . . . ; for real—in a big mutha fuckin way. . . . That boy's looking very large; he even walks in stereo. . . ." When he spots Radio Raheem, Mister Señor Love Daddy's ubiquitous voice chimes through his window at radio station WE LOVE across the street, joining the chorus as he responds over the air waves, "Radio Raheem blasting that big box, cold rocking scene." No one messes with Radio Raheem.

Later, when Raheem, in his transcendent status, avoids participating in the scene where the fire hydrant is opened to "cool" the community, the event callers acknowledge him and allow him to have the right of way without getting wet. In this scene, there is a tension between the water's cooling of the community, and Raheem's "natural cool." "Coolness" is a stylistic manifestation of the spiritual power Raheem possesses. He is depicted as too "cool" to get wet. "Cool" becomes his way to assert his power. Raheem's status as spiritual agent is even more clearly affirmed when the intruder Charlie and his new car are *not* allowed to pass through the scene without getting wet. Most importantly, beneath Raheem's cool militance is a fundamental belief in the value of harmony and unity in his community.

Da Mayor affirms his role as a spiritual agent in several scenes. Though a drunkard, Da Mayor possesses spiritually-derived powers as sage and promoter of harmony and unity; these powers show up in one scene in which he saves a child from death, and in another scene in which he defines the community ethic.

An important prerequisite for this spiritual gift is the love of human life and the community. Da Mayor explicitly affirms this love during a heated exchange with Mother Sister, when she challenges his character by ignoring him and he asserts his ethic by saying, "I love everybody." Da Mayor's most important role is to relay the proverb that provides the film's title to Mookie: "Always do the right thing." Here, however, we have a character who is partially ineffective in his role, because he does not use his spiritual power to resist alcohol, and he does not take the responsibility of acting as a mentor to his community.

The film addresses this conflict between the ideal and the real when the youthful Ahmad attacks Da Mayor's character. He accuses him of being drunken and irresponsible. Da Mayor retorts by calling Ahmad disrespectful—an allusion to his "natural" power as a community elder. What the film does in creating this conflict is point out how the natural power of spiritual agents is weakened by the hierarchical structures, and how the conflict between spiritual power and the dominant power ends in the eventual loss of the spirit. Da Mayor is no more than the man he is, but he clings to his belief in harmony and unity through love; "I love everybody, even you," he asserts to Mother Sister. He never lets go of this value, despite the fact that he is physically and spiritually broken. Both Mother Sister and Da Mayor serve to exemplify the stripping of this power, and the weakening of the spirit that results from living under oppression.

Nommo: *The Power of the Spoken Word*

We have discussed Afrocentric and Eurocentric orientations to life and language and alluded to the distinctive goals of each. In the Afrocentric view, less emphasis is placed on categories and structures. Instead there is emphasis upon the power of the divine spirit, which leads to a special emphasis on the spoken word as a spiritually enriched communicative form. From an Afrocentric view, the spoken word is power governed by the natural rhythm of life. Through the spoken word, or *nommo*, "I am in tune with the rhythm of the universe" (Asante, 185). The goal of life is to strive for harmony and unity, and oral language becomes a mechanism for transmitting life and spirit to, and sharing them with, others. Living language is the legacy of Afrocentrism.

Historically, orality has been the major communicative instrument in African-derived cultures. Compared to Eurocentric cultures, these cultures place less emphasis on the structures that accompany written language and more on the natural power of speaking and the inherent spiritual power of the human voice. The human voice gains its power from natural rhythms that each individual learns by looking inward, toward a relationship with the rhythm of the universe. Malcolm X's revelation about dance applies to language as well. To be in tune with the natural rhythm of life means that spoken language can become an instrument of improvisation. Unlike Eurocentric language that uses external structure as a means of control, the Afrocentric spoken word emphasizes spiritual- and self-governance. The aim is harmony and unity with the universe, and oral language permits "connections, interactions, and meetings that lead to harmony" (Asante, 185).

Nommo, for both callers and responders, does not depend upon a linear, structured way of presenting the spoken word. Afrocentric rhetoric may incorporate seemingly disparate ideas into the unfolding of a verbal work. This is because there may be voices that speak in harmony rather than a single voice uttered at any given moment. While one speaks, another joins in. While one event occurs, another event occurs.

Two fundamental components of Afrocentricity that apply to the spoken word are rhythm and styling. We have already discussed rhythm. Styling refers to a "conscious or unconscious manipulation of language or mannerisms to influence favorably the hearers of a message" (Mitchell-Kernan, 314). These gestures are both nonverbal and verbal, but the focus here is on the verbal. A specific verbal example of styling is signifying (see Chapter 4, pages 150–151). Signifying "incorporates essentially a folk notion that dictionary entries for words are not always sufficient for interpreting meanings or messages, or that meaning goes beyond such interpretations. Complimentary remarks may be delivered in a left-handed fashion. A particular utterance may be an insult in one context and not another" (Knowles-Borishade, 497).

The power of *nommo* as an instrument for signifying lies in its ability to stretch the normal limits of language semantically, linguistically, formally, and structurally. This understanding of language goes back to an Afrocentric view that (1) structure is negotiable, and (2) the human voice should be in tune with natural rhythms, not inflexible structures. The language of *nommo* is marked by ambiguities. "Stretching" the language may involve using a combination of metaphors, sentence reversals, punning, and vituperations on a person's character or the qualities of something—all to create an effect. Signifying implies repetition and indirection (saying one thing and meaning another, or using evasive language before making the point). Linguistic performance becomes ritualistic and rhythmic. When someone signifies, another may respond immediately with a "Back at you." Signifying, then, implies a call-and-response dynamic in African-derived cultures—a form of talking back.

Consider this call-and-response among M. L., Sweet Dick Willie, and Coconut Sid, in which the strategy of indirection operates:

M. L.:   Sweet Dick Willie . . .

Willie: That's my name.

M. L.:   Damn man, do I have to spell it out?

Sid: Come on man, make it plain.

M. L.:   Okay, but listen up. I'm gonna break it do-o-o-wn.

Willie: Let it be broke, mutha fucka!

M. L.:   Can you dig it?

Willie: It's dug.

This signifying dialogue precedes the Corner Men's discussion of the African-American condition. Following this dialogue, M. L. proceeds with his point about the Korean business in the neighborhood. Here, however, the participants are speaking indirectly, dealing with the nuances of language before making a point. From a Eurocentric view, this interaction seems to waste time and detract from the point.

Another characteristic of signifying is vituperation—heaping insults on a victim. In one scene, Sweet Dick Willie leads the spewing forth of insults as he signifies on Mike Tyson. Willie begins his vituperative ritual with

Fuck Mike Tyson. Mike Tyson ain't shit. I remember when he mugged that woman right there on Lexington. . . . I ain't scared of no goddamn Mike Tyson. I'll drop him like a bad habit. . . . If Mike Tyson dream about whuppin' my ass, he'd better wake up and apologize.

The heaping of insults proceeds as Willie goes onto signify M. L., who has a vision of owning a boat (a mechanism of escape from the hot day). Willie says,

> You fool, you thirty cents away from having a quarter, how in the fuck you gonna get a boat? . . . Look at you, you raggedy as a roach, eat the holes outa donuts. . . . Not in them raggedy-ass shoes; shoes so run over, he gotta lay down to put 'em on.

Mister Senor Love Daddy also exemplifies Afrocentric styling through the signifying of rap. He is a master of sentence reversals (a rhetorical trope known as *epanados*):

> Wake up. Wake up, wake up, wake up. Up you wake, up you wake, up you wake, up you wake. . . . Here I am, am I here? You know it, it you know. . . . What can I say? Say what I can. I saw it, but I didn't believe it; I didn't believe it what I saw. Are we gonna live together? Together are we gonna live?

The power of *nommo* rings through Love Daddy's frequent play on the word *truth*: "t-ruth, Ruth." Love Daddy's style of delivery transforms the word *truth* from "Double Truth-Ruth" to "Triple Truth-Ruth," and finally to "Quintessential Truth-Ruth," each form going further in its play with rhythmic and rhyming sounds. *Nommo* is about natural, spiritual power. Its aim is harmony and unity, which means that its language form and voice conflict with the hierarchical voice of Eurocentric persuasion. The best example of this conflict is the exchange between Charlie and Da Mayor in the fire hydrant scene. Charlie rejects the proverbial wisdom of Da Mayor who says, "Those that'll tell don't know; those that know won't tell," rejecting Da Mayor's words as "voodoo" language. Eurocentric culture often perceives specifically Afrocentric uses of language as unclear, indirect, and mysterious. But the Afrocentric orientation remains a special power in discourse, and it has influenced the style of many charismatic orators of our time, including Martin Luther King, Jr., and Malcolm X.

The Responders

The call-and-response tradition in African oral discourse is the root of performances that encourage audience participation. Responders "are secondary creators in the event, containing among them a vital part of the message." They hear the call from the initiator and contribute to the completion of the act. This relationship between artist and audience is one of the most significant features retained in both sacred and secular discourse forms by African-American communities. The most familiar forum for this exchange is black religious worship, where there is frequent interaction between the minister and the congregation. But call-and-response is a defining feature of many African-derived art forms, including music and dance.

Responders contribute to the cycle of action and reaction in numerous ways. This means that a critic can look at the role of responders and responses in the creation of discourse at different levels. At one level, a critic might do a close analysis of the interaction between the caller and the actual audience for the discourse during a live event. A critic might provide the context for the rhetorical event and record when and where calls and responses come during the course of the event; he or she could then analyze and interpret how this interactive dynamic functions to achieve the goal of harmony and unity. At another level, a critic might identify a watershed, or pivotal, moment of action within a rhetorical piece where, for instance, a crucial decision is made and responders, either those referred to in the discourse or the actual audience for the rhetoric, participate in the event.

Do the Right Thing provides an important watershed moment of action that can be read as calling both the audience within the film *and* the audience in the theater to respond. That moment follows the New York City police officers' brutal killing of Radio Raheem. The conflict that leads to Raheem's death at the hands of that controlling agency develops because of the Wall of Fame controversy. When Buggin' Out finds support from Radio Raheem in demanding the inclusion of famous African Americans on the Wall, both men confront Sal. In this scene, Sal's weapon, the baseball bat, is used to crush Radio Raheem's boombox, a symbolic voice of the Bedford-Stuyvesant community. A physical fight follows the destruction of the boombox, and the New York City police arrive at the scene. When these regulators arrive, Buggin' Out and Radio Raheem are taken in custody as Buggin' Out yells, "You're taking me down; you're not taking Vito or Pino or Sal out!" Eventually, one police officer kills Radio Raheem by choking him with a nightstick. The killing of Raheem is a symbolic attempt to kill the community's spirit—an act that stirs the community to a response that attempts to regain the objective of harmony and unity.

Sal inadvertently sanctions Mookie's choice to throw the garbage can through his window by saying, "You gotta do what you gotta do," a phrase he echoes twice to Mookie during the story. Da Mayor affirms Mookie's decisive choice to "always do the right thing." Mookie finds himself the leader and liaison between the community's weakened spiritual power, symbolized by the destruction of the boombox, and the transcendent truths that counter an oppressive power structure. The community joins in the ritual act and reclaims its voice by destroying the Wall of Fame and the property where this symbol of oppressive power resides. It is a moment of frustration that symbolizes the miscommunication between the orientation by which these community members live and the Eurocentric orientation.

The film seizes this moment to show what happens when the power structure breaks the last vestiges of the spirit of harmony and unity. The act of throwing the garbage can into the window is followed by further destruction of the property and finally, the burning of Sal's Famous Pizzeria. The firefighters who come to the scene spray the restaurant and turn the hoses violently on the community members. The community repeatedly chants the words "Howard Beach," a reminder to the audience of the racially-motivated killing of a black youth in Queens. The African-American community claims its place in this scene when firefighters tell members of the community to "Go home" and they respond, "This is our home!"

A powerful moment follows the ritual act of the destruction of Sal's, in the symbolic resurrection of the community voice through the resounding song,

"Fight the Power", which is played over the closing scene of the charred boombox. The playing of this song, along with the placement of the photographs of Malcolm X and Martin Luther King, Jr., in the ruins of the pizzeria by Smiley (who, for the first time, smiles) assert the communal spirit and the resilience of the black community, despite the oppressive power structure that surrounds it. Two prominent spiritual agents, Da Mayor and Mother Sister, continue to "stand." Mother Sister makes clear that "we're still standing," even though the block's buildings may be destroyed. The community's resilience can be read as a sign of the continuation of the cycle of oppression and resistance.

Conclusion

The cycle of racial violence in New York City did not begin with the 1986 Howard Beach incident, and it will not likely end with another single incident. But culture-centered criticism can help explain the rhetoric inspired by the Howard Beach incident and other racial crimes. At the core of one culture-centered perspective, Afrocentrism, is the value of harmony and unity. There are several other important theoretical tenets of Afrocentric theory, some of which are still being developed. This chapter has focused on several components of Afrocentric theory in its analysis of Spike Lee's *Do the Right Thing*.

This film can be read as a story that plays out the clash between two orientations toward life and discourse—one that encourages a linear, hierarchical structure in life and language, and another that resists the emphasis upon this structure and instead emphasizes improvisation. Lee develops strong characters who can be read as callers, responders, and spiritual agents that ascribe to *nommo* and are guided by the central value of harmony and unity. Lee portrays these roles (of caller, responder, and spiritual agent) as a natural part of his characters' lives as they are played out in routine community encounters. There is a clash between the spiritually empowered discourse that these characters assert and the hierarchical orientation of the agents (such as the police) who monitor the community, exerting dominance over the values of the black community. These intrusive outsiders assume a lack of discipline and respect within the African-American community, monitoring and controlling that community with little knowledge of, or respect for, its cultural orientation.

Do the Right Thing does not represent an in-depth investigation of community understanding, nor does it demonstrate clear-cut solutions to the problem of racial violence. It functions instead as a response to racial violence by portraying the events of everyday experience in an African-American urban community. The film's characters present life as experienced in an African-derived culture, and they often simply do not respond to the serious questions of racial discord. From an Afrocentric view, these questions are left for audience response. The audience must complete the circle. Closure, or problem-solving, within a work is a Eurocentric concept. All in all, an Afrocentric interpretation of *Do the Right Thing* highlights the value of harmony and unity, and asserts the importance of community participation amidst perceived threats of annihilation at the hands of the existing power structures.

Stepping Back From the Critique of *Do the Right Thing*

This chapter has provided an illustration of one approach to culture-centered criticism, one grounded specifically in Afrocentricity. We have noted previously that culture-centered criticism can proceed from grounding in *any* culture. Afrocentricity was chosen as the mode of analysis here because of the nature of the film and the cultural orientations of those who made it.

We all belong to one or more cultures, and we all have perspectives based on those cultural groundings. So one way you might react to the criticism presented in this chapter is to disagree with it on the basis of your own cultural background. Perhaps you do not know exactly *why* you disagree, just that you do. Think about why your own cultural background might cause you to read the film differently. What about your cultural orientation might cause you to ask different questions or come to different conclusions than those presented in this chapter?

What we are trying to stress here is the fact that not only is *Do the Right Thing* controversial, but ways of understanding it, of saying what it means, are controversial as well. Consider just one example. The author of this critique argues that the dramatic scene in which Mookie throws a garbage can through the window of the pizzeria shows a move *away* from violence. Yet others may well read that action as a move *toward* violence. What is the source of those different readings? Can the conflict between these two readings be resolved? Should it be? Think about other readings of the film presented here and, if you disagree with them, try to explain what the source of that disagreement is. You might remember, as you do so, this author's argument that an Afrocentric reading of the film *serves* the African-American community as a way to resist and respond to racial violence. Is that what you want your reading of the film to do? If not, you might use the film in a different way, for a different purpose. What might the purpose be?

Bibliography
● ● ● ● ● ● ● ● ● ● ● ● ● ● ●

Chapters 1–4

Adorno, T. W. 1973. *The jargon of authenticity.* Evanston, IL: Northwestern University Press.

Altheide, D. L. 1985. *Media Power.* Beverly Hills, CA: Sage Publications, Inc.

Altheide, D. L. and R. P. Snow. 1979. *Media logic.* Beverly Hills, CA: Sage Publications, Inc.

Althusser, L. 1971. *Lenin and philosophy and other essays.* Trans. B. Brewster. New York: Monthly Review Press.

Asante, M. K. 1987. *The Afrocentric idea.* Philadelphia: Temple University Press.

Brummett, B. 1981. Gastronomic reference, synecdoche, and political image. *Quarterly Journal of Speech* 67:138–45.

———. 1984. Burke's representative anecdote as a method in media criticism. *Critical Studies in Mass Communication* 1:161–76.

Bryant, D. C. 1953. Rhetoric: Its function and its scope. *Quarterly Journal of Speech* 39:401–24.

Buhle, P. 1987. *Popular culture in America.* Minneapolis: University of Minnesota Press.

Burke, K. 1937. *Attitudes toward history.* New York: The New Republic.

———. [1935] 1965. *Permanence and change.* Reprint. Indianapolis: The Bobbs-Merrill Company, Inc.

———. 1966. *Language as symbolic action.* Berkeley: University of California Press.

———. [1945] 1969a. *A grammar of motives.* Reprint. Berkeley: University of California Press.

———. [1950] 1969b. *A rhetoric of motives.* Reprint. Berkeley: University of California Press.

———. 1973. *The philosophy of literary form.* 3d ed. Berkeley: University of California Press.

Cha, T. H. K., ed. 1980. *Apparatus.* New York: Tanam Press.

Chambers, I. 1986. *Popular culture: The metropolitan experience.* New York: Methuen.

Daniel, J. and G. Smitherman. 1976. How I got over: Communication dynamics in the black community. *Quarterly Journal of Speech* 62:26–39.

Derrida, J. 1978. *Writing and difference.* Trans. A. Bass. Chicago: University of Chicago Press.

Fisher, W. K. 1984. Narration as a human communication paradigm: The case of public moral argument. *Communication Monographs* 51:1–22.

———. 1985. The narrative paradigm: An elaboration. *Communication Monographs* 52:347–67.

Fiske, J. 1989a. *Reading the popular.* Boston: Unwin Hyman.

————. 1989b. *Understanding popular culture*. Boston: Unwin Hyman.

Frye, N. 1964. *The educated imagination*. Bloomington, IN: Indiana University Press.

Gates, H. L., Jr. 1988. *The signifying monkey: A theory of African-American literary criticism*. New York: Oxford University Press.

Gerbner, G., L. Gross, M. Morgan, and N. Signorielli. 1980. The "mainstreaming" of America: Violence profile no. 11. *Journal of Communication* 30:10–29.

Hall, S. 1985. Signification, representation, ideology: Althusser and the post-structuralist debates. *Critical Studies in Mass Communication* 2:91–114.

Heath, S. and G. Skirrow. 1986. An interview with Raymond Williams. In *Studies in entertainment: Critical approaches to mass culture*, ed. T. Modleski, 3–17. Bloomington: Indiana University Press.

Jameson, F. 1981. *The political unconscious: Narrative as a socially symbolic act*. Ithaca, NY: Cornell University Press.

Kinneavy, J. 1972. *A Theory of Discourse*. Englewood Cliffs, N.J.: Prentice Hall, Inc.

Kramer, C. 1974. "Women's Speech: Separate But Unequal?" *Quarterly Journal of Speech* 60:14–24.

Kuhn, A. 1985. *The Power of the Image*. London: Routledge and Kegan Paul.

Leff, M. C. and F. J. Kauffeld, eds. 1989. *Texts in context: Critical dialogues on significant episodes in American political rhetoric*. Davis, CA: Hermagoras Press.

Meyrowitz, J. 1985. *No sense of place: The impact of electronic media on social behavior*. New York: Oxford University Press.

Modleski, T., ed. 1986. *Studies in entertainment: Critical approaches to mass culture*. Bloomington, IN: Indiana University Press.

Mukerji, C. and M. Schudson. 1986. Popular culture. *Annual Review of Sociology* 12:47–66.

Nelson, C., and L. Grossberg, eds. 1988. *Marxism and the Interpretation of Culture*. Urbana, IL: The University of Chicago Press.

Postman, N. 1985. *Amusing ourselves to death: Public discourse in the age of show business*. New York: Penguin Books.

Richards, I. A. 1936. *The philosophy of rhetoric*. New York: Oxford University Press.

Rogin, Michael P. 1987. *Ronald Reagan the movie, and other episodes in political demonology*. Los Angeles: University of California Press.

Snow, R. P. 1987. Interaction with mass media: The importance of rhythm and tempo. *Communication Quarterly* 35:225–37.

Toulmin, S. 1958. *The Uses of Argument*. London: Cambridge University Press.

Treichler, P. A. and C. Kramarae. 1983. "Women's Talk in the Ivory Tower." *Communication Quarterly*, 31:118–132.

Williams, R. 1976. *Keywords: A vocabulary of culture and society*. New York: Oxford University Press.

————. 1977. *Marxism and literature*. New York: Oxford University Press.

Chapter 5

A time to weep. Oct. 22, 1987. *Milwaukee Journal*, A8.

Ahlgren, P. Oct. 15, 1987. Mother of fire victims always wanted many children, relative says. *Milwaukee Journal*, A16.

Bargren, P. Oct. 15, 1987. Drawn together: Spaulding, Carr long crossed paths. *Milwaukee Journal*, B1–2.

Bednarek, D. I. Oct. 22, 1987. Integration lawsuit settled. *Milwaukee Journal*, A1.

———. Oct. 25, 1987. Education of minorities emerges as top priority. *Milwaukee Journal*, B1–2.

Breyfogle, W. Oct. 22, 1987. The good servant: St. Mark's AME Church is a bastion of concern. *Milwaukee Journal*, D19–20.

Christopulos, M. Oct. 1, 1987. Loss of grandson brought back a painful memory. *Milwaukee Sentinel* Part 1, 12.

Cole, J. Nov. 5, 1987. Study details barriers to minority gains. *Milwaukee Sentinel* Part 1, 1.

Conrad, K. Oct. 25, 1987. Direct payments might help [Letter]. *Milwaukee Journal*, J20.

Cunibert, B. Oct. 11, 1987. Quiet death to freedom. *Milwaukee Journal*, J1–2.

Cuprisin, T. and M. Lisheron. Oct. 25, 1987. Stabbing victim dies; had gone to clinic first. *Milwaukee Journal*, B1–2.

Davidian, G. Oct. 22, 1987. Sister of fire victims blames gas rates, heaters. *Milwaukee Journal*, A8.

Davidian, G. and J. L. Katz. Oct. 15, 1987. Smoke alarm rule backed. *Milwaukee Journal*, A16.

De Atley, R. Oct. 6, 1987. The musical genius is an eccentric man-child. *Milwaukee Journal* XTRA, 10.

Deger, R. Nov. 12, 1987. Shaw defends free tuition plan as youth incentive. *UWM Post*, 1.

Deshotels, M. M. Oct. 25, 1987. Aid cuts hit families hard [Letter]. *Milwaukee Journal*, J20.

Differences need not be divisive; society works best with racial harmony [collection of untitled letters]. Nov. 15, 1987. *Milwaukee Journal*, J12.

Dlugi, J. Nov. 15, 1987. Letters to the Editor. *Milwaukee Journal*, J13.

Esposito, K. Oct. 16, 1987. 300 protest racism, response on UW-Madison campus. *Milwaukee Journal*, A12.

———. Nov. 9, 1987. 2 stories of pain, prejudice. *Milwaukee Journal*, A1.

Faust, P. Oct. 15, 1987. Brewers' Sheffield is arrested again. *Milwaukee Journal*, C2.

Funeral set for woman slain in Northwest Side apartment. Nov. 11, 1987. *Milwaukee Journal*, B11.

Gilbert, C. Oct. 11, 1987. Fire victims at rest at last. *Milwaukee Journal*, B1.

———. Nov. 9, 1987. Blacks count the reasons for long bus ride. *Milwaukee Journal*, B1–2.

Gill, B. and R. Romell, Nov. 5, 1987. Diverse social ills had role in tragedy. *Milwaukee Sentinel* Part 1, 1.

Gribble, J. Oct. 15, 1987. 2nd of 3 charged with killing vendor arrested in Arkansas. *Milwaukee Journal*, B1–2.

Guensberg, C. Oct. 6, 1987. Who's that man in the mirror, Michael? *Milwaukee Journal* XTRA, 10.

Hajewski, D. Oct. 16, 1987. Poverty forces families to double up. *Milwaukee Journal*, B1–6.

Jackson, D. Oct. 22, 1987. An American place. *Milwaukee Journal*, D11.

Jankowski, M. E. Oct. 25, 1987. Reporters showed sensitivity [Letter]. *Milwaukee Journal*, J20.

Jones, R. P. Nov. 1a, 1987. Dean defends UW action in cases of racism. *Milwaukee Journal*, A1.

———. Nov. 1b, 1987. Racist incidents hurt UW recruiting efforts. *Milwaukee Journal*, A1.

———. Nov. 9a, 1987. 2 stories of pain, prejudice. *Milwaukee Journal*, A1.

———. Nov. 9b, 1987. UW dean stays calm in storm over racism. *Milwaukee Journal*, A6.

Kasten, Jr., R. W. Oct. 25, 1987. Heat assistance vital [Letter]. *Milwaukee Journal*, J20.

Kissinger, M. Oct. 16, 1987. Blueprint for tragedy. *Milwaukee Journal*, A1.

Kissinger, M. and G. C. Rummler. Oct. 15, 1987. Once again, 5 firemen feel helpless. *Milwaukee Journal*, B1–2.

Knoche, E. Nov. 5, 1987. Mother in filthy home didn't know how to flush toilet. *Milwaukee Sentinel* Part 1, 5.

Kren, M. Oct. 15a, 1987. A refrain of grief resounds. *Milwaukee Journal*, B1–2.

———. Oct. 15b, 1987. Suffering called heart, soul of King, Malcolm X. *Milwaukee Journal*, D2.

Lynch, K. A. Oct. 22, 1987. A new cornerstone. *Milwaukee Journal*, D4.

McCallister, M. Nov. 12, 1987. Milwaukee Urban League study. *UWM Post*, 1.

Mitchard, J. Oct. 15, 1987. Grief will come, but not just yet. *Milwaukee Journal*, A1.

———. Oct. 23, 1987. Rise up: Family privately recalls 5 lives. *Milwaukee Journal*, B1.

Morvay, J. E. Oct. 1, 1987. Grandmother didn't get last goodby. *Milwaukee Sentinel* Part 1, 1.

Mulvey, M. Nov. 5, 1987. Peer pressure called main obstacle for black students. *Milwaukee Sentinel* Part 1, 5.

News at six. Oct. 15, 1987. Television broadcast. Milwaukee: WITI-TV.

News 4. Milwaukee Oct. 15, 1987. Television broadcast. Milwaukee: WTMJ-TV.

Norris, T. Oct. 8, 1987. Taking a chance on love. *Milwaukee Journal*, D1–2.

Richfield, I. Oct. 25, 1987. High birth rates unhealthy [Letter]. *Milwaukee Journal*, J20.

Romell, R. Oct. 1, 1987. Loss of life is worst in 104 years. *Milwaukee Sentinel* Part 1, 1.

Romell, R. and B. Gill. Nov. 4, 1987. Fatal fire wasn't the first tragedy for family plagued by poverty. *Milwaukee Sentinel* Part 1, 1.

Schultze, S. Oct. 25, 1987. Learnfare may mean turmoil for schools. *Milwaukee Journal*, 1A.

Short, C. R. Nov. 15, 1987. Colleges should show intolerance of racism [Letter]. *Milwaukee Journal*, J13.

Six children killed in house fire. Oct. 15, 1987. *Milwaukee Journal*, A1.

Survivor goes home. Oct. 7, 1987. *Milwaukee Journal*, A1.

Sussman, L. Oct. 16, 1987. School hears pupils' fears about fire. *Milwaukee Journal*, A6.

Sykes, Jr., L. Nov. 17, 1987. Things had been looking up before slaying, husband says. *Milwaukee Journal*, B1.

The ten o'clock channel 12 news. Oct. 15, 1987. Television broadcast. Milwaukee: WISN-TV.

Tessler, R. Oct. 25, 1987. Fathers shirk responsibility [Letter]. *Milwaukee Journal*, J20.

Thomas, J. C. Oct. 25, 1987. Landlords too often blamed [Letter]. *Milwaukee Journal*, J20.

Ward, M. Nov. 15, 1987. Grim echoes. *Milwaukee Journal, Milwaukee Magazine*, 6.

Wilkerson, L. Oct. 25, 1987. Child and fire experts sort through the flames. *Milwaukee Journal*, G5.

Chapter 6

ABC Television Network. Aug. 8, 1984. 1984 Summer Olympic Games.

Althusser, L. 1971. *Lenin and philosophy and other essays.* Trans. B. Brewster. New York: Monthly Review Press.

Altman, R. 1986. Television/sound. In *Studies in entertainment: Critical approaches to mass culture*, ed. T. Modleski, 39–54. Bloomington: Indiana University Press.

Augst, B. 1980. The lure of psychoanalysis in film theory. In *Apparatus*, ed. T. H. K. Cha, 415–37. New York: Tanam Press.

Barthes, R. 1980. Upon leaving the movie theater. In *Apparatus*, ed. T. H. K. Cha, 1–6. New York: Tanam Press.

Baudry, J.-L. 1980a. The apparatus. In *Apparatus*, ed. T. H. K. Cha, 41–66. New York: Tanam Press.

———. 1980b. Ideological effects of the basic cinematographic apparatus. In *Apparatus*, ed. T. H. K. Cha, 25–40. New York: Tanam Press.

Coakley, J. 1986. *Sport in society: Issues and controversies.* St. Louis: Times Mirror/Mosby.

Comisky, P., J. Bryant, and D. Zillman. 1977. Commentary as a substitute for action. *Journal of Communication* 27:150–53.

Dorr, A. 1986. *Television and children: A special medium for a special audience.* Beverly Hills: Sage Publications, Inc.

Duncan, M. C. and B. Brummett. 1987. The mediation of spectator sport. *Research Quarterly for Exercise and Sport* 58:168–77.

———. 1989. Types and sources of spectating pleasure in televised sports. *Sociology of Sport Journal* 7:195–211.

ESPN Television Network. Dec. 1, 1985. Great Alaskan shootout: Purdue University–University of Arizona [televised basketball].

Ellis, J. 1982. *Visible fictions: Cinema, television, video.* London: Routledge and Kegan Paul.

Featherstone, M. 1991. *Consumer culture and postmodernism.* London: Sage Publications, Inc.

Fiske, J. 1987. *Television culture.* London: Methuen.

———. 1989a. *Understanding popular culture.* Boston: Unwin Hyman.

———. 1989b. *Reading the popular.* Boston: Unwin Hyman.

Flitterman-Lewis, S. 1987. Psychoanalysis, film, and television. In *Channels of discourse: Television and contemporary criticism,* ed. R. C. Allen, 172–210. Chapel Hill: University of North Carolina Press.

Gantz, W. 1981. An exploration of viewing motives and behaviors associated with television sports. *Journal of Broadcasting* 25:263–75.

Hall, S. 1985. Signification, representation, ideology: Althusser and the post-structuralist debates. *Critical Studies in Mass Communication* 2:91–114.

———. (1988). The toad in the garden: Thatcherism among the theorists. In *Marxism and the interpretation of culture,* eds. C. Nelson and L. Grossberg, 35–57. Urbana, IL: University of Illinois Press.

Kuhn, A. 1982. *Women's pictures.* London: Routledge and Kegan Paul.

Lacan, J. 1977. *Écrits.* Trans. A. Sheridan. New York: Basic Books.

Metz, C. 1981. The fiction film and its spectator: A metapsychological study. In *Apparatus,* ed. T. H. K. Cha, 373–414. New York: Tanam Press.

Meyrowitz, J. 1985. *No sense of place: The impact of electronic media on social behavior.* New York: Oxford University Press.

Morris, B. S. and J. Nydahl. 1983. Toward analyses of live television broadcasts. *Central States Speech Journal* 34:195–202.

Morse, M. 1983. Sport on television: Replay and display. In *Regarding television,* ed. E. A. Kaplan, 44–66. Los Angeles: American Film Institute/University Publications of America.

Mulvey, L. 1975. Visual pleasure and narrative cinema. *Screen* 16:6–18.

NBC Television Network. July 4, 1986. Wimbledon Lawn Tennis Championships: Women's Doubles Semi-finals.

NBC Television Network. July 6, 1986. Wimbledon Lawn Tennis Championships: Men's Doubles Finals.

NBC Television Network. July 10, 1988. McDonald's United States Gymnastic Championships.

Nichols, B. 1981. *Ideology and the image.* Bloomington: Indiana University Press.

Nielsen Company, A. C. 1988. Sports Report (based on total network television sports viewing for 1987 and drawn from personal communication with K. Polanski, Media Department, July 26).

Novak, M. 1976. *The joy of sports.* New York: Basic Books.

Pressdee, M. 1986. Agony or ecstasy: Broken transitions and the new social state of working-class youth in Australia. *Occasional Papers,* S. Australian Center for Youth Studies, S.A. College of A.E., Magill, S. Australia.

Prisuta, R. H. 1979. Televised sports and political values. *Journal of Communication* 29:94–102.

Rojek, C. 1985. *Capitalism and leisure theory*. London: Tavistock Publications Ltd.

Shields, R. 1989. Social spatialization and the built environment: The West Edmonton mall. *Environment and Planning D: Society and Space* 7:147–64.

Silverman, K. 1983. *The subject of semiotics*. New York: Oxford University Press.

Sewart, J. L. 1986. The commodification of sport. In *Media, audience, and social structure*, eds. S. J. Ball-Rokeach and M. G. Cantor, 174–88. Beverly Hills, CA: Sage Publications, Inc.

Urry, J. 1990. *The tourist gaze: Leisure and travel in contemporary societies*. London: Sage Publications, Inc.

Williams, B. R. 1977. The structure of televised football. *Journal of Communication* 27:140–49.

Chapter 7

Asante, M. K. 1987. *The Afrocentric idea*. Philadelphia: Temple University Press.

Haley, A. [1965] 1987. *The autobiography of Malcolm X*. Reprint. New York: Ballantine.

Knowles-Borishade, A. F. 1991. Paradigm for classical African orature: Instrument for a scientific revolution? *Journal of Black Studies* 21:488–500.

Mitchell-Kernan, C. [1973] 1990. Signifying. In *Mother wit from the laughing barrel: Readings in the interpretation of Afro-American folklore*, rev. ed., A. Dundes, 310–328. Jackson, MS: University Press of Mississippi.

Suggested Readings
●●●●●●●●●●●●●●●●●●●●●

Marxist Criticism

Allor, M. 1988. Relocating the site of the audience. *Critical Studies in Mass Communication* 5:217–33.

Baudrillard, J. 1981. *For a critique of the political economy of the sign.* St. Louis: Telos Press.

Becker, S. L. 1984. Marxist approaches to media studies: The British experience. *Critical Studies in Mass Communication* 1:66–81.

Centre for Contemporary Cultural Studies. *Culture, media, language.* London: Hutchinson.

Collins, R., J. Curran, N. Garnham, P. Scannell, P. Schlesinger, and C. Sparks, eds. 1986. *Media, culture, and society.* Beverly Hills, CA: Sage Publications, Inc.

Corcoran, F. 1984. Television as ideological apparatus: the power and the pleasure. *Critical Studies in Mass Communication* 1:131–45.

Eagleton, T. 1983. *Literary theory.* Minneapolis: University of Minnesota Press.

Fiske, J. 1983. The discourses of TV quiz shows or, school + luck = success + sex. *Central States Speech Journal* 34:139–50.

———. 1986. Television and popular culture: Reflections on British and Australian critical practice. *Critical Studies in Mass Communication* 3:200–216.

———. 1986. Television: polysemy and popularity. *Critical Studies in Mass Communication* 3:391–408.

———. 1988. Meaningful moments. *Critical Studies in Mass Communication* 5:246–51.

Gramsci, A. 1971. *Selections from the prison notebooks.* Trans. Q. Hoare and G. N. Smith. New York: International Publishers.

Grossberg, L. 1984. Strategies of Marxist cultural interpretation. *Critical Studies in Mass Communication* 1:392–421.

Gurevitch M., T. Bennett, J. Curran, and J. Wollacott. 1982. *Culture, society and the media.* New York: Methuen.

Hebdige, D. 1979. *Subculture: The Meaning of style.* London: Methuen.

Lentricchia, F. 1983. *Criticism and social change.* Chicago: University of Chicago Press.

McGee, M. C. 1982. A materialist's conception of rhetoric. In *Explorations in rhetoric:*

Studies in honor of Douglas Ehninger, ed. R. E. McKerrow, 23–48. Chicago: Scott, Foresman and Company.

————. 1987. Power to the <people>. *Critical Studies in Mass Communication* 4:432–37.

Morley, D. 1980. *The "nationwide" audience: Structure and decoding*. London: British Film Institute.

Feminist/Psychoanalytic Criticism

Beauvoir, de, S., 1953. *The second sex*. New York: Alfred A. Knopf.

Connell, R. W. 1987. *Gender and power*. Stanford, CA: Stanford University Press.

Gilligan, C. 1982. *In a different voice*. Cambridge, MA: Harvard University Press.

Hall, C. S. 1954. *A primer of Freudian psychology*. New York: Mentor Press, Inc.

Irigaray, L. 1985. *This sex which is not one*. Ithaca, NY: Cornell University Press.

Keohane, N. L., M. Z. Rosaldo, and B. C. Gelpi, eds. 1981. *Feminist theory: A critique of ideology*. Chicago: University of Chicago Press.

Kuhn, A. 1982. *Women's pictures*. London: Routledge and Kegan Paul.

Lacan, J. 1977. *Écrits*. Trans. A. Sheridan. New York: W. W. Norton.

Nichols, B. 1981. *Ideology and the image*. Bloomington: Indiana University Press.

Young, I. M. 1990. *Throwing like a girl and other essays in feminist philosophy and social theory*. Bloomington, IN: Indiana University Press.

Dramatistic/Narrative Criticism

Brown, R. H. 1987. *Society as text: Essays on rhetoric, reason, and reality*. Chicago: University of Chicago Press.

Brummett, B. 1980. Symbolic form, Burkean scapegoating, and rhetorical exigency in Alioto's response to the "Zebra" murders. *Western Journal of Speech Communication* 44:64–73.

————. 1981. Burkean scapegoating, mortification, and transcendence in presidential campaign rhetoric. *Central States Speech Journal* 32:254–64.

————. 1982. Burkean transcendence and ultimate terms in rhetoric by and about James Watt. *Central States Speech Journal* 33:547–56.

————. 1985. Electric literature as equipment for living: Haunted house films. *Critical Studies in Mass Communication* 2:247–61.

Burke, K. 1961. *The rhetoric of religion*. Berkeley: University of California Press.

————. [1931] 1968. *Counter-statement*. Reprint. Berkeley: University of California Press.

Campbell, K. K. and K. H. Jamieson. 1978. *Form and genre: Shaping rhetorical action*. Falls Church, VA: Speech Communication Association.

Cawelti, J. 1973. *The six-gun mystique*. Bowling Green, OH: Popular Press.

Goffman, E. 1972. *Strategic interaction*. New York: Ballantine Books.

————. 1974. *Frame analysis*. New York: Harper Colophon.

Warnick, B. 1987. The narrative paradigm: Another story. *Quarterly Journal of Speech* 73:172–82.

Culture-centered Criticism

Basso, K. 1990. *Western Apache language and culture.* Tucson: University of Arizona Press.

Carbaugh, D., ed. 1990. *Cultural communication and intercultural contact.* Hillsdale, NJ: Lawrence Erlbaum.

Dundes, A., ed. 1984. *Mother wit from the laughing barrel: Readings in the interpretation of Afro-American folklore.* Englewood Cliffs, NJ: Prentice Hall.

Gates, H. L., Jr. 1986. *Figures in black: Words, signs, and the "racial" self.* New York: Oxford University Press.

Geertz, C. 1973. *The interpretation of cultures.* New York: Basic Books.

Griefat, Y. and T. Katriel. 1989. Life demands *Musayara:* Communication and culture among Arabs in Israel. In *Language, communication and culture.* S. Ting-Toomey and F. Korzenny, eds., 121–138. Newbury Park, CA: Sage Publications, Inc.

Kincaid, D. L., ed. 1987. *Communication theory: Eastern and western perspectives.* San Diego: Academic Press.

Mullen, R. W. 1982. *Black communication.* Washington, D.C.: University Press of America.

Smitherman, G. 1977. *Talkin' and testifyin': The language of black America.* Boston: Houghton Mifflin.

Vanderwert, W. C., ed. 1971. *Indian oratory.* Norman, OK: University of Oklahoma Press.

Media-centered Criticism

Bennett, W. L. 1988. *News: The politics of illusion.* 2d ed. New York: Longman.

Blumler, Jay G. and E. Katz, eds. 1974. *The uses of mass communications: Current perspectives on gratifications research.* Beverly Hills, CA: Sage.

Brummett, B. 1988. The homology hypothesis: Pornography on the VCR. *Critical Studies in Mass Communication* 5:202–16.

Chesebro, J. W. 1984. The media reality: Epistemological functions of media in cultural systems. *Critical Studies in Mass Communication* 1:111–30.

Gumpert, G. and R. Cathcart. 1982. *Inter/Media.* New York: Oxford University Press.

———. 1985. Media grammars, generations, and media gaps. *Critical Studies in Mass Communication* 2:23–35.

Haynes, W. L. 1988. Of that which we cannot write: Some notes on the phenomenology of media. *Quarterly Journal of Speech* 74:71–101.

Levy, M. R. 1987. VCR use and the concept of audience activity. *Communication Quarterly* 35:267–75.

Mander, J. 1978. *Four arguments for the elimination of television.* New York: William Morrow.

McLuhan, M. 1964. *Understanding media: The extensions of man.* New York: McGraw-Hill.

Newcomb, H. 1982. *Television: The critical view.* 3d ed. New York: Oxford University Press.

Piccirillo, M. S. 1986. On the authenticity of televisual experience: A critical exploration of para-social closure. *Critical Studies in Mass Communication* 3:337–55.

Rosengren, Karl E., L. A. Wenner, and P. Palmgreen, eds. 1985. *Media gratifications research.* Beverly Hills, CA: Sage Publications, Inc.

Index
● ● ● ● ● ● ●